1989.
Galileo probe launched without mishap.
Technical difficulties permanently damage spacecraft.
49.25 pounds of plutonium are on board.

1990.
Ulysses probe launched
with 24.2 pounds of plutonium on board.

November 1996.
Russian Mars space probe crashes back to Earth on Chile
and Bolivia, with a half-pound of plutonium on board.
Amount of plutonium which is released: unknown.

January 1997.
Delta II rocket explodes* on lift off.
Residents as far away as 73 miles are asked to stay inside
with windows closed and air conditioning turned off.
No plutonium is on board.

October 1997.
Cassini space probe is scheduled for launch.
72.3 pounds of plutonium on board.

After 1997.
More launches involving
plutonium payloads are planned.

August 1999.
Cassini space probe, on its way to Saturn,
is scheduled for a return "flyby" 312 miles above Earth.

Number of people, estimated by NASA, who "could
receive 99 percent or more of the radiation exposure" in
the event of an "inadvertent reentry":
5 billion…

THE WRONG STUFF

THE SPACE PROGRAM'S NUCLEAR THREAT TO OUR PLANET

KARL GROSSMAN

COMMON COURAGE PRESS   MONROE, MAINE

Library of Congress Cataloging-in Publication Data
Grossman, Karl.
The wrong stuff: the space program's nuclear threat to our
planet/Karl Grossman.
p. cm.
Includes index.
ISBN 1-56751-125-2 (cloth).—ISBN 1-56751-124-4 (paper)
1. Radioactive pollution.
2. Space vehicles—Nuclear power plants—Environmental aspects.
3. Plutonium as fuel. 4. Plutonium—Toxicology.
I. Title.
TD196.R3G76 1997
363.17'99—dc21   97-11915
CIP

Common Courage Press
Box 702
Monroe, ME 04951

207-525-0900 fax: 207-525-3068

First Printing

TABLE OF CONTENTS

CHAPTER ONE

"CANBERRA...
WE'VE GOT A PROBLEM."

Or...
If a rocket fell to Earth and only the
Developing World heard it,
did it really crash?

Sunday afternoon, November 17, 1996. President Bill Clinton, vacationing in Hawaii, is interrupted by an urgent message from the U.S. Space Command. The Russian Mars 96 space probe—with a half-pound of deadly plutonium on board—is falling back to Earth. The rocket's fourth stage misfired after the launch the previous day from the Baikonur Space Center in Kazakhstan. Based on its "tracking data," the U.S. Space Command advises Clinton that it "estimates the spacecraft will reenter the Earth's atmosphere" in a matter of hours "with a predicted impact point in east-central Australia." Clinton calls Australian Prime Minister John Howard—who, coincidentally, the president plans to visit the very next day on his first stop before an Asia tour—and promises "assets we have in the Department of Energy" to deal with any radioactive contamination.[1]

It is early morning in Australia. Howard places the Australian government, military and Emergency Management Australia on full alert. Preparations are made to implement the

Australian Contingency Plan for Space Re-Entry Debris, acronymed SPRED, developed in 1988 after concerns of a Soviet nuclear-powered satellite, the Cosmos 1900, coming down that year on Australia.[2] At a press conference Howard informs his country that, "I can't tell you where it is going to land. I can't tell you when."[3] Howard thanks the U.S. president for his phone call while criticizing Russia for failing to provide Australia with any warning about the impending re-entry of the car-sized space probe. "It is obviously one of those situations where there is a proper obligation to share that kind of information in the interests of people taking adequate preparation," says Howard.[4] He warns that Australians should use "extreme caution" if they come in contact with remnants of the plutonium-bearing Russian probe.[5]

The White House issues a press release stating:

> Russian space authorities believe there is no danger of nuclear contamination. Nevertheless, in what is considered to be the extremely unlikely event that one or more of the [plutonium] batteries break open, the United States is prepared to offer all necessary assistance to any nation to deal with any resulting problems.[6]

But the situation is potentially much worse than needing to scoop up bits of plutonium that might crash land. The 270 grams of Plutonium-238 are contained in four cannisters—sources of electricity for robotic landing vehicles. The plutonium could vaporize into fine dust particles, spreading widely and maximizing the number of lethal doses.

The potential of a spaceborne nuclear device impacting on Australia becomes global headline news. Reporting "Mars probe expected to fall within hours," CNN presents Robert Bell, senior director for defense policy of the U.S. National Security Council. He says the U.S. Space Command "believes the size of the probe is large enough to give pieces of it a chance of surviving reentry, though most of the spacecraft will burn up in the atmosphere before impacting."[7]

Reuters news service reports Bell saying that there are "a couple of scenarios that could be a worst case" including "if some cloud of dispersal were formed at a lower altitude and inhaled by humans, it could be lethal." [8]

"We've got a problem," Russian Space Agency spokesman Vladimir Ananyev asserts in a Reuters dispatch. "The probe had been due to leave the Earth's orbit last night but is still there. We are trying to sort it out." [9]

Reuters also quotes a Russian "nuclear scientist who declined to be named" as noting: "This plutonium isotope is several hundred times more radioactive than the plutonium used for military purposes...If it is spread over the Earth it is highly dangerous and leads to an established increase in cancer diseases."[10]

Russian NTV television reports: "Unburned bits of the station could hit the Earth. To make matters worse the station has four thermoelectric generators fueled by radioactive plutonium."[11]

Meanwhile, Australia "hit the panic button when President Clinton rang the Prime Minister," reports *The Irish Times* from Adelaide. A "national crisis" had been "sparked by this interplanetary ballistic bungle."[12] Some Australians hit the bottle or turn to betting. "A barkeeper in the tiny outback town of Tibooburra," reports the Associated Press from Sydney, "offered his customers free beer after officials announced the probe might land in a nearby swamp. A bookmaker in central Australia's Alice Springs said dozens of gamblers tried to place bets on where the Russian probe would crash. The Australian government, military and civil defense teams went on full alert amid warnings that a crash could produce a cloud of radioactivity."[13]

Confusion reigns over where exactly the space probe will fall.

As the hours pass into late evening Sunday, the U.S. Space Command issues an updated projection from its headquarters in Colorado Springs, Colorado. The probe will now be coming down in the Pacific Ocean, *east* of Australia.[14] However, Russian Rossiiskiye Vesti news maintains the probe "crashed to its doom in the Pacific Ocean, *west* of Australia."[15] But the Russians are at a disadvantage: as a result of economic problems, the ship they use to track space launchings is not out to sea. Yuri Koptev, general director of the Russian Space Agency, would later tell ITAR-TASS that sending the tracking ship out to its station in the Indian Ocean would have cost about 15 billion rubles or $2.7 million, a significant sum for the cash-strapped Russian space program. "We lost the necessary data because of our poverty," he said.[16]

In contrast, being central to U.S. military efforts to expand into space and very well-funded, the U.S. Space Command has an extensive program tracking thousands of objects in space.

The *New York Times* prepares its next day's edition with the latest word when it goes to press Sunday night New York time November 17, 1996: the probe will miss Australia and instead come down *off* New Zealand. The *Times* says in its November 18 edition, which features a front page headline "Russian Space Probe Falls Back To Earth," that "United States Space Command calculated that debris from the Russian Mars 96 spacecraft, which was carrying canisters of radioactive plutonium, would reenter Earth's atmosphere...over the Pacific Ocean 500 miles southeast of New Zealand."[17]

But while the *Times* is rolling off the press, the U.S. Space Command has a new announcement: the probe *has fallen* far east of Australia *and* New Zealand, in the Pacific west of South America—between Easter Island and the coast of Chile.[18]

The Russians also say the probe fell east of Australia and west of South America, although in a different patch of Pacific than that claimed by the U.S. Space Command. Reports the Russian news service ITAR-TASS: "Fragments of the Russian Mars 96 probe...fell down in the Pacific hundreds of kilometers off South America inflicting no damage to Chile or any other country."[19]

"The one thing both agree on is that the Mars 96 probe landed in the water," heralds *USA Today*. "That means the radioactive batteries in its lander vehicles, with their seven ounces of potentially lethal plutonium, lie at the bottom of the ocean."[20]

Prime Minister Howard goes before Australia's House of Representatives and states: "It does appear that what we all have is a happy ending to the saga of the Russian spacecraft....It has been assumed widely for some time that it would touch down in Australia and some of the debris might have exposed Australian citizens to risk—a matter that the government has to take contingency arrangements against." [21]

Back in Hawaii, the anchorperson on KFC-TV Channel 2 news at 10 p.m. intones: "Vacation for the president doesn't necessarily mean he's not working. While here on Oahu President Clinton has been on the phone...keeping tabs on the seven-ton Russian Mars space probe which launched yesterday and, due to a misfired booster rocket, crashed into the southern Pacific Ocean this afternoon. There were predictions that it would fall somewhere in Australia, the country Clinton will head for tomorrow."[22]

The broadcast cuts to CNN's John Holliman from CNN Center in Atlanta, Georgia: "The launch was beautiful and the Russian rocket left the Earth for a year-long journey to Mars. The problem came when the fourth stage was scheduled to fire. It misfired," Holliman relates, "causing the nuclear-powered satellite to stay in orbit around Earth, rather than traveling at more than 17,000 miles an hour toward Mars. The worry was that the four nuclear power plants, each the size of a

35mm film canister, might break open in a populated area, releasing radiation. The Russians quickly said the cannisters were built to prevent that from happening but still there was worry. It's hard to predict where an orbiting object will reenter the Earth's atmosphere and at one point Sunday it was expected to come down in Australia." Then came the "new U.S. Space Command estimate of impact zone [and] as evening continued the point of predicted impact was moved more and more to the east until finally Space Command put it here," says Holliman. A graphic is shown displaying the estimated drop site, "a third of the way between Easter Island and the west coast of Chile, at least 800 miles from any populated area."[23]

"Crippled Mars Probe Crashes Harmlessly To Earth In South Pacific Waters," headlines the following day's *Florida Today* front page.[24] "Errant Russian Spacecraft Crashes Harmlessly After Scaring Australia," is the headline of the *Washington Post*.[25]

But eleven days later, the U.S. Space Command completely revises its account of what happened, changing not only its description of *where* but also *when* the probe fell—not far *off* South America but *on* Chile and Bolivia, and not on Sunday November 17, but on November 16, the night before Clinton called Howard.

"U.S. Space Command has developed new information indicating that the Russian Mars 96 spacecraft likely came down on Nov. 16 instead of Nov. 17 as earlier reported," says the news release issued November 29 by the Directorate of Public Affairs of the U.S. Space Command.

"Any debris surviving the heat of this re-entry would have fallen over a 200-mile long portion of the Pacific Ocean, Chile, and Bolivia. We now believe that the object that reentered on Nov. 17, which we first thought to be the Mars 96 probe, was in fact the fourth stage of the booster rocket. The area where any debris surviving this reentry could have fallen is located along an approximately 50-mile-wide and 200-mile-long path, oriented southwest to northeast. This path is centered approximately 20 miles east of the Chilean city of Iquique and includes Chilean territory, the border area of Bolvia and the Pacific Ocean."[26]

This conforms to Chilean eyewitness accounts of a fireball coming down from the sky in northern Chile. John Van der Brink, an electronics specialist from, ironically, Australia, recently retired from the European Southern Observatory in Chile, and he and his wife, Katrina, were in the mountains of northern Chile looking for meteors on the night of November 16. Van der Brink, who worked with NASA during the 1960s tracking rockets over Australia, tells the Boston Globe that it was immediately obvious that what he saw was a spacecraft burning up. "I had no illusions it was anything other than a piece of space debris." It was brighter than the brightest star, he said, had a trail about 12 times the width of the full moon, and had "sparkling bits sort of coming off the back of it. This was an extraordinarily spectacular event."[27]

Leo Alvarado had been riding in a car with four other geology students from the Universidad Catolica del Norte when they saw what appeared to be a blazing fire in the sky above northern Chile that same night. It traveled "almost horizontal, not like a meteorite," Alvarado tells the Christian Science Monitor: "We watched it break up into many pieces and burn."[28]

Alvarado passed on word about the siting to Luis Barrera, an astrophysicist at the Astronomy Institute at the Universidad Catolica del Norte. Dr. Barrera also heard from a family traveling in the area who saw what they describe as a comet-like object flying horizontally, then breaking apart and changing colors as it fell.[29]

"The news is bad. I think it vaporized," Barrera concludes.[30]

The attention of the world is far, far lighter than it had been when the probe appeared to be headed for a fall on Australia. Reporter David L. Chandler notes in the *Boston Globe*: "Chilean officials are especially offended because Australia, at first thought to be in the path of the failing Russian spacecraft, got a warning phone call from President Clinton, while they heard nothing for a week and a half." Chandler quotes Houston aerospace engineer James Oberg, who specializes in following Russian space missions, as saying: "You can clearly see the double standard...Australia got a phone call from the president, and they [Chile] got a two-week-old fax from somebody."[31]

Chandler writes: "Fumbling by the U.S. Space Command, which tracks objects in orbit, led to a two-week delay that could have endangered the lives of anyone who might encounter Mars 96's half-pound of deadly plutonium without realizing what it was."[32]

Manuel Baquedano, director of the Institute for Ecological Policy in Chile, asks in the Chilean newspaper *Diario la Epoca*, "are the lives of Australians worth more than the lives" of Chileans?[33]

The *New York Times* relegates the story to a five-paragraph Reuters dispatch under "World News Briefs" deep inside its December 14 edition.[34]

There is also scant attention from the U.S. or Russian governments. Dr. Barrera recounts that people from NASA e-mailed him early on, congratulating him on gathering eyewitness accounts of the probe's disintegration. (He ultimately collected accounts from thirteen people.) But then the agency's interest subsided. Barrera suspects that NASA did not want too much attention paid to a situation that might impact NASA's plans for an October 1997 launch of the Cassini space probe with 72.3 pounds of Plutonium fuel—nearly 150 times the amount which was on the Mars 96 space probe. And the Russian government has been "uncooperative," said Barrera, still not giving Chile a description of the canisters so that searchers would know what to look for—if the batteries remained intact.[35]

The regional government for northern Chile, at the start of 1997, meanwhile, asks its "Ministries of Defense and Interior and the Chilean Nuclear Energy Commission to conduct a study to determine with absolute certainty [if there was] radioactive contamination," reports *El Mercurio*, the major newspaper in Chile. "This is something that requires a very complex investigation...an investigation of high quality."[36]

El Mercurio recounts the observations of those seeing the Mars 96 probe coming down looking "like a brilliant object in the sky, similar to a comet, that was disintegrating until it exploded in the air and spread out over the [northern] region" of Chile and southern Bolivia. The possible spread of plutonium represents, it said, "a dangerous situation."[37]

A unit of Bolivian police was reported in December 1996 to have found debris of the Mars 96 space probe in Bolivia near the Chilean border,[38] but that report is subsequently termed "unofficial" by the Bolivian Embassy in the U.S.[39]

As to why the U.S. is not providing South America with the kind of help Clinton had promised Australia, Gordon Bendick, director of legislative affairs of the U.S. National Security Council, declares in an interview from the Old Executive Office Building adjacent to the White House: "It's not the United States' responsibility to protect the world from this."[40]

"We told Bolivia and Chile that we would provide technical assistance, but they haven't requested any," Bendick goes on. "They asked for technical data and we provided [information on] the radioactive combination of the air, the ground and the water, and we said it is negligible. Radiation from the probe is so low and doesn't even exceed that natural background in the areas where this thing went down."[41]

"If [the cannisters] burned up in the atmosphere, bottom line here, if they weren't heat resistant enough to stand what I would call a non-standard re-entry pattern, the release was maybe up to 200 grams of plutonium, which is like a drop of blood in the Pacific Ocean," Bendick declares. "There is no environmental problem with a couple of hundred grams....If in fact this thing survived reentry into the atmosphere and these things came down and crash-impacted on the Earth...they were meant to penetrate the Earth, much as the containers with the Plutonium-238 were meant to penetrate Mars, their original target—they'll never be found. And even if they did and were found, people could walk around with them in their pants pockets for their rest of their lives and never be bothered....If it became particulate matter after diffusing in the atmosphere, burned plutonium would be much similar to open air testing that the French did in the Pacific as recently as a few years ago." And that possibility was not dangerous either, said Bendick, because "we can find no positive causal link" between radioactivity released in atomic bomb testing done by the United States in Nevada, for example, and cancer in people downwind, the NSC official claims.[42]

Space News, the space industry publication, meanwhile reports that it was told by a "U.S. government source" that "specially-equipped Department of Energy aircraft capable of spotting from the air the nuclear material carried in the Russian spacecraft...were not deployed as the aircraft cannot operate at the altitudes and terrain where Mars 96 may have hit Earth."[43]

Space News also quotes a "government source" as saying the reporting by the U.S. Space Command on the Mars 96 probe's fall to Earth was "a real black eye for the U.S. Space Command and their space tracking abilities."[44] Army Major Steve Boylan, chief of media relations for the U.S. Space Command, defends its performance emphasizing that when a space device falls, "as soon as it starts reacting with the Earth's atmosphere, it can skip, it can slow down, it can bounce...especially things that aren't designed for reentry."[45]

But Steven Aftergood, senior research analyst for the Federation of American Scientists, is not impressed: "The fact that the U.S. government initially missed the reentry of the Mars 96 space probe is embarrassing and worse. It calls into question the quality of our space tracking abilities. When you consider that this issue reached all the way up to The White House and had the president contacting the prime minister of Australia over a reentry that already occurred, it's border-line scandalous."[46] Nor is Aftergood reassured by the Russian performance.

"The way it was played out was disgraceful," he tells *Space News* adding that it "makes the Cassini safety issues tangible in a way that [they] might not have been otherwise."[47]

Despite all the technology that goes into launching rockets, and the sophisticated devices used to track their trajectory, when a nuclear-fueled satellite falls back to Earth, its impact becomes a game of Chernobyl roulette.

What Goes Around Comes Around

But just how likely is such an accident? To date, three out of the twenty-six U.S. missions involving nuclear material have ended in mishaps. The most serious U.S. accident happened on April 21, 1964, when a U.S. navigational satellite, Transit 5BN-3, powered by a SNAP-9A plutonium-fueled radioisotope thermoelectric generator (RTG) failed to achieve orbit and fell from the sky, disintegrating as it burned up in the atmosphere.

The SNAP-9A was fueled with 2.1 pounds of Plutonium-238. It and other early SNAP (for Systems for Nuclear Auxiliary Power) RTGs were actually "designed to vaporize the Plutonium-238 metal fuel in the stratosphere during reentry" in the event of an accident, according to the 1990 publication *Emergency Preparedness for Nuclear-Powered Satellites*, a report of

Europe's Organization for Economic Cooperation and the Swedish National Institute of Radiation Protection. "Dispersion of the radioisotope as very small particles at high altitude," it was believed at the time, "would preclude high activity debris in localized areas."[48]

In other words: NASA designed the early SNAP nuclear power systems to break apart and have their plutonium vaporize in the event of a fall to Earth so as to spread the plutonium globally rather than have it come down on one place on Earth. This mirrored a notion at the time: "The solution to pollution is dilution."

A NASA listing of its record with its nuclear-fueled spacecraft—"U.S. History of RTG Power Source Use"—states that the 1964 misguided SNAP-9A "burned up on reentry" into the atmosphere.[49] *Emergency Preparedness for Nuclear-Powered Satellites* states the SNAP-9A plutonium system

> ...burned up over the West Indian Ocean north of Madagascar....In August 1964, the U.S. sampling program detected Plutonium-238 in the stratosphere....The radioactive dust was also detected in the Northern Hemisphere in May 1995 at aircraft altitudes, but the greater concentrations were observed at high altitudes within the Southern Hemisphere, with about four times as much Plutonium-238 as in the Northern Hemisphere. By November 1970, about five percent of the original Plutonium-238 still remained in the atmosphere...A worldwide soil sampling program carried out in 1970 showed SNAP-9A debris to be present at all continents and at all latitudes.[50]

Dr. John Gofman, professor emeritus of medical physics at the University of California at Berkeley, has long maintained that the resulting spread of Plutonium-238 around the world contributed to global lung cancer rates. An M.D. and Ph.D. who developed some of the first methods for isolating plutonium for the Manhattan Project, the co-discoverer of several radioisotopes including Uranium-233, and former associate director of the U.S. government's Lawrence Livermore Laboratory, Gofman stresses that "although it is impossible to estimate the number of lung cancers induced by the accident, there is no question that dispersal of so much Plutonium-238 would add to the number of lung cancers diagnosed over many subsequent decades."[51]

The SNAP-9A accident "is the main source of Plutonium-238 in the environment," according to *Emergency Preparedness for Nuclear-Powered Satellites*.[52]

Plutonium, a man-made element, has been described repeatedly as the most toxic substance known.

Dr. Helen Caldicott, president emeritus of Physicians for Social Responsibility, writes in *Nuclear Madness*, "Named after Pluto, god of the underworld, it is so toxic that less than one-millionth of a gram, an invisible particle, is a carcinogenic dose. One pound, if uniformly distributed, could hypothetically induce lung cancer in every person on Earth."[53]

The health threat of plutonium is primarily as a fine particle—as vapor or dust—that is inhaled. It is not water-soluble and once in the lung it lodges there, irradiating that portion of the organ and, very likely, slowly inducing cancer. Some of it may split off and irradiate other parts of the body, causing other forms of cancer and leukemia.

Explains Dr. Caldicott:

When lodged within the tiny airways of the lung, plutonium particles bombard surrounding tissue with alpha radiation. Smaller particles may break away from the larger aggregates of the compound to be absorbed through the lung and enter the bloodstream. Because plutonium has properties similar to iron, it is combined with the iron-transporting proteins in the blood and conveyed to iron-storage cells in the liver and bone marrow. Here, too, it irradiates nearby cells, inducing liver and bone cancer, and leukemia. Plutonium's iron-like properties also permit the element to cross the highly selective placental barrier and reach the developing fetus, possibly causing teratogenic damage, and subsequent gross deformities in the newborn infant. Plutonium is also concentrated in the testicles and ovaries where it inevitably will cause genetic mutation to be passed on to future generations and, in some cases, cancer of the testicles.[54]

Further, the plutonium used in space devices—Plutonium-238—is 280 times more radioactive than Plutonium-239, the plutonium used as fuel in atomic bombs and built up as a by-product in the operation of nuclear power plants. Plutonium-238 does not fission (split in a nuclear reaction) like Plutonium-239. It has a far shorter "half-life" (the period in which half its radioactivity is expended) of 87.8 years—compared to 24,500 years for Plutonium-239.[55] This more rapid decay is what causes Plutonium-238 to be 280 times more radioactive than Plutonium-239—and also to produce considerable heat as it breaks down. When nuclear scientists looked for uses for plutonium in addition to fuel in atomic weapons, they saw Plutonium-238 and the heat it produces as a source of electrical power. The concept: translate the heat of Plutonium-238 into electricity. The downside: this quick decay and 280 times the radioactivity make Plutonium-238 an even more intensely toxic nuclear poison.

The SNAP-9A accident was a major spur for NASA to develop solar energy on satellites. Indeed, accounts of the history of solar power will often describe NASA as a pioneer in developing solar photovoltaic energy systems—panels drawing electricity directly from the sun. (Little electricity is involved: the SNAP-9A for instance, was to produce a miniscule 25 watts of electricity.)[56] And so, despite the insistence of those involved in promoting nuclear power that it was an essential power source for satellites and all other spacecraft, because of the 1964 SNAP-9A mishap NASA began turning to solar systems to power satellites.

Still, notes *Emergency Preparedness for Nuclear-Powered Satellites*, the legacy of the SNAP-9A series of space nuclear power systems is still with us—looming overhead.

Two SNAP-9A's and two SNAP-3A's, a previous model also with a purposely designed "dispersable plutonium" system, are "still in orbit with lifetimes in the order of 500-1,000 years," on four U.S. Transit series navigational satellites, the publication points out.[57]

"Navigational satellites"—although their name sounds benign—were, beginning with the Transit series, "especially developed" by the U.S. "for use by submarines in the event of their needing to launch missiles against enemy objectives," notes *The Complete Encyclopedia of Space Satellites*. "For such submarines it would be essential to know their exact position in order to deploy the rockets they carried with utmost effectiveness and precision."[58]

The next accident involving a space nuclear device occurred on May 18, 1968, when a NASA Nimbus-B-1 meteorological satellite with a SNAP-19 model RTG on board with 4.2 pounds of Plutonium-238 fuel "did not reach orbit due to a booster guidance failure at launch," according to *Emergency Preparedness for Nuclear-Powered Satellites*. "The booster was destroyed by the range safety officer at an altitude of 30 kilometers and the spacecraft with the RTG fell into the Santa Barbara Channel off the coast of California."[59] This time, fortunately, the RTG did not break up and was "retrieved" from the water.[60]

We're Glowing to the Movies

Then came the ill-fated Apollo 13 mission to the moon two years later and the largest amount of plutonium that has so far come falling back to Earth—although the blockbuster movie *Apollo 13* failed to mention that part of the drama. However, three pages of the book on which *Apollo 13*, the film, is based, *Lost Moon, The Perilous Voyage of Apollo 13*, co-authored by Apollo 13 mission commander Jim Lovell and Jeffrey Kluger, focus on the situation.[61]

Taken on the Apollo 13 mission, carried up in the Lunar Excursion Module or LEM connected to the command module, was a plutonium-fueled RTG—a SNAP-27 model—to be left on the moon to fuel experiments, including meteorological readings. "On the surface of the moon," relates *Lost Moon*, "the tiny generator posed no danger to anybody. But what, some people worried when the system was first proposed, would happen if the little rod of nuclear fuel never made it to the moon? What if the Saturn 5 rocket blew up before the spacecraft even reached Earth orbit, dropping the [plutonium] who knows where....Now Apollo 13's LEM was on its way home, heading for just the fiery reentry the doomsayers had feared."[62]

The Apollo 13 mission was launched successfully on April 11, 1970, but on the way to the moon a liquid oxygen tank on board exploded, resulting in a desperate effort to return the three astronauts back to Earth alive. Avoided by the film but not in *Lost Moon*: the effort by NASA to prevent lives on Earth from being lost because of the 8.3 pounds of plutonium in the SNAP-27.

The three astronauts had made the LEM their temporary in-space lifeboat for most of the ride back, then threaded their way back into the damaged command module for the perilous reentry through the Earth's atmosphere. At that moment in the film, the LEM is jettisoned and actor Tom Hanks, playing Lovell, declares "farewell Aquarius" (the name given to the LEM)— and it seems to float off peacefully into the void.

In fact, what NASA decided to do was to aim the command module containing the astronauts to one area of the Pacific to hopefully be scooped up by a helicopter and taken aboard a

U.S. Navy aircraft carrier, and aim the LEM and the SNAP-27 that was left in it to another area of the Pacific: the "deepest water we can find...an especially bottomless patch of ocean...a spot off New Zealand," recounts *Lost Moon*. [63]

The LEM, which had no heat shield, came crashing down. According to NASA, the SNAP-27 somehow survived reentry and sank. As the NASA "U.S. History of RTG Power Source Use" describes, "In conjunction with the safe recovery of the three astronauts, the SNAP-27 was successfully targeted to deposit intact in the Tonga Trench in the South Pacific, where it is effectively isolated from man's environment."[64] As to a patch of Pacific Ocean being "isolated from" humanity's environment, that is, of course, highly debatable. According to *Emergency Preparedness for Nuclear-Powered Satellites*, "The Plutonium-238 in the RTG is now at the bottom of the Tonga Trench in approximately 6,000 meters [19,680 feet] of water. No attempt has been made to recover the RTG because the exact location is unknown and the water is too deep."[65]

As to why the plutonium story was left out of *Apollo 13*, Michael Rosenberg, executive vice-president of Imagine Entertainment, which produced the film, said the omission was an "artistic decision."[66] NASA, whose personnel served as advisors for the film, was no doubt grateful that the movie confined itself to the threat to the lives of the three astronauts, and not the danger to life on Earth posed by the falling plutonium.

Chernobyl Roulette

The most recent U.S. mission in which nuclear power was used, as of this writing, was that of the Mars Pathfinder launched two weeks after the fall of the Russian Mars space probe. Sent up on December 2, 1996, it dropped to Mars on July 4, 1997 and sent out the Sojourner rover containing 10.4 grams of Plutonium-238.[67]

The 12 percent failure rate of U.S. space missions with nuclear material is paralleled by a similar failure rate for the former Soviet Union and now Russia. There have been at least forty-one known Soviet and now Russian missions involving nuclear power and out of these at least six have failed.[68]

The Soviet space program avoided the U.S. reliance on plutonium as a power source out of concern that an explosion during launch would disperse the highly lethal substance. Instead, the Soviets stressed the development of nuclear reactors for space—smaller versions of land-based nuclear plants—which would be made to "go critical," to begin fissioning their nuclear fuel, only after they got to what the Soviets considered high enough above the Earth.

(Of the 26 U.S. nuclear space missions, only one involved a reactor, the SNAP-10A, launched on April 3, 1965. It soon broke down but remains in orbit.) [69]

The uranium in a nuclear reactor is only feebly radioactive until fission—or atom-splitting—begins. Then, once a reactor begins fission, "fission products"—Cesium-137, Strontium-90, Iodine-131, among 200 radioactive substances—are built up. They are all poisons to life. (And are what is considered nuclear waste.) Also, there is production of Plutonium-239 (out of Uranium-238 which upon taking on a neutron transmutes to Plutonium-239).

The problem with the Soviet approach: a space nuclear reactor falling back to Earth once it has been operating can result in the spread of these poisonous substances on Earth. And although the Soviets claimed they only started up their space reactors when they were high enough above the Earth, what they considered "high" was not very high at all, often only 150 or so miles up. A satellite must be thousands of miles above the Earth to achieve a relatively safe and stable orbit and not be drawn down to Earth.

The most serious accident involving a Soviet space nuclear device happened on January 24, 1978 and involved the

Cosmos 954 satellite. Cosmos was the name given by the Soviet Union to a series of mainly military satellites, most of which were used for reconnaissance.[70] Cosmos 954, launched on September 18, 1977, "belonged to a series of remote sensing satellites called RORSAT (Radar Ocean Reconnaissance Satellite) and carried radar equipment to monitor marine traffic. The radar equipment was powered by a nuclear reactor."[71]

The Cosmos satellites were placed in very low orbit in order to better survey the Earth.[72] Cosmos 954's orbit was just 156 to 165 miles overhead.[73] In fact, the orbits were so low and precarious that the "original mission" of a Cosmos satellite lasted only a matter of months. Then a "safety system" was activated to "separate the radioactive core from the body of the satellite and boost the core into a higher orbit," ostensibly a safer one, notes *Emergency Preparedness for Nuclear-Powered Satellites*. But the higher orbit was generally only 560 to 625 miles high,[74] far short of a safe and stable orbit.

And although the boosting procedure "had been done 13 times before with satellites in the Cosmos series," relates *Emergency Preparedness for Nuclear Powered Satellites*, when it came time for the reactor on Cosmos 954 to be moved upward, "the separation apparently failed and the satellite tumbled out of control."[75]

> In the early morning hours of January 24, 1978, Cosmos 954 commenced reentering the Earth's atmosphere over the Pacific Ocean. The satellite, glowing from the friction of the atmosphere at high altitude, was first spotted by telescopic camera observation from the Maui Observatory in Hawaii…
>
> The object was breaking up and heading toward northern Canada over the Queen Charlotte Islands. It continued for another 12 minutes and 5,500 km before impacting over the Canadian Northwest Territories. Eyewitnesses near the impact zone reported seeing a brilliant, glowing object accompanied by at least a dozen smaller glowing fragments…

During the first weeks of search, it became apparent that sizeable amounts of radioactive debris had survived reentry and was spread over a 600 km path from Great Slave Lake to Baker Lake. Along the path more than fifty large radioactive fragments were recovered [and there were] other chunks, flakes and slivers [found. But] this represents only a small fraction of the total satellite mass of several tons. Most of the satellite material had probably been vaporized and dispersed globally. In addition to the fragments, which fell along a well defined track, a wide area stretching southwards from Great Slave Lake was affected by scattered small particles (0.1 - 1 mm) from the enriched fuel in the reactor core. [Ultimately, the] total search area [for radioactive material from Cosmos 954] covered about 124,000 square kilometers [of the Northwest Territories].

A balloon sampling program detected enriched uranium, presumed to come from Cosmos 954, the following June and September. A large part (75 percent) of the reactor fuel is thus assumed to have been suspended as fine dust in the atmosphere. This has gradually descended to the Earth giving a small contribution to worldwide fallout.[76]

There were 110 pounds of highly-enriched (nearly 90 percent) uranium fuel on Cosmos 954.

Five years later, another nuclear-powered Cosmos satellite, Cosmos 1402, came falling from space. On this satellite, too, "the safety system...had failed to boost the reactor core into a higher orbit," relates *Emergency Preparedness for Nuclear-Powered Satellites*. Parts of the Cosmos 1402 began dropping on December 28, 1982 and again on January 23, 1983 and "the reactor core was predicted to reenter in the night between 7 and 8 February. An unforeseen eruption of solar flares, however, increased the atmospheric density and the reentry prediction had to be adjusted to an earlier point of time, about half a day," the publication continues. "The final reentry took place over the South Atlantic Ocean on 7 February."[77]

"The consequences of the uncertainty in the reentry prediction resulted in nearly world-wide threat even on the last day," relates *Emergency Preparedness for Nuclear-Powered Satellites*. "If the flight of the [reactor core] would have been around 20 minutes longer, the reentry would have taken place over central Europe." It then adds something similar to what was said about the Russian Mars space probe fall years later: "From the Cosmos 1402 incident it can be concluded that a reentry of a satellite with a nuclear power source on board is likely to raise world-wide concern because of the large ground areas covered by the orbital tracks and the uncertainty in the prediction of the reentry point."[78]

The RORSAT series of Cosmos satellites were "one of the most error-plagued elements of the Soviet space program," says *The Encyclopedia of Soviet Spacecraft*. "The majority of difficulties stems from its reliance upon nuclear power and the resulting danger of contamination." [79]

In addition to Cosmos 954 and 1402, other failed Soviet spacecraft with nuclear power were: the Cosmos 300 and Cosmos 305, believed to be lunar probes, that fell back to Earth in 1969—burning up in the atmosphere and releasing radiation; a RORSAT satellite that came tumbling down north of Japan on April 25, 1973 releasing radiation. And then came the Russian Mars 96 space probe.[80]

Also, Cosmos 367 in 1960, Cosmos 785 in 1975 and Cosmos 1266 and Cosmos 1299 in 1981 were Soviet satellites with reactors that had to be prematurely boosted to higher orbit after undergoing a "malfunction," according to *The Encyclopedia of Soviet Spacecraft*.[81] They are in orbit—for now—with the other used Soviet space nuclear reactors, at 560 to 625 miles high, with the four old U.S. SNAP reactors at 500 to 1,000 miles overhead. All can be expected to re-enter Earth's atmosphere in the next several hundred years, carrying radioactive poisons with the potential for dispersal.

CHAPTER TWO

"THE MOTHER
OF ALL ACCIDENTS"

Despite the poor record of using nuclear power in space, there is a continuing push to deploy it.

Among the space projects to use nuclear power now under-way or planned is the Cassini space probe mission. It involves more plutonium—72.3 pounds—than has ever been used on a space device.

The purpose of the $3.4 billion Cassini mission is to survey Saturn, its rings and moons—including its largest moon, Titan. NASA has named the mission after Jean-Dominique Cassini, a French-Italian astronomer who in the late 17th Century discovered four of Saturn's moons. Saturn is an inhospitable planet, one on which people could never land because it is "gaseous" and "unlike rocky inner planets such as Earth" has "no surface on which to land," says NASA's *Fact Sheet: The Cassini Mission*. "A spacecraft pilot foolhardy enough to descend into its atmosphere would simply find the surrounding gases becoming denser and denser, the temperature progressively hotter; eventually the craft would be crushed and melted."[1]

An accident during the launch from Earth is the initial Cassini mission concern. Fearful of using a space shuttle because of the 1986 Challenger accident—indeed, the ill-fated Challenger's next mission was to loft a plutonium-fueled space probe—NASA intends to send Cassini up on a Titan IV rocket. This is despite the spotty record of Titan rockets. In 1993, a

Titan IV blew up just 101 seconds after launch from Vandenberg Air Force Base in California, blasting to smithereens its $800 million spy satellite payload. Fragments of the satellite system and rocket scattered over the Pacific.[2]

"Workhorse, My Foot," was the title of a *Space News* editorial about the Titan IV rocket after that accident. "The Titan frequently is referred to by its misnomer, the workhorse launcher. But it has proven to be more of a temperamental and ornery show horse than the rugged and reliable pack mule the military needs," said the space industry trade newspaper. It described the Titan IV as "costly to build, inefficient to assemble" and said it should not be seen as a "long-term solution" to "launch needs."[3]

And in August 1999...*it's coming back*

Then in 1999 there is to be a scenario with Cassini that could be even more lethal than an accident during the scheduled October 1997 launch. In August 1999 NASA intends to have Cassini make an extremely dangerous Earth "flyby."

The Titan IV is to loft Cassini to Earth orbit. From there the space probe would separate from the Titan IV and be propelled by a small chemically-fueled rocket, a Centaur. The plutonium on board is to generate an average of just 745 watts of electricity to power instruments. The plutonium has nothing to do with propulsion.

Because Cassini does not have the propulsion power to get directly from Earth to Saturn, NASA plans a "slingshot maneuver"—to fly the probe to Venus, have it circle Venus twice and then send it hurtling back at the Earth. Cassini and its 72.3 pounds of plutonium fuel would, under the NASA plan, come flying towards Earth at 42,300 miles per hour and then do a "flyby" or "swingby" just 312 miles overhead. The idea: use the pull of the Earth's gravity to increase the velocity of Cassini. After the "slingshot maneuver" using Earth and then one more "flyby," of Jupiter in 2000, NASA says Cassini would be able to reach Saturn in 2004.

But after many millions of miles in space, if there is a miscalculation on the 1999 Earth "flyby," the probe could make what NASA, in its *Final Environmental Impact Statement for the Cassini Mission,* calls an "inadvertent reentry" and fall into the 75-mile high Earth atmosphere, disintegrating and releasing plutonium. If this occurs, NASA says "approximately 5 billion of the estimated 7 to 8 billion world population at the time…could receive 99 percent or more of the radiation exposure."

In the event of such an "inadvertent reentry," says NASA, "the potential health effects could occur in two distinct populations, the population within and near the reentry footprint and most of the world population within broad north to south latitude bands."[4]

NASA, in its public relations promotion for Cassini, claims the plutonium on Cassini would be contained in an accident. The three plutonium-fueled radioisotope thermoelectric generators (RTGs) to be on Cassini "are safe," insisted NASA PR man Doug Isbell in a December 1996 *Christian Science Monitor* story about the Mars 96 probe's fall. The plutonium will be shielded in "modules" that "have been tested to contain their plutonium." Cassini's plutonium system and that of the Russian Mars probe are two different things, he said. Cassini was "designed by us, as opposed to a foreign country."

That PR pitch is completely contradicted in the *Final Environmental Impact Statement for the Cassini Mission,* a report NASA was forced to prepare under the National Environmental Policy Act or NEPA, a law passed in 1969. Under NEPA, every U.S. government agency has "the obligation to consider every significant aspect of the environmental impact of a proposed action [and to] inform the public that it has indeed considered environmental concerns in its decision-making process."[5]

The *Final Environmental Impact Statement for the Cassini Mission* admits that a sizeable amount of the 72.3 pounds of plutonium on Cassini would likely be released in a "flyby" accident—and as "vapor or respirable particles."[6] This would maximize the health impacts.

"For all the reentry cases studied," says the document, "about 32 to 34 percent of the fuel from the three RTGs is expected to be released at high altitude. An evaluation was performed...to determine the reentry response of fuel particles as a function of reentry conditions. Based on this analysis and the expected initial particle size distribution of the fuel, the particle size distribution of the fuel released during reentry was calculated as a function of the reentry angle. The fraction of the fuel particles released during reentry estimated to be reduced to vapor or respirable particles less than 10 microns ranges from 66 percent for very shallow reentries (8 degrees) to about 20 percent for steep (90 degree) reentries."[7]

Also, NASA, in the *Final Environmental Impact Statement*, details how the plutonium could be dispersed in other stages of the flight, in an explosion at lift-off and if the Titan IV and Centaur malfunction later in launch and the "modules" of plutonium fall to a hard Earth surface—such as rock.

Dr. Horst Poehler, a twenty-two year veteran of working for NASA contractors at the Kennedy Space Center, describes the shielding of the plutonium as hardly shielding at all.

"It's fingernail thin," said Dr. Poehler. "It's a joke."[8]

The so-called "shielding" consists, he said, of an iridium alloy shell with a thickness of 0.022 inches or 3/128 inch housing the plutonium pellets followed by two graphite shells each less than a quarter-inch thick, insulating foil and finally 1/16th-inch thin aluminum.[9] In response to Dr. Poehler's description of the "shielding," NASA admits in an addendum to its *Final Environmental Impact Statement* that the thin protective layer is, in fact, basically the extent of it.[10]

The long-time scientist for NASA said an accident involving Cassini could be "the mother of all accidents" because of
the large amount of plutonium it is to be carrying and the
potential of the 1999 "flyby" to disperse substantial amounts of
plutonium all over the Earth.[11]

"I support NASA when they do the right things," Poehler
said, but with Cassini "they convict themselves with their own
reports." Some thirty NASA reports, said Poehler, acknowledge
the release of plutonium in various impact situations.[12]

"Remember the old Hollywood movies when a mad scientist would risk the world to carry out his particular project?"
declared Dr. Poehler. "Well, those mad scientists have moved
to NASA."[13]

What Harm Plutonium?

"The way Cassini would burn up," explains Dr. Michio
Kaku, professor of nuclear physics at the City University of
New York, is "as it flies by Earth...if there is a small misfire" of
Cassini's "rocket system it will mean that it will penetrate into
the Earth's atmosphere and the sheer friction will begin to
wipe out the heat shield and it will, like a meteor, flame into
the Earth's atmosphere...This thing, coming down into the
Earth's atmosphere, will vaporize, release the payload and then
particles of plutonium dioxide will begin to rain down on populated areas, if that is where the system is going to be hitting."
Pulverized as dust, the plutonium "will rain down on people's
hair, people's clothing, get into people's bodies. And because it
is not water soluble, there is a very good chance that it could
be inhaled and stay within the body causing cancer over a
number of decades."[14]

As for the death toll, NASA says in its *Final Environmental
Impact Statement* that despite the radiation exposure which, it
acknowledges, could affect a huge number of people, only
"2,300 health effects could occur over a 50-year period to this
exposed population" and these "latent cancer fatalities" are

"likely to be statistically indistinguishable from normally occurring cancer fatalities among the world population."[15]

However, Dr. Ernest Sternglass, professor emeritus of radiological physics at the University of Pittsburgh School of Medicine, after his review of the data contained in NASA's *Final Environmental Impact Statement*, said that "they underestimate the cancer alone by about 2,000 to 4,000 times. Which means that not counting all the other causes of death—infant mortality, heart disease, immune deficiency diseases and all that—we're talking in the order of ten to twenty million extra deaths." Considering the additional potential causes of death, the total death toll "may be as much as thirty to forty million people."[16]

What NASA has failed to do, said Dr. Sternglass, is acknowledge the research over recent decades showing that what are considered low levels of radioactivity are disproportionately more damaging than high levels. What NASA did, said Dr. Sternglass, was to use old data on the impacts of the high amounts of radioactivity suffered by victims of the atomic bombing of Hiroshima "and divide."[17]

"It's hogwash!" says Dr. Caldicott of NASA's low human death toll claim. "If the cloud blows over a heavily populated area like New York or London and the plutonium comes down as dust, it could be millions and millions" of people who breathe in that dust ending up "condemned to developing lung cancer and other cancers."[18]

Dr. Caldicott says NASA has failed to understand the especially dangerous characteristics of plutonium, its super-lethal Plutonium-238 variety and the health impacts from "chronic, long-term exposure. This is incredibly deadly stuff." Also, she said, NASA has drastically underestimated the impact by basing it on an "average dose for the overall world population," not providing for those who would receive larger doses.

Further, NASA calculated the impact of the radiation from the plutonium as a "whole body dose" rather than acknowledging the concentrated dose many victims would receive in their lungs after inhaling plutonium. A "hot spot" will develop, said Dr. Caldicott, "among the cells in the vicinity" of where a speck of plutonium lodges and the outcome "for many people will be cancer."[19]

A dispersal of plutonium from Cassini "would be a terrible event," said Dr. Karl Z. Morgan, one of the first five health physicists in the world, often described as the "father" of health physics, and the former director of the Health Physics Division at Oak Ridge National Laboratory. "Each of these plutonium particles would deliver a terrific dose—hundreds or thousands of rems—to the tissue close up against the particle. There would be numerous cancers as a result." NASA, he said, is "just hoping that there won't be another event" like the SNAP-9A.[20]

Dr. Alice Stewart, who in 1958 did the landmark study showing the deadly effects of radiation on fetuses after pregnant women received X-rays, calls the Cassini mission with its payload of plutonium "an altogether hazardous procedure."[21]

Dr. Richard E. Webb, a nuclear reactor physicist and author of The Accident Hazards of Nuclear Power Plants, said that lofting 72.3 pounds of Plutonium-238 fuel into space is the equivalent of sending seventeen operating large-sized commercial nuclear power plants up, each with their inventories of a thousand pounds of Plutonium-239, and hoping they do not drop from the sky, disintegrate and spread their plutonium. "It would be like 17,000 pounds of Plutonium-239 falling," he said.[22]

And there are more scientists sounding the alarm over the Cassini mission and the consequences to life on Earth if the plutonium fuel on board is dispersed in an accident.

Even NASA officials themselves have voiced concern over the Cassini mission. The agency's chief scientist, Frances

Cordova, conceded in a 1994 issue of *Space News* that the Titan IV "does not have a 100 percent success rate" and that using it for the Cassini mission "is truly putting all your eggs in one basket—your 18 instruments on one firecracker." She said: "We can't fail with that mission. It would be very, very damaging for the agency."[23]

After the 1993 Titan IV explosion in California, the White House ordered NASA to reconsider using a Titan IV to launch. The White House Office of Management and Budget cited "reliability questions" in the wake of that Titan IV blow-up.[24] For a time, NASA thought about launching Cassini on a space shuttle. But the agency remained concerned over the reliability of the shuttle, too, because of the Challenger accident demonstrating that shuttles were far less safe than NASA had once estimated.

"Is a Titan 4 launch any riskier than a shuttle launch?" asked *Space News* during the months of reconsideration. "NASA's own statistics indicate the probability of another catastrophic accident like Challenger is about one in 75. NASA is understandably nervous about losing an entire generation's work on one spacecraft again, but every launcher currently in use around the world has had problems at one time or another, including the shuttle. If a shuttle is lost or seriously damaged at any point in the months leading up to the Cassini mission the fleet could be grounded indefinitely, delaying the Saturn probe well past its October 1997 launch window."[25]

Also, said *Space News*, "any cost overrun could easily prompt Congress to cancel Cassini...That leaves the most important question of all. Why not stick to a plan 13 years in the works? There comes a point in every program when it is time to stop studying and start building."[26]

Space News was saying, and NASA finally concluded: there would be danger on the Cassini launch either way—with a Titan IV or a shuttle.

The Special Interest Calculation:
Factoring in Corporate Power

The article in *Space News* that told of Cordova's concerns also reported: "The high risk and cost of the Cassini mission to Saturn trouble NASA Administrator Daniel Golden so much that he would cancel the program if it were not so important to planetary science." Cordova was quoted as revealing that the prior week "Goldin said if he had a choice, he would have cancelled Cassini—if there hadn't been all these other constraints."

What are these constraints? One became apparent in 1995 when *Space News'* fear that Congress would drop Cassini on financial grounds materialized. A subcommittee of the House Appropriations Committee recommended cancelling the Cassini mission because of its cost. The move was led by members of the new Republican majority of the House. "The effort to kill Cassini is taking place in a remote corner of the wider battlefield pitting GOP reformers against the federal government it wants to hack down to size," reported the *Orlando Sentinel*. The time had come for Congress to start making "tough choices," said Representative Jerry Lewis, a California Republican and chair of the Subcommittee on Veterans Affairs and Housing and Urban Development and Independent Agencies.[27]

The Subcommittee inserted a passage into the Appropriations Committee report which stated that the panel "agrees in general with the goal of the Cassini mission to Saturn but the projected total cost of the mission"—then $2.6 billion—"is viewed as too expensive in the current budgetary environment."[28]

But almost immediately the full House Appropriations Committee overturned the subcommittee's recommendation. After the subcommittee action, "lobbyists from Lockheed and NASA were all over us," said an aide to the House Appropriations Committee, who asked for anonymity because of how "hot" the situation was.[29]

Lockheed Martin, the U.S. government's largest military contractor, manufactures the Titan IV rocket ("almost exclusively used for military missions," said a Lockheed representative). And since Lockheed and Martin Marietta merged in March 1995, Lockheed Martin has manufactured the plutonium-fueled RTG systems.[30] Two years before, Martin Marietta had gobbled up the General Electric Company's Aerospace Division, which, starting in the 1950s, had made the devices.

So, despite the danger and the dollars, the Cassini project has kept going.

The Solar Alternative NASA Rejects

The key issue, of course, is the nuclear one. Any space launch, any space mission, carries the possibilities of mishap and many are expensive, too, although Cassini stands to be the single most expensive NASA project to date. With more than 72 pounds of plutonium as part of the Cassini equation, and with the risks on launch and especially during the Earth "flyby," what would be just an accident on a non-nuclear flight could be a catastrophe of unprecedented proportions on Cassini—indeed, as Dr. Poehler says, "the mother of all accidents."

And perhaps the most outrageous aspect of it all: plutonium power, and thus the enormous risk to life, is not necessary for the Cassini mission.

Like the plutonium-powered SNAP systems, the RTGs on Cassini have nothing to do with moving the spacecraft, no connection with propulsion. They are there just to generate an average of 745 watts of electricity—or the amount needed for seven light bulbs.[31]

In 1994 the European Space Agency (ESA) reached a "technology milestone," made a "breakthrough"—new "high efficiency" photovoltaic solar cells specifically for use on deep space probes. Declared the ESA announcement: "Under contract with ESA, European industry has recently developed high efficiency solar cells for use in future demanding deep space missions."[32]

The new solar cells reach a 25% efficiency "under deep space conditions," stressed ESA, "The 25% mark represents the highest efficiency ever reached worldwide." (What is considered "efficiency" in a solar energy system, noted ESA, "is the ratio between the electrical energy produced by the cell and the incoming solar energy...The higher the efficiency, the 'better' the solar cell."[33])

Although satellites "are normally powered by solar cells arrays, spacecraft operating at a very large distance from the Sun" have had difficulty using solar power because the sunlight is dimmer at such great distances. The temperature, typically minus-100 degrees Celsius in deep space, has complicated the use of solar systems. So space probes in this "demanding" deep space environment, have had "to use power sources other than solar panels, because their electrical performance degrades too much at these low light intensities and low temperatures. Until now, deep space probes had to use thermonuclear power generators, like the so-called RTGs (Radioisotope Thermoelectric Generators)," said the ESA announcement. "As RTG's technology is not available in Europe, ESA therefore attempted to develop a power source based on very high-efficiency solar cells."[34]

ESA and an industrial team led by Deutsche Aerospace (DASA) of Germany with CISE of Italy as sub-contractor pulled off the technological feat, "ESA expects that the new high-performance silicon solar cells could profitably be used in deep space missions."[35]

"If given the money to do the work, within five years the European space agency could have solar cells ready to power a space mission to Saturn," *Florida Today* was told by ESA physicist Carla Signorini in 1995.[36]

A combination of solar power and long-lived fuel cells could easily provide all the electricity that Cassini would require, says Dr. Kaku. "NASA is putting ideology ahead of the laws of physics because the amount of energy that you could generate from solar cells is clearly sufficient to energize Cassini. We are only speaking about a modest amount of electricity. It is well within engineering specifications to use solar cells and, if necessary, fuel cells—batteries—to supply the electricity needed. But NASA is ideologically committed to using nuclear." Kaku acknowledged that "retrofitting Cassini with solar cells would cost more and might delay the mission a bit, yet that is a small price to pay for the lives of people who could be killed if there is a tragedy."[37]

Still NASA, along with the other proponents of a nuclear-powered Cassini—including the U.S. Department of Energy, DOE's national nuclear laboratories, of course Lockheed Martin and the other corporations involved in the production of nuclear hardware for space missions—insists on sticking with atomic power on Cassini.

Rejecting solar energy for Cassini, in its initial *Draft Environmental Impact Statement for the Cassini Mission*, issued in October 1994, NASA said:

> In general, the present level of the technology would necessitate the use of large, heavy arrays of solar cells. The added mass of the solar arrays necessary to power the systems on complex planetary exploration spacecraft, such as Cassini, pushes the total mass of the spacecraft, including its propellants and scientific instruments, above the launch capability of the current generation of U.S. launch vehicles for a launch trajectory to Saturn."[38]

Bruce Gagnon, co-coordinator of the Global Network Against Weapons & Nuclear Power in Space, and others sent comments to NASA—about why the European solar break-through, announced six months before, had not even been considered. That forced NASA to revisit the issue—but it stuck to its nuclear position. In an addendum in its *Final Environmental Impact Statement for the Cassini Mission*, issued in

June 1995, NASA acknowledged that the European "cells thus far have tested favorably under simulated environments." An analysis by its engineers showed that, yes, they provided "improved performance." But "even if a heavy-lift booster and a suitable upper stage could be made available, the severe field-of-view problems, greatly increased turn times, and greater operational complexity and programmatic risk associated with an all-solar Cassini design makes such a design, from both mission engineering and scientific perspective, infeasible."[39] *Infeasible*, not impossible.

"Infeasible?" commented Dr. Kaku. "Using solar on Cassini is only infeasible if safety is not the primary concern."[40]

And in the body of the final report, NASA left its rejection of solar energy word-for-word as it appeared in its draft report.

Saturn will be around for a while, so why not wait and arrange a safe flight to it rather than taking the colossal chance of contaminating Earth with radioactivity from a plutonium-fueled Cassini mission?

Similar NASA insistence on nuclear power for a space probe and the claim that solar energy could not serve as a sub-stitute for plutonium-fueled electricity came in connection with Galileo, the space probe that, until Cassini, had been loaded with the most plutonium ever used on a space device— 49.25 pounds. In the three years of controversy prior to the Galileo launch in 1989, NASA also insisted that plutonium power was essential and solar-generated electricity was not an alternative. Only after its launch were reports suddenly released from NASA's Jet Propulsion Laboratory (JPL) telling a different story. As one NASA-funded JPL analysis concluded: "The Galileo mission could be successfully performed with a concentrated solar array power source. While the concentrat-ed array concept still requires extensive development effort, no insurmountable system-level barriers preclude the use of a concentrated solar array on this difficult mission."[41] And that study was based on solar systems available in 1981, thirteen years before the European Space Agency's "technology milestone" in the development of high-efficiency solar cells for deep space missions.

The Facts on the Ground

Meanwhile, the radioactive consequences from a nuclear Cassini mission have already begun.

"Radioactive Mishaps Rising At LANL," was the headline in July 1996 of a front-page story in *The New Mexican*. "Mishaps in which workers or equipment have been contaminated with radioactive substances are on the rise at Los Alamos National Laboratory," the Santa Fe newspaper reported. "Lab officials say the rise in radiation exposure and radioactive mishaps since 1993 has one primary cause: the Cassini project [and] an ongoing effort to build radioactive heat sources" for it. Being worked with, it was noted, was "an isotope of plutonium that is particularly difficult to handle, Plutonium-238, which is many times more radioactive than the better known Plutonium-239 used in nuclear bombs."[42]

"The number of reports of contaminations at the [Los Alamos] lab's plutonium facility—Technical Area 55—jumped 75 percent between 1993 and 1995, from 139 to 244," said *The New Mexican*, and the "total amount of radiation that the entire laboratory work force was exposed to in 1995 was higher than in any other year this decade save 1990."[43]

Greg Mello of the Los Alamos Study Group, an organization which monitors Los Alamos National Laboratory, commented in the article that "increased work with plutonium will cause increases in worker exposures and an increased danger of more widespread accidents."[44]

Exploding Confidence

In preparation for an accident during Cassini's scheduled launch, representatives of NASA, other federal agencies, and of Florida and Brevard County, where Cape Canaveral is located, have been holding meetings since 1995. "Their plans include a worst-case scenario in which a rocket explosion would vaporize the probe's plutonium pellets and send a radioactive mist over Brevard," reported *Florida Today*.[45]

The plans include "training of local hospital staff to handle cases of radiation exposure." Ray Gann, radiological officer and operations specialist for Brevard County Emergency Management, was quoted as saying, "I feel very comfortable with it and I think it's going to be a very good launch. Even if something unfortunate should take place, I feel very confident that the response would be swift."[46]

Ten days prior to that *Florida Today* article, a Delta II rocket exploded at the Cape Canaveral Air Station, just where the Titan IV carrying Cassini is to lift off. The twelve-story $55 million rocket blew up thirteen seconds into launch—a photo of the explosion is featured on the cover of this book. The Florida winter sky was transformed into a distinctly unpatriotic Fourth of July-style fireworks display.

Duck and Cover

The explosion of the Delta II sent streams of smoke and flaming wreckage over the launch site. Its aftermath impacted a wide area of Florida. "'Take cover immediately from falling debris,' an Air Force officer announced over loudspeakers at the base. 'I say again, take cover immediately from falling debris,'" related a *Florida Today* account the day after the explosion. "'I saw this fire cloud, and then we just ran,' said Gerhard Daum, an aerospace reporter with the *Darmstadter Echo* in Germany...'Man, it was scary,' added Justin Ray, a freelance journalist...'I personally never want to see something like that again.' Spectators a few miles away at Jetty Park at Port Canaveral were equally frightened."[47]

A cloud of toxic chemicals formed and began drifting out to sea, then back to land and then south down Florida's East

Coast.[48] It included nitrogen tetratoxide and monomethylehydrazine (MMH), both components of the rocket's fuel described in NASA documents as "deadly if a person comes into contact" with them.[49] Residents as far south as Vero Beach, 73 miles away, were told by the Cape Canaveral officials to stay inside, close all windows and doors, and to turn off air conditioning and heating units.[50] At the Cape Canaveral Elementary School, Brad Smith, a 4th and 5th grade teacher, described the cloud as having "weird purples and reds." He said he pushed wet paper towels under the door to his classroom to keep the rocket fumes away from his students.[51]

Gagnon, who in addition to being co-coordinator of the Global Network Against Weapons & Nuclear Power in Space is coordinator of the Florida Coalition for Peace & Justice, commented to *Florida Today* that the fall back to Earth of the Mars 96 space probe and then two months later the fiery explosion of the Delta II rocket made "real and imaginable" to people how accidents involving space systems "can happen."[52]

In the Garden of NASA

The Cape Canaveral Air Station and adjacent Kennedy Space Center make Florida the major area (followed by California, where the Vandenberg Air Force Base is located) for U.S. space launches—including those involving nuclear power. Looking into the consequences of plutonium being dispersed over the Florida landscape in the event of an accident involving a plutonium space system, in 1985, the U.S. government conducted a study summarized in a report, *Behavior of Plutonium Oxide Particulates in a Simulated Florida Environment.* "Radioisotope heat sources containing Plutonium-238 oxide are used in many space missions to provide power for instrument operation and data transmission...One concern that needs to be evaluated for the risk analysis is the possibility that a launch accident might disperse plutonium oxide heat sources into the area surrounding the Kennedy Space Center."[53]

"An environmental test chamber" was obtained, "samples of soil from various locations in orange groves adjacent to the Kennedy Space Center" were gathered. Plutonium taken from a space system was scattered over the soil. A climate emulating that of Daytona Beach, Florida was maintained based on "temperature and humidity rates" from "meteorological data for Daytona Beach." Over the nine-month experiment, done at Los Alamos National Laboratory, scientists conducted "more than 60 simulated rainfalls."[54]

The study found the plutonium usually stayed on the soil's surface although "especially at the beginning of a rainfall" particles did become airborne. The study determined: "Plutonium concentrations in the air are dramatically higher during the simulated rainfalls than at any other time."[55]

The *Final Environmental Impact Statement for the Cassini Mission* is an inch-thick document providing an analysis of not only what is expected to happen if plutonium falls on Florida soil in a Cassini accident but describing in detail all of what NASA sees as the potential impacts of the mission.

Destruction by Choice

The first concern: launch mishaps. A main worry: a deliberate blowing up of the Titan IV and its payload by the flight control officer "if the launch vehicle threatens land or populations." In other words, if it looks like the Titan IV is going haywire in the minutes after lift-off, what NASA terms a "Command Shutdown and Destruct" can be "initiated." The flight control officer at the Cape Canaveral Air Station would trigger an explosion of charges placed inside the Titan IV and the Centaur (which is to sit on top of the Titan IV, the Cassini probe on top of it).[56] Plutonium, it is admitted, could end up being released in the process.

This "Command Shutdown and Destruct" can be ordered, says the document, "any time during Phases 1 through 5" of the launch. Phase 1 is zero to eleven seconds after blast-off, Phase 2 eleven to twenty-three seconds, Phase 3 twenty-three to 56 seconds, Phase 4 is 56 to 246 seconds and Phase 5 is 246 to 688 seconds.[57]

The *Final Environmental Impact Statement* says:

> At any time during Phases 1 through 5, the Flight Control Officer could elect to activate the command shutdown and destruct system and destroy the launch vehicle...Destruct mechanisms would be in place on the launch vehicle, including the core vehicle, the Centaur, and the SRMUs [an acronym for Solid Rocket Motor Upgrades, the Titan IV's rockets]. These destruct mechanisms would ensure that the propellant tanks and/or the solid rocket motor cases split, thrust terminates and propellants disperse....The most significant environments threatening the RTG's from a CSD [Command Shutdown and Destruct] scenario would be the blast overpressures (shock waves) from the explosion of the liquid propellants and fragments generated by the breakup of the Cassini spacecraft, the Centaur, and the SRMUs.[58]

In a "Command Shutdown and Destruct," the three RTGs containing the plutonium "will be damaged and will either fall to the launch pad, ground, or ocean surface." NASA says "the blast overpressures alone are not expected to seriously threaten the integrity" of the containers holding the plutonium fuel but "a secondary impact of the damaged RTG on a hard surface could result in a fuel release."[59]

NASA doesn't consider Phases 2 to 4 a problem time-span for a "Command Shutdown and Destruct" because the RTGs and their plutonium would end up falling into "ocean waters and sinking with no release expected."[60]

It is part of Phase 5 that is the next big concern, when the Titan IV would be back over land: Africa. NASA has set a trajectory for the Titan IV following lift-off from Florida to go over the Atlantic and then over Africa on its way up to orbit.

If a "Command Shutdown and Destruct" is called while Cassini is over Africa, NASA says "reentry heating" from the fall through then more of the Earth's atmosphere would strip the RTGs of their "housings." Each RTG is to contain eighteen "modules" or canisters of plutonium pellets. Each module is called a General Purpose Heat Source or GPHS by NASA. With the housings gone, the individual modules of plutonium would "reenter individually by design." Then "GPHS modules could impact rock surfaces" on the African continent with "fueled clad failure possible" and plutonium being released.[61]

Destruction Without Choice

Other kinds of explosions of the Titan IV during launch would *not* be on purpose. The failure of one of the Titan IV rockets to ignite could end up causing the Titan IV to blow up and involve the Cassini probe and the Centaur in the conflagration. If a "Fail-to-Ignite" mishap occurred:

> The entire launch vehicle would probably begin a rigid body tipover. At about 4 seconds, the vehicle would have tipped to between 25 and 29 degrees from the vertical, and the nonignited SRMU [Solid Rocket Motor Upgrade] would physically separate from the rest of the launch vehicle. At about 6 seconds, the aft end of the motor would contact the ground first, with the rest of the vehicle then rolling over and crashing. The ground impact would cause the Cassini spacecraft, Centaur, and core vehicle propellant tanks to rupture, and the propellants would mix and explode. The payload fairing would be blown apart by the explosion. The shock wave from the explosion of the Centaur propellants would completely remove the RTG converter and possibly the graphite components of the RTG, thereby releasing bare-fueled clads.

But, it is postulated, "only" if the plutonium containers are "struck by the most energetic" rocket motor "nose cone fragment" could they "possibly fail and release fuel to the environment."[62]

Then there is a launch accident involving the Centaur rocket fuel tank. "Equipment failures, exceedance of operating or processing requirements, and software or human error could cause the Centaur tank failure/collapse," says NASA. "The Centaur tank assembly could rupture in three ways, resulting in mixing the liquid hydrogen and oxygen propellants: the liquid oxygen tank could rupture to the external surroundings, the liquid hydrogen tank could rupture to external surroundings, or the immediate bulkhead between the oxygen and hydrogen tanks could fail resulting immediately in rupture to external surroundings. These failures could result in an explosion of the Centaur propellants."[63]

Still, the "shock waves from the explosion of the Centaur propellants...are not expected to result in a release of plutonium fuel" in the first four minutes of the flight. But if the Centaur rocket explodes in this way during Phase 5, when it, the Titan IV and Cassini are over Africa, that is a different situation, says NASA.[64]

"In Phase 5, a Centaur tank failure/collapse would probably result in the breakup of the spacecraft. Upon atmospheric reentry, the RTG aluminum casing would melt by design releasing the GPHS modules, which would enter as discrete bodies" and "those GPHS modules which impact a rock hard surface on the African continent could release fuel."[65]

Then there are the "potential failures" that could cause the Titan IV, Centaur and Cassini to make an "inadvertent reentry"—to fall back to Earth—after the Titan IV makes it up to Earth orbit, designated as Phase 6. "Some potential failures associated with Phase 6 could result in the breakup of the spacecraft and the RTGs, with the GPHS modules independently reentering the Earth's atmosphere intact and impacting the surface of the Earth. Failures leading to reentry during Phase 6 include the failure of the Centaur to ignite for its second burn, mechanical and electronic failures, and guidance malfunctions. The types of trajectories that could result from such failures include escape from Earth orbit, gradual orbit decay, reentry, and a powered reentry." Falling to Earth from orbit, "the Cassini spacecraft (including the RTGs) would undergo thermal and mechanical breakup." Again, the "modules" that "strike a rock surface" would release plutonium. "Impact on soil or water is not expected to result in a fuel release."[66]

The Impact of Gravity

Then Cassini would be sent on its way to Venus for two swings around that planet in an initial move to boost its velocity.

And in June 1999, Cassini and its 72.3 pounds of plutonium are to be directed by NASA to begin hurtling back at the Earth in a "slingshot" or "gravity assist" maneuver this time involving Earth, to further increase its velocity. The Earth "flyby" or "swingby" 312 miles high at 42,300 miles per hour is scheduled to happen on August 19, 1999.

If on the Earth "flyby" Cassini makes an "inadvertent reentry" into the Earth's atmosphere, NASA acknowledges that the high-speed impact would cause it to break up. Some of the "modules" of plutonium would likely disintegrate, NASA concedes, and, depending on the angle of reentry, some of the plutonium would be released as "vapor or respirable particles" which would rain down on Earth.[67]

As the *Final Environmental Impact Statement* explains: "Based on reentry analyses, it was concluded that for both shallow (7-20 degrees) and steep (20-90 degrees) reentry angles, the 54 GPHS modules (i.e., 18 modules per RTG) would reenter independently and that the response of each GPHS module to the thermal and mechanical stresses of deceleration during reentry could vary significantly, depending on the reentry angle and motion of the GPHS during reentry. The preliminary modeling indicated that complete burn-through of the graphite aeroshell could occur if the GPHS module reentered in a broadside stable orientation. This could lead to the release of the graphite impact shells (GISs) and possibly the release of fuel particles at high altitude."[68]

In any event, "the mechanical and thermal stresses resulting from the reentry heating at high altitude is expected to result in the failure of the RTG housing and release of the 54 GPHS modules. The variations in the reentry conditions that these 54 GPHS modules experience is predicted to result in a range of fuel end states, including damaged and undamaged GPHS aeroshell modules, GISs, fuel chunks, and fuel particles and vapor."[69]

NASA variations as to what could then happen include:

• "Intact GPHS Modules." Here, canisters of plutonium manage to "survive reentry intact" and "strike the Earth's surface. The release of fuel from the fueled clad is not expected unless the GPHS modules strike a hard surface, such as rock. For rock impacts, the assumed release fraction is 25 percent."[70]

• "Intact But Damaged GPHS Modules With Intact GISs [Graphite Impact Shells]." Here the "total release of fuel is assumed to occur" for modules "impacting rock surfaces and a release of 25 percent is assumed if they strike soil."[71]

• "Fuel Particle and Vapor." Here is where NASA says: "For all the reentry cases studies, about 32 to 34 percent of the fuel from the three RTGs is expected to be released at high altitude" and depending on the "reentry angle," the amount of plutonium released as "vapor or resirable particles" would range from "about 20 percent for steep" dives to "66 percent for very shallow reentries." "The remainder of the fuel is released in particulate form."[72]

A Breath of Fresh Air

The *Final Environmental Impact Statement* considers the "individual and collective radiological dose"—the impacts on people—from the release of plutonium in a Cassini accident. "Exposure to plutonium dioxide from an accident could occur in several ways," NASA says.

> Following an accident, exposure could result from inhalation of respirable particles of plutonium dioxide in the immediate vicinity of the accident....The very small respirable particles would be the principal hazard because they can remain in the body for many years if inhaled....These small particles or vapor could also present an exposure hazard downwind of the accident when the radioactively contaminated plume passes. This is a concern for both Phase 1 launch pad accidents and Phases 5 and 6, and Earth swingby accidents....For an inadvertent Earth swingby accident, exposure could also result from inhalation of plutonium dioxide vapor and small particle fallout from a high altitude release. Most of the vapor released at high altitude would be expected to fall back to the Earth's surface within 5 years. Because most of the plutonium dioxide inhaled would reside in the body for a long time, the body would be continuously exposed as long as the plutonium remained.[73]

> In addition, exposure to plutonium dioxide deposited in the environment after an accident could be possible, either from inhalation of resuspended small plutonium-bearing particles or from ingestion of contaminated food. Inhalation of resuspended particles is the dominant long-term exposure pathway....For ground-level releases from impacts on hard surfaces, most of the long-term dose commitment would occur during the first 2 years after release....Long-term dose estimates for the populations outside CCAS [Cape Canaveral Air Station] boundaries and worldwide include dose contributions from inhalation of resuspended material and ingestion of contaminated food products over a 50-year period following the accident.[74]

Under a heading "Potential Radiological Impacts to the Global Area," NASA says that accidents occurring in the launch's Phase 5 when the Titan IV and Cassini are over Africa "could result in limited land contamination over Africa" and with a fall from orbit in Phase 6 there could be land contamination "in indeterminate locations within the global area"[75]

It adds: "Should an accident result in a release in territories outside the jurisdiction of the United States, the Federal Government would respond if requested with the technical assistance and support needed to clean up and remediate affected areas and to recover the plutonium fuel if necessary."[76]

If Cassini drops into the Earth's atmosphere and breaks up during the "flyby," the impact area could be extremely large: "Intact or damaged GPHS modules, GISs, particles of fuel, or vapor from a high altitude release" would cover a "footprint tens to thousands of square kilometers in area, depending on the reentry angle. The vapor fraction, as well as some of the very small particulates would remain in the atmosphere for several years" and slowly descend over the Earth.[77]

With Enough Shovels

Among the most astounding charts in the *Final Environmental Impact Statement* is one headed "Range of Decontamination Methods for Various Land Cover Types." You have to see it to believe it, so we reprint it here on page 47. Notice the categories—"Natural Vegetation, Urban, Agriculture, Wetland, Inland Water, Ocean"—and how "decontamination" would ostensibly be carried out in each.[78]

Each and every category provides for: "Locate and remove any detectable particles" and, as you will note, there are separate columns for "Low-range Cost Decontamination/Mitigation Methods" and "High-Range Cost Decontamination/Mitigation Methods."[79]

The full-page chart begins with "Natural Vegetation," for which NASA says actions might range from: "Rinse vegetation with water, Impose recreational and other use restrictions" to "Remove and dispose all vegetation, Remove and dispose topsoil, Relocate animals, Restore habitat."[80]

Then consider the next category, "Urban," where NASA says the range could be from "Rinse building exteriors and hard surfaces, Rinse ornamental vegetation, Deeply irrigate lawns, Relocate affected population temporarily" to "Remove and dispose all vegetation, Impose land use restrictions, Demolish some or all structures, Relocate affected population permanently."[81] Yes, *Relocate affected population permanently.*

Under "Agriculture," NASA lists possible actions from "Deeply irrigate cropland, Destroy first-year crop, including citrus crops, Rinse citrus and other growing stocks, Plow (shallow) pasture and grain crop areas" to: "Destroy citrus and other perennial growing stocks, Ban future agricultural land uses."[82] Yes, *Ban future agricultural land uses.*

Under "Wetland," NASA proposes: "Rinse emergent vegetation, Impose recreational and other use restrictions" to "Remove and dispose of all vegetation, Dredge and dispose sediments, Restore Habitat."[83]

Under "Inland Water," it goes—after the constant "Locate and remove any detectable particles"—to "Impose boating and recreational restrictions" and then "Dredge and dispose of contaminated sediments, Impose commercial and recreational fishing restrictions."[84]

And under "Ocean," the range could be "Impose shoreline use restrictions" to "Dredge and dispose of contaminated sediment, Impose commercial and recreational fishing restrictions."[85]

The Greatest Job Creation Program in History

What kind of financial cost is NASA talking about?

The *Final Environmental Impact Statement* uses as one basis for economic consequences, a 1990 analysis by the Environmental Protection Agency on cleaning up land contaminated with radioactive materials.[86] This study found "that cleanup

Land Cover	Low-Range Cost Decontamination/Mitigation Methods	High-Range Cost Decontamination/Mitigation Methods
Natural Vegetation	Locate and remove any detectable particles. Rinse vegetation with water. Impose recreational and other restrictions.	Locate and remove any detectable particles. Remove and dispose all vegetation. Remove and dispose topsoil. Relocate animals. Restore habitat.
Urban	Locate and remove any detectable particles. Rinse building exteriors and hard surfaces. Rinse ornamental vegetation. Deeply irrigate lawns. Relocated affected population temporarily	Locate and remove any detectable particles. Remove and dispose all vegetation. Impose land use restrictions. Demolish some or all structures. Relocate affected population permanently.
Agriculture	Locate and remove any detectable particles. Deeply irrigate cropland Destroy first-year crop, including citrus crops. Rinse citrus and other growing stocks. Plow (shallow) pasture and grain crop areas.	Locate and remove any detectable particles. Destroy citrus and other perennial growing stocks. Ban future agricultural land uses.
Wetland	Locate and remove any detectable particles. Rinse emergent vegetation. Impose recreational and other use restrictions.	Locate and remove any detectable particles. Remove and dispose all vegetation. Dredge and dispose sediments. Restore habitat.
Inland Water	Locate and remove any detectable particles Impose boating and recreational restrictions.	Locate and remove any detectable particles. Dredge and dispose of contaminated sediment. Impose commercial and recreational fishing restrictions.
Ocean	Locate and remove any detectable particles. Impose shoreline use restrictions.	Locate and remove any detectable particles. Dredge and dispose of contaminated sediment. Impose commerical and recreational fishing restrictions.

RANGE OF DECONTAMINATION METHODS FOR VARIOUS LAND COVER TYPES
Final Environmental Impact Statement for the Cassini Mission,
National Aeronautics and Space Administration,
Solar System Exploration Division, Office of Space Science, June 1995, Table 4-16.

(remediation) costs for contaminated soils in the United States could range from approximately $250,000 to $5 million per square kilometer ($1,000 to $20,000 per acre), if removal and disposal were not required. Removal and disposal of contaminated soil at a near-surface facility could cost from approximately $37 million to $50 million per square kilometer ($150,000 to $200,000 per acre)." Then a Department of Energy analysis is cited which gives a "decontamination cost" of $200 million per square kilometer or $800,000 per acre that "includes the cost of cleanup and disposal of contaminated materials, reclamation costs, costs associated with relocation of residents, and long-term surveillance."[87]

As to how much land might need "decontamination," NASA says if a launch accident and the area around the Cape Canaveral Air Station is involved, a square half-mile could become contaminated and the "cost for cleanup" could range from "about $7 million" to—for a more thorough clean-up with "removal and disposal"—of "approximately $70 million."[88]

But if it is damage "to the global area," if Cassini falls during the 1999 Earth "flyby" and the "reentry footprint" of dispersed plutonium "occurred over land, the potential costs would be high," says NASA.[89]

"Since the estimated size of the footprint could range up to about 50,000 square kilometers (19,305 square miles) for the shallowest reentry angles and could be greater than the 10 square kilometers (3.9 square miles) for even steep reentry angles, all of this land would require surveillance and monitoring to locate the detectable particles (e.g., larger components and the larger particles)," says NASA. "Initial surveys would likely include low-altitude air overflights with sensitive radiation detectors. These would be expected to identify the hot spots (e.g., most of the GPHS modules and GISs and some of the larger particles) of surface plutonium contamination...Initial costs of the surveys could easily be in the tens to hundreds of millions of dollars."[90]

Also "the activities that might occur after the initial survey would vary a great deal," states NASA, "depending on the extent of the contamination and the location...Larger components would be recovered, to the extent practical. In some types of land areas, the environmental impacts of attempts to recover single particles might be much greater than leaving the particles in place." And "in the unlikely event that such an accident occurred, it is reasonable to assume that not all the particles would be detected and recovered."[91]

The *Final Environmental Impact Statement* provides a dollar figure for decontamination of a half-acre around the Cape Canaveral Air Station. But NASA does not offer a cost estimate when it comes to decontamination of the potentially impacted "global area."

The multiplication of the DOE projected "decontamination cost" of $200 million per square kilometer with the 50,000 square kilometers NASA says could be impacted involves a staggering number which most calculators don't have room to display: $10,000,000,000,000 or $10 trillion for this worst case "decontamination" scenario.

It is probably unlikely that the entire 50,000 acre "footprint" for potential plutonium fall-out would all be impacted severely. Still, if just one-hundredth of it needed complete "decontamination," the dollar total would still be enormous— $100 billion.

As for the cost to life—what NASA terms the "health risk" cost—the *Final Environmental Impact Statement* admits the number of people that could be impacted could range from large to another stupendous number.

For a mishap on launch, NASA says "the population at risk from a Phase 1 accident involving a release of plutonium dioxide would be the population in the vicinity of CCAS [Cape

Canaveral Air Station], estimated to be in the order of 100,000 people."[92]

"For a Phase 5 accident with impact in Africa, the predicted health effects" could impact on "an assumed reference population of about 1,000 people."[93]

For a fall from orbit in the launch's sixth phase, "assuming average world population densities in the latitude bands likely to be impacted by such an accident," there would be 5,000 people in the "reference population."[94]

What Price Titan?

Then comes the total of people that might be affected by an "inadvertent reentry" of the Cassini probe in the "flyby"—and "the expected number of health effects due to the risk of radiological accidents associated with the overall mission is dominated by Earth swingby reentry accidents," NASA admits. It is here the *Final Environmental Impact Statement* says "the potential health effects could occur in two distinct populations, the population within and near the reentry footprint and most of the world population within broad north to south latitude bands" and goes on: "In the unlikely event that [an] inadvertent reentry occurred, approximately 5 billion of the estimated 7 to 8 billion world population at the time...could receive 99 percent or more of the radiation exposure."[95]

Yet, insists NASA, only a small fraction of this number—2,300 people—would suffer "health effects."[96] In the narrative of the *Final Environmental Impact Statement*, NASA does not specify what "health effects" are. But on another one of the report's full-page charts, it acknowledges: "Health effects are incremental latent cancer fatalities."[97]

The chart also says "Health effects, or excess latent cancer fatalities for the short-term inadvertent reentry accidents are evaluated based on collective exposure of approximately 5 billion persons worldwide. Most of the persons exposed would receive an individual radiation dose of 1.0×10^{-5} Sv (1.0×10^{-3}

rem) per year."[98] That formula looks quite mysterious but the intricate code physicists have set up is not hard to break. The Sv in the formula stands for sievert, a measure of radiation. One sievert equals 100 rems. A rem is an acronym for "roentgen equivalent man." (Roentgen is another measure of radiation, named for the German physicist W.C. Roentgen, who discovered X-rays.) What NASA is claiming is that "most of the persons exposed" to plutonium from a Cassini flyby accident would receive one thousandth of a rem of radioactivity—a millirem. NASA does not deal with the issue of those people who would not be among the "most"—those who would receive more than one millirem—for the distribution of plutonium would not be uniform.

Beyond that, NASA's claim about "health effects" is that because a millirem is considered a low dose of radioactivity, not many people, relatively, would end up dying: 2,300 estimates NASA. This would be "over a 50-year period in this exposed population" of 5 billion and be "statistically indistinguishable from normally observed cancer fatalities around the world since approximately 1/5 or 1 billion people would die of cancer due to other causes" during that time.[99]

Thus the "risks are clearly low when compared to the health risks from many large projects and the daily risks faced by individuals," NASA asserts.[100] It seeks to buttress this with another chart, of "Calculated Individual Risk Of Fatality By Various Causes In The United States," which lists the number of fatalities in 1991 from motor vehicle accidents (43,500), drownings (4,600), lightning (64), "homicide and executions" (22,909), suffocation (2,900) and so on.[101] If auto travel is worth 43,500 certain deaths every single year, surely the news of Titan is worth the risk of 2,300. Or so the reasoning goes.

According to Dr. Sternglass, NASA's Cassini death toll estimate "completely ignores," research done over the past twenty-five years on the real consequences of low-level radioactivity.

"They are grossly underestimating the effect of low doses of radioactivity given over a long period of time," said Dr. Sternglass, the author of *Secret Fallout: Low-Level Radiation from Hiroshima to Three Mile Island*[102] and numerous articles in scientific journals on low-level radiation and its impacts. "They know this work. They read the scientific papers. But it is the policy of the U.S. government to ignore these findings because if the true effects of low levels of radioactivity were accepted, it would mean a shutdown of the nuclear industry."[103]

"The dose response to low-level radiation turns out to be logarithmic," explains Sternglass. There is a "very sharp rise" in health impacts when the body is impacted by low levels of radioactivity and at higher levels the rate of health impacts "flattens out."[104]

This is the reason, said Dr. Sternglass, for recent findings that have shown that people far from the 1986 Chernobyl accident have suffered from a higher rate of maladies that exposure to radioactivity can cause. "Children in Greece, for example, have died at a higher rate from infant leukemia and thyroid cancer because of the radioactivity that blew to Greece from Chernobyl in the Ukraine—even though that radioactivity was considered to be at a low level," he said. "There is an enormous difference between internal, ingested isotopes giving a radiation dose at very low levels over long periods of time compared with the risk from an intense but short burst," he said. "This has now been demonstrated overwhelmingly."[105]

But rather than integrate these new findings in the analysis of the health impacts of plutonium being dispersed in a Cassini accident, NASA simply based its analysis "on old studies on the effects of the massive amounts of radiation received in one burst by victims of the Hiroshima atomic bombing," he said. They figured that the radioactivity from a Cassini accident would constitute a fraction of that radioactivity and then claimed that the health impacts would be a correspondingly tiny fraction.[106]

A Cassini accident releasing plutonium to be inhaled by people will mean that "millions will die. They will not die all at once," said Dr. Sternglass. "The plutonium will lodge in their bodies and over time do its damage. There will be cancer. There will be a weakening of immune systems and deaths from other diseases. Millions upon millions will suffer." [107]

"And those people at NASA know this. But the decision to send out this damn thing [the Cassini space probe] was made long ago. There are billions of dollars at stake. There is the fiction of 'safe' nuclear power to uphold. So they deny, deny, deny, ignore, ignore, ignore."

"For NASA to make the calculation knowing what we all know now," said Sternglass, "is a crime against humanity."[108]

Dr. Caldicott challenged the basis of the NASA methodology—that "most of the persons exposed" would receive a one millirem—a presumed "average dose for the world," as she put it. This does not allow for those who would end up with higher doses, she stressed. Further, she said, NASA was premising an individual's exposure on a "whole body" dose when, in fact, if the plutonium is inhaled there would be an intense dose, a "hot spot" in that portion of the lung where it is lodged.[109]

"To take the dose from that tiny piece of plutonium and average it out over the whole body with its trillions and trillions of cells is mad," said Dr. Caldicott. "It is pathologically incorrect. If we operated like that, we'd be killing patients every day."[110]

Further, said Dr. Caldicott, NASA is premising the consequences on a 50-year exposure to the dispersed plutonium when, in fact, the plutonium would be radioactive and in the environment for more than a thousand years. And, she said, if "someone were to die of lung cancer induced by that plutonium and were cremated, contaminated smoke might carry plutonium particles into someone else's lungs. If an animal died, its polluted carcass may be eaten by other animals or its poisoned dust could be scattered by the winds and inhaled by other creatures."[111]

Those involved in assembling the *Final Environmental Impact Statement* approached the medical consequences of plutonium being dispersed by "claiming *de minimus*. They use the term *de minimus* over and over again," she noted. "In other words, they looked at the minimal effects. When engineers design a bridge they consider the worst case scenario; when we in medicine look at the prospects for a patient, we must always consider the worst thing that could happen to a patient. These people are taking this *de minimus* approach, violating the fundamental ethics of engineering and medicine."[112]

She termed those involved in asserting that only 2,300 people would die as a result of plutonium dispersed in a Cassini flyby accident as "apologists for the nuclear industry, prostitutes."[113]

Dr. Morgan, the pioneer health physicist who taught radiation physics as a professor at the Georgia Institute of Technology, said that "undoubtedly, on a statistical basis, many of those plutonium particles" dispersed in a Cassini accident "would end up in the respiratory systems of people all over the Earth" and give a highly concentrated and prolonged radiation dose near to where they are lodged.[114]

Of the one millirem dose average claimed in the NASA report, he said, "Absurd, of course, because some particles will be deposited in the respiratory system, the lower lungs" and emit "hundreds or thousands of rems" of radioactivity "up close." Further, what NASA did "in averaging the dose" of plutonium "to the whole body—70 kilograms, that's ridiculous."[115]

Of the Cassini mission, Dr. Morgan said "I'm very interested in getting the data, in exploring our solar system" but he does not like the risk. "I never like to gamble."[116]

Dr. Alice Stewart said that "nobody knows how dangerous" the Cassini mission could be if its plutonium fuel is dispersed.

She noted that not only cancer but pulmonary fibrosis would be a likely consequence in those impacted by plutonium in their lungs. "These particles get up in the bronchis and will cause cancer and can also cause pulmonary fibrosis."[117] NASA's *Final Environmental Impact Statement for the Cassini Mission* does not consider pulmonary fibrosis.

"What is the benefit?" asked Dr. Stewart, "against such a big risk?"[118]

Dr. Edward Lyman, a physicist and scientific director of the Nuclear Control Institute based in Washington, D.C., a group deeply involved in challenging the use of plutonium, said that an additional focus should be on ingested doses of plutonium. NASA is principally concerned in its *Final Environmental Impact Statement for the Cassini Mission* with inhaled doses of plutonium. "The nuclear industry claims that plutonium is not absorbed in the gut, that a person can actually eat plutonium. This is absurd. It is less injurious than when inhaled but only comparatively. Plutonium is incredibly carcinogenic."[119]

Further, he said, although plutonium is "not easily soluble" in water, once dispersed into the environment it can mix with organic substances "forming compounds that can enable it to be taken up in the body. This is something that international boards when they put out the standards for plutonium don't take into account."[120]

Dan Hirsch, former director of the Adlai E. Stevenson Program on Nuclear Policy at the University of California at Santa Cruz and president of the Los Angeles-based Committee to Bridge the Gap, was amazed by the six to twenty-one pounds of plutonium that NASA admits could be released as "vapor or respirable particles" in a Cassini flyby accident. "That amount is roughly equivalent in curies to the amount of plutonium released in atmospheric nuclear weapons tests. Because this is Plutonium-238, with a shorter half life, it wouldn't be around as long [as the Plutonium-239 component of the fallout], but for the first century or so the impacts would be comparable. This is a remarkable amount of plutonium."[121]

Further, said Hirsch, "people always focus on the lung cancer dose, breathing in the plutonium. But the plutonium doesn't disappear in the environment. It would fall on agricultural land and go into the next season's crops, and if the field is burned off it would be resuspended in the atmosphere. It will get washed off into rivers and get into fish and people will eat the fish; there are, in fact, scores of environmental pathways bringing plutonium to people other than people breathing it in."[122]

"The permissible concentration in drinking water is less restrictive but it still constitutes a problem," said Hirsch. "This plutonium would get into potable water, it would sprinkle down on apple orchards, on corn fields. Nobody is able to calculate what this all means."[123]

Dr. Steve Wing, an epidemiologist at the School of Public Health at the University of North Carolina in Chapel Hill, whose study on the long-time impacts of radioactivity released in the Three Mile Island accident received considerable attention when it was released in 1997, said that plutonium dispersed in a Cassini accident "is clearly of great concern. If material is dispersed and people are exposed, there is danger, and that's the issue."[124]

There is also a problem in analyzing the long-term effects on people that would be caused by the dispersed plutonium, said Dr. Wing. In a succession of studies commissioned by the U.S. Atomic Energy Commission, tests on beagles demonstrated that infinitesimal amounts of plutonium cause cancer in the dogs. "Beagles are an animal species with a maximum life span of about twenty years. This is shorter than some of the latency periods we would be talking about in people."[125]

NASA in its *Final Environmental Impact Statement* principally examines the health impacts on people—not on all life which the plutonium would impact. Yet its estimates are predicated on animal tests which, said Dr. Wing, as lethal as they concluded plutonium is, might have underestimated its effects on life forms—including human beings—with longer lifetimes.

Of NASA's death toll estimate, Dr. Caldicott declares: "They are guessing."[126]

The Odds of a Plutonium Release: Cross Your Fingers

And that is exactly what Dr. Michio Kaku also says about NASA's projection of the accident probabilities. NASA in its *Final Environmental Impact Statement for the Cassini Mission* maintains the likelihood of an accident involving the release of plutonium is very small. It bases its projections on "Monte Carlo analyses." Says NASA: "The Monte Carlo simulation was performed with random selections of failure mode confidence levels, effects of the failure mode on imparting an Earth-impact trajectory change, and the probability of recovering spacecraft control given the failure and time of occurrence in the simulated mission. A total of 1,000 Monte Carlo runs or simulated missions were performed." The probability of a launch accident is given in a range, depending on the phase of the launch, from one-in-600,000 for the need for a "Safety Destruct" during Phase 1 to one-in-112 for an Earth "reentry" on Phase 4.[127] The odds of an "inadvertent reentry" during the flyby are set at one-in-1.3 million. [128]

"They're guessing," says Dr. Kaku.[129]

"The methodology" that NASA is using "comes from the nuclear reactor program," Kaku explains. "It's called a fault tree analysis: if one valve breaks, that one valve can cause perhaps two other pipes to break, causing four to break, and so on. You can get numbers out of this but what do those numbers mean: absolutely nothing." This is because major accidents, says Dr. Kaku, are regularly the result of "multiple failure, and multiple failure is almost impossible to model on a computer with accuracy." Human error is equally problematic to anticipate. "In real life you cannot quantify human stupidity. How do you put a number on incompetence?" Yet NASA "has imported from the nuclear industry a discredited technology." [130]

The sort of oddsmaking NASA is doing on Cassini is pegged not on empirical evidence but on guesswork, says Kaku. In short, he says of the estimate, it's "Garbage In, Garbage Out." When "we have the numbers one-in-1.3 million," says Kaku, NASA "cooked those numbers...That is scientifically fraudulent...That is what NASA is doing." [131]

The nuclear physicist, author of the best-seller *Hyperspace* and seven other books, a Phi Beta Kappa graduate of Harvard University with a Ph.D. in theoretical physics from the University of California at Berkeley, says, "It is scientifically dishonest to tell the American people that they know the odds of a major failure in their system when we have had major failures in other systems, like Titan rocket booster failures. We've had the Mars probe which simply disappeared off our radar screens one day as it was about to enter Mars orbit. A billion dollar Mars satellite simply disappeared off our radar screen and we still don't know the reason why. So I think that we have to have a reality check. It has been scientifically dishonest for the NASA scientists to claim that they know the probability of a major rocket failure when, in fact, we are dealing with Russian roulette. We are simply playing the odds. They are crossing their fingers and hoping that there will not be a misfire of the Cassini rocket." [132]

CHAPTER THREE

ONE-IN-100,000
BECOMES ONE-IN-76

I became involved in the issue of nuclear power in space in 1985. As is my practice through years of doing investigative reporting, I was spending the evening in an easy chair thumbing through reports, articles and various and sundry pieces of paper from a (usually towering) pile alongside. It's amazing, I tell my journalism students, what you can find looking through written material, especially government publications.

One government publication I was reading was *Energy Insider*, a monthly journal of the U.S. Department of Energy. There on its front page was an article headlined: "DOE's Nuclear Power Sources Scheduled For Shuttle Missions to Jupiter and the Sun."[1]

The article told of NASA space shuttles to be used the following year, 1986, to loft space probes containing "nuclear isotope power sources." It told of the space probes each receiving electrical power to run instruments from a "122-pound advanced plutonium-fueled generator."[2] While the article did not provide a weight figure for the plutonium involved, the suggestion was that it would be substantial, considering the overall weight of the generating system—substantial that is, if one was aware of the extreme toxicity of plutonium.

I was familiar with plutonium and nuclear technology, having five years before authored *Cover Up: What You Are Not Supposed To Know About Nuclear Power*[3] I had also written numerous newspaper and magazine articles on nuclear technology through the years as well as having written and narrated television programs on the subject.[4]

There was a paragraph towards the end of the article that said "safety and environmental considerations are a major factor in the design" of the plutonium-fueled space devices, and how "a major design requirement includes provision for...such postulated accidents as launch vehicle aborts, reentry, and impact and post impact situations."[5] The government was saying that it had "postulated accidents" involving the plutonium systems, including "launch vehicle aborts, reentry, and impact and post impact situations." Most interesting—and potentially quite an important issue, I thought, considering that plutonium was involved.

Let me note that I was not suspicious about NASA and the U.S. space program at the time. Indeed, along with other journalists, I had recently been sent a NASA application to be a "Journalist In Space"—and considered filling it out. Announced the offer:

> ONLY ONE WILL GO. NASA has a reserved seat on the Space Shuttle for one professional journalist, and the Association of Schools of Journalism and Mass Communication is acting as travel agent...If selected, you will not be paid by NASA but serve as a pool reporter from the time of the announcement [of your selection] in the Spring of 1986, through training during the Summer, and until 30 days after the flight in the Fall of 1986, sharing your observations with your earthbound colleagues.[6]

Having the year before worked on a book about strife in Central America which included visiting the war zone on the Honduras-Nicaraguan border, I figured that a flight on the shuttle had to be far less dangerous.[7] The space shuttle, I assumed, was a trustworthy vehicle; and I like to fly on airplanes. I even took the application to school to show it to my students so they could see one of ways that journalists get into a story.

Also, although I had, in my years of investigative reporting, looked into governmental agencies and found chaos, confusion and corruption, my impression was that NASA was an exception. Watching Neil Armstrong stepping down onto the moon, for example, gave me, like virtually everyone else viewing that scene on television in 1969, quite a thrill. (Armstrong too, had been an Eagle Scout, like me, and years later, as a reporter, I covered him back on Earth. In person he seemed just as apple pie and can-do.) NASA, I thought, was a different kind of government agency: squeaky clean, efficient. (Years later, I am astounded about how wrong I was, how misled by NASA public relations. And based on the information I subsequently obtained about the shuttle, it became evident that a shuttle flight is extremely risky, and NASA's attempts to dragoon journalists, politicians and schoolteachers like Christa McAuliffe onto the shuttle for its PR interests were outrageous.)

Meanwhile, seeing that article in the *Energy Insider*, made curious by the disclosures of planned launches of shuttles with plutonium systems on board and the government's acknowledgement that it had looked into various sorts of accidents which might occur, I sent a request for detailed information under the U.S. Freedom of Information Act.[8]

The Department of Energy and the Myth of Sisyphus

I sent seven separate requests: to the Department of Energy, NASA and to what the *Energy Insider* said were the "five DOE installations—Oak Ridge National Laboratory, Savannah River Laboratory, Mound Facility, Los Alamos National Laboratory and Sandia National Laboratories...participating in the project." [9]

I asked for "any and all information you have concerning the consequences" if the plutonium-fueled space probes planned to be launched aboard NASA shuttles crashed back to Earth or underwent an explosion "in the atmosphere of the Earth," and about "preparations being made in the event of this."[10]

I use the Freedom of Information Act or FOIA—the journalist's best tool since the invention of the typewriter—with regularity. The act, which became law in 1968 and was strengthened in 1973 in the wake of the Watergate scandal, was designed to open up government, to raise the curtains of secrecy and help cut through the bureaucratic mazes that have developed as the U.S. government became bigger and bigger.

From that FOIA request to DOE, NASA and the national labs in 1985 through now, more than a decade later, I have never had such a tough time using FOIA or getting information at all from the federal government as I have had in exploring the use of nuclear power in space.

The Department of Energy wrote back questioning my "willingness to pay any fees incurred for researching, copying or certifying the requested documents."[11] This was highly unusual in my experience. The letterhead of my stationery clearly identified me as journalist. Journalists are supposed to be granted "fee waivers" on FOIA requests. As a journalist, as a matter of principle, I would not accept the denial. Meanwhile, DOE also advised that it would be handling the parallel requests to NASA and the national laboratories.

I sought advice from the Fund for Open Information and Accountability, an organization formed to defend FOIA—indeed to fight to keep it alive—during the Reagan administration. With the help of the group's Andrea Weiss, a specialist in the use of FOIA, I drafted a letter stressing the "Attorney General's Guidelines Regarding Fee Waivers." The material I was seeking was in the "genuine public interest," I noted, information on how the government was "preparing to deal with" an accident "involving a plutonium-fueled generator to be sent aboard a NASA shuttle in 1986," had great "value to the public," was "not available in the public domain" and I had no "'personal interest' in this information but only seek the facts to present them journalistically."[12] These are the elements of the "Attorney General's Guidelines."

The answer back from DOE: No. "Your request does not appear to involve records that would be useful in their present form to the public," I was told. "In this regard, much of the responsive material consists of highly technical data." Also, my "publication of the requested information would result in commercial benefit."[13]

Now the government was really getting outrageous, I thought. I lecture on the Freedom of Information Act and its history. And nowhere, ever, was there a notion of limiting the release of information or barring a fee waiver because information was "highly technical." There are nine exemptions under FOIA that permit the government to withhold information—such as information involving an ongoing criminal investigation, protected by privacy laws or a matter of national security. (Exception 1 of the FOIA is the ban on the release of information impacting on national security). As for denying a fee waiver to the press because "publication of the requested information would result in commercial benefit," that was just more nonsense—and unprecedented, too.

Meanwhile, it was becoming clear that what I thought would be a straightforward, routine FOIA request—information on a study that the government had admitted doing in one of its own publications—was becoming something else. I smelled the smoke of a cover-up which, as a journalist, I knew will often cover the fire of a hot story.

I bluntly charged cover-up in a letter appealing the fee waiver denial. My strategy when facing stone-walling by the government is to take a strong stand signalling that I have no intention of meekly going away. "It appears to us that the Department of Energy is attempting to cover up on this serious matter," I wrote. On the issue of the information being technical, I noted that FOIA "was not designed to allow government bureaucrats to withhold information on the basis of whether that information, in their view, would 'be useful in their present form.' Why the cover-up? Let's have the information, as technical as it might be, and let journalists and the people decide whether it is useful." On the information resulting in "commercial benefit," I asked: "Is the Department of Energy now claiming that simply because newspapers are sold, radio stations receive advertising, it can limit information which would be obtained by them through the Freedom of Information Act because they are commercial enterprises?"[14]

"The issue of a nuclear-fueled object in space crashing back on Earth is of great public interest," I stated, and I compared the reluctance of the U.S. government to provide information to how a "totalitarian government" might try to "cover up on such an important issue."[15] This, I figured, would get the DOE's attention.

Two months later, DOE gave in. I won the appeal. "This information is of public interest," decided George B. Breznay, Director of the DOE Office of Hearings and Appeals, in a five-page singled-spaced "Decision and Order of the Department of Energy." "In previous cases, we have consistently found that the public interest is involved in the control and management of radioactive material." On the matter of the documents being "technical," he ruled that "the fact that the information is in technical form does not make it useless to the public in that form" and cited prior cases in which it was determined that "access to raw scientific and medical data [was] crucial to informed debate." And, said Breznay, "It also appears that Mr. Grossman has the qualifications and ability necessary to interpret, analyze and prepare articles from the requested information." Also, he said "we find no overriding commercial interest in the present case that warrants a denial of the free waiver request."[16]

In fact, when I finally got the information, it was immediately apparent that it was *not* "highly technical data"—anyone could understand the graphic accounts in the documents about all the ways shuttles can blow up or crash and the problems created by inserting atomic power into the equation.

But that would be nearly a half year later. Because the cover-up would continue.

A week after being notified I won the appeal, I received a letter from the DOE official who had given me the original no, acknowledging the ruling on appeal and saying: "The Office of Nuclear Energy will correspond with you directly with a response to your request. If you need further assistance, please contact Dan Butler." This was someone with whom I would have many conversations in the months ahead as I sought to obtain the information I had been promised. [17]

Each week I would call Butler, who turned out to be a PR guy for the DOE, asking him what was happening. In an early conversation, he excoriated me for "going the Freedom of Information route. We would have given you the stuff if you asked." (*Sure* they would have.) He claimed, week after week, that the documents would be mailed out "soon." Then one day there was a change: DOE had decided, Butler told me, that the material was "pre-decisional" so there would be no release after all. What was pre-decisional? The "decisions" about what the impacts would be if there were accidents involving the plutonium-fueled space probes were not in "final" form. So the government, said the DOE representative, would not be providing me with any of the material. Period. [18]

My journalistic juices were flowing now—clearly, I had struck a nerve. And I was outraged over DOE's subversion of the Freedom of Information Act. Just following the formal FOIA route was not going to get anywhere.

To do something about what was happening, to bring pressure to bear on government refusing to abide by the law, I went the media and political routes. In a syndicated newspaper column I write, I told about the situation. Traces of plutonium had just been found in the water supply of New York. "We may soon be looking skyward to worry about new sources of danger from this manmade element," I said, telling about the two planned plutonium-fueled space probe shuttle missions and then the story that I've told here: my reading the article in the *Energy Insider*, the fee waiver obstacle and then the flat-out refusal of the government to release the information. "Last week I was advised that DOE, joined by NASA, flatly refuse to release it," I wrote in the August 1985 column. "Our government is covering up schemes which could cause serious loss of life."[19]

The potential problems of using nuclear powered space devices were—and still are—bigger than any one reporter, and I sent out a press release to the media nationally outlining my situation and urging other journalists to jump in and also seek the information.

The Fund for Open Information asked me to be the speaker at an annual dinner they were sponsoring and talk about this refusal by government to comply with FOIA. I did. I urged the audience to send complaints to members of Congress, the DOE and NASA. I sought assistance from U.S. senators and representatives from my home state of New York. Letters were sent by several of them to then U.S. Energy Secretary John Herrington.

By September, the pressure appeared to be finally breaking the cover-up. I started getting telephone calls from the DOE to "hold on." The claim was that a "special" DOE-NASA team was putting an FOIA reply together. In October 1985, in the mail one day, came several hundred pages of government documents.

How Disaster Could Occur:
Let NASA Count the Ways

It turned out that 49.25 pounds of plutonium, according to the documents, was to be sent up on the Galileo mission to Jupiter. The International Solar-Polar Mission (subsequently renamed the Ulysses mission), to have a space probe orbit the Sun, would have 24.2 pounds of plutonium on it.

The documents were nearly all *completed* in 1984— putting the lie to the claim the data was pre-decisional. The principal document was *Updated Safety Analysis Report for the Galileo Mission and the International Solar-Polar Mission*. It said on its cover that it was "Prepared for the U.S. Department of Energy" by General Electric. The corporation which was the government contractor to build the plutonium-fueled generators had also been given the assignment of somehow objectively analyzing the risks.[20]

This report started by telling—in detail—how the shuttle could explode, and how the plutonium could be dispersed as a result. As with Cassini, launch mishaps were described as the initial problem.

> Launch vehicle accidents that occur on the launch pad or during launch up to the time the STS [Space Transportation System, what the shuttle was often dubbed in the report] clears the launch tower (t = +7 sec.) are probably the most critical from the viewpoint of potential nuclear fuel release. Because of the large quantities of liquid propellants involved and the proximity of the nuclear payload, most launch pad accidents result in explosions of a magnitude that are very severe in terms of their effect on the nuclear payload.[21]

There were concerns about "overpressurization" of the fuel tanks of liquid oxygen and liquid hydrogen resulting in a launch explosion. Of special worry: "Tipover" and "Pushover" accidents. A "Tipover" accident would occur if only one of the two solid rocket boosters—acronymed SRBs—the reddish brown-colored rockets attached to the sides of the shuttle, ignited. If one SRB ignited

> but the other SRB fails to ignite then the Shuttle will tip over in a partial sidewise motion onto the launch pad. Impacting on the pad, the Shuttle will topple over the edge of the mobile launch platform. On reaching the deck of the mobile platform, the ET [external tank] will break at the intertank region and the SRB's will break at their segments. The LOX [liquid oxygen] and LH2 [liquid hydrogen] from the ruptured tanks will mix on the ground surface and explode.[22]

A "Pushover" accident would be caused by both SRB's not igniting, and then "the Shuttle will be pushed over or toppled forward....The ET would impact first, with the result that the LOX tank would break off and fall about 95 feet into the flame trench. Quickly following the broken LOX tank into the trench would be a large quantity of liquid hydrogen from the ruptured LH^2 tank."[23]

It was quickly becoming obvious that taking a ride on a shuttle was not like flying on a 747. Going on a shuttle was comparable to taking a ride on a gargantuan Roman candle firecracker. Being a "Journalist In Space" was vanishing as an interest.

Then there were the ways the shuttle could explode after launch, such as a "Premature SRB Separation." Here, if the solid rocket booster separated from the main rocket too early, it "generally will lead to either tumbling (cartwheel) flight or to separation at the forward attach point or both."[24]

A major concern with explosions was a secondary explosion of the rocket that would be propelling both the Galileo and Ulysses space probes, a liquid-fueled Centaur rocket, also the propulsion source for Cassini. The report devoted pages to the Centaur, which would be sitting in the shuttle's cargo bay, exploding on its own, or the main shuttle rocket, the SSME (for Space Shuttle Main Engine) blowing up and causing the

Centaur to explode. An "explosive failure of a SSME or an explosion anywhere in the aft end" of the shuttle would cause "serious consequences" due to a "major shrapnel hazard," said the report in describing one accident, an "SSME Compartment Explosion." The flying shrapnel could puncture the Centaur and cause it to blow up. "Centaur accidents and the SSME compartment explosion represent...most critical failure response modes," said the report. [25]

And on and on it went. More graphic descriptions. Plenty of charts including one called "Explosion Yields Used for Space Shuttle Accidents" and another "Shock Wave Characteristics for Space Shuttle Accidents." [26]

As to the consequences if plutonium were released in an accident, there was a separate 241-page report called "Nuclear Risk Analysis Document" also done by General Electric.

DOE and/or NASA personnel had evidently spent considerable time and bottles of Liquid Paper® before sending this report to me because all the figures that had been there for the numbers of people expected to be affected had been whited-out and "Exemp. 1" hand-written in. "Exemp. 1"—meaning the first exemption of the Freedom of Information Act, the bar on disclosing matters of national security—had been written over what had been totals for items like: "Dose Through Inhaled Vapor-Lung Expected No. of Persons," "Dose Through External Radiation (Fallout)-Whole Body Expected No. of Persons," "Dose Through External Radiation(Ground Release)-Whole Body Expected No. of Persons," "Radioactivity Released In Shallow Water. Dose Through Salt Water Fish or Shellfish Expected Number of Persons," "Radioactivity Released In Shallow Water. Dose Through Fresh Water Supply. Expected Number of Persons." [27]

As to why these numbers were being censored, there was a covering letter sent with the documents from James J. Lombardo, Acting Director, Division of Special Applications,

Office of Defense Energy Projects and Special Applications,
Office of Nuclear Energy. He wrote:

> Exemption 1 of the FOIA provides that an agency may exempt
> from disclosure information specifically authorized under crite-
> ria established by an Executive Order to be kept secret in the
> interest of the national defense or foreign policy and that are in
> fact properly classified pursuant to such Executive Order.
> Portions of Volume III are being withheld pursuant to
> Exemption 1 of the FOIA. The information deleted on certain
> pages of Volume III pertain to the safeguarding of classified
> population exposure data and the reference to geographical
> sites, and is classified...It has been determined that release of
> the information could reasonably be expected to cause damage
> to the national security.[28]

Now that, I thought, was just a hell of a thing: deleting the
number of people to be affected by the plutonium in the event
of an accident on grounds of national security. The numbers
should be disclosed, I felt, on the grounds of national *insecurity*.

And speaking of numbers, this report was my first exposure
to estimates of the likelihood of an accident involving a space
nuclear mission. For Galileo and the Ulysses mission—from
prelaunch through launch and "early ascent," "final ascent,"
orbit and so on, the numbers were preceded by a decimal point
and then two or three zeroes. It was a .00079 chance for either
a Galileo or Ulysses launch accident, a .0043 chance for an
accident once in orbit, etc.[29]

A second report I received a few weeks later done by NASA
and its Jet Propulsion Laboratory insisted: "The launch of the
Galileo Payload would involve a very small risk of releasing
Plutonium-238 into the environment because of the possibility
of malfunction of the Space Shuttle. This risk would be small
due to the high reliability inherent in the design of the Space
Shuttle."[30]

It was in this report that I first came across the "U.S. History of RTG Power Source Use," the listing of earlier plutonium-fueled space device missions and their records, which acknowledged that there were three failures out of a total twenty-two flights involving RTGs up to then. First the SNAP-9A accident in 1964 and the admission that it "burned up on reentry" into the Earth's atmosphere. Then the SNAP-19 accident in 1968 in which the "heat source [was] retrieved." And then the incident involving the SNAP-27 on board Apollo 13 and the statement that "in conjunction with the safe recovery of the three astronauts, the SNAP-27 was successfully targeted to deposit intact in the Tonga Trench in the South Pacific, where it is effectively isolated from man's environment."[31] Surely, I thought, no 100% safety record, despite the claims that the likelihood of an accident was extremely low. And what did the claim that the South Pacific "is effectively isolated from man's environment" reflect about NASA's environmental consciousness?

NASA, I had begun to learn, was no special exception from other governmental bureaucracies. It and DOE were like other government agencies I had encountered through the years, given to insensitivity, duplicity and arrogance—and having their review functions done by the very corporations that were supposed to be working for the government, not visa-versa.

Well, I kind of got what I wanted after nearly a year and I began to mull over how to use it. Clearly, an enormous danger was involved. Accidents *could* happen, and in a variety of ways, and lethal plutonium could be released and impact on life, it was being admitted. As the "Nuclear Risk Analysis" document stated: "As a result of the mission failure evaluations, several situations have been identified that present conditions severe enough to breach some of the fuel capsules allowing release of some of the plutonium fuel."[32]

"Space isotope nuclear systems might release radioactivity into the environment under certain postulated accident conditions, resulting in risks to the population in the form of radiation doses and associated health effects," it acknowledged.

Still, I was troubled by the probability issue. High risk, low probability—that was the NASA line, and still is. I now had learned of the myriad ways that the space shuttles could blow up. Importantly, the Galileo and Ulysses missions were to be the first nuclear missions for the shuttle. Yet, there had been twenty-four shuttle flights up to that point and...no accident so far. People had to find out about the potential dangers of the planned Galileo and Ulysses missions; the information I had obtained had to get out. But I wondered how to frame it considering that the likelihood of an accident was said to be so remote. A catastrophic shuttle accident was said by NASA to be about one-in-100,000 as far as I could determine from the jumble of probability figures. On the other hand, there was the listing of the twenty-two earlier U.S. plutonium space missions out of which three failed. That was not a one-in-100,000 or one-in-a-million situation. And the plutonium flights were being readied, including one to be flown by the shuttle Challenger in May, 1986.

Meanwhile, I got a contract to write a second book about land-based nuclear power—and quick. The lights on Long Island, New York, where I live, went off for more than a week after Hurricane Gloria struck in Fall 1985 and that was being perceived widely by Long Islanders as due to the ineptness of the area's utility, the Long Island Lighting Company, in re-establishing service. LILCO, meanwhile, was in the process of building a nuclear power plant, Shoreham, a story of—as the New York State Public Service Commission concluded—"pervasive mismanagement." I had been reporting for some time on the mess at Shoreham, which was to be the first of seven to eleven nuclear plants LILCO wanted to build to become, from

Long Island, the wholesaler of nuclear-generated electricity of the U.S. Northeast. Barney Rosset, head of Grove Press, sitting by a kerosene lantern in his blacked-out East Hampton home, phoned one night and asked me to write a book—right away—about LILCO. While working on that book, which became *Power Crazy*,[33] I kept mulling over how to handle the nuclear power-in-space story.

NASA: Scientific Agency or Gambling Addict?

I was on the way to teach my course on investigative reporting on January 28, 1986 when, over the car radio, came the report about the shuttle Challenger blowing up. I stopped at a P.C. Richard appliance store in Riverhead, New York and there, in front of scores of television sets, I saw that horrible image which has since become imprinted on all our minds.

As I watched that fiery explosion on the TV sets, what I was thinking was that as tragic and terrible as the Challenger catastrophe was, it could have been much, much worse. It could have happened on the Challenger's next scheduled mission in May, four months later—with a plutonium-fueled space probe on board. Then, I thought, looking at those TV sets, it wouldn't have been seven astronauts dying but many more people.

I went immediately to a pay telephone and called an editor at the *Nation* magazine with whom I had been working on a story on LILCO and Shoreham. Did the folks at the *Nation*, I asked, know about the planned nuclear shuttle missions ahead, know that the Challenger's next mission was a plutonium-fueled space probe mission? They did not. I was asked to assist in the preparation of a *Nation* editorial on the subject.

The following day I called Butler of DOE to check on whether, in the wake of the Challenger disaster, the plans were still underway to proceed with the plutonium flights. "Sure," he replied, although he said there might be a postponement while an investigation into the accident was conducted. I commented that the accident would have been far more serious if plutonium had been aboard the Challenger. "I don't know," Butler said scornfully. There was not a bit of concern expressed.[34]

The government intended, Butler made very clear, to push ahead with the two plutonium shuttle flights even though the odds of a catastrophic shuttle accident had just been shown not to be anything like one-in-100,000 but more like one-in-twenty-five. After all, it was the twenty-fifth shuttle launch and disaster had struck. In fact, NASA was soon to change the odds of a catastrophic shuttle accident to one-in-78 and later to one-in-76, where they are today.[35]

One-in-100,000 to suddenly odds nothing like that. In science, one only knows real probabilities through empiricism, a sufficient number of experiments. It had become apparent then that NASA had been basing its projection of likelihood and probability on insufficient evidence and a lot of self-interest and wishful thinking. And that continues to this day.

"The Lethal Shuttle" was the title of the *Nation* editorial. It ran on the front page and opened with, "Far more than seven people could have died if the explosion that destroyed Challenger had occurred during the next launch, which had been played for May." The editorial asserted that "an explosion like the one that disintegrated Challenger" could have dispersed plutonium if the accident happened on the May flight. It related my effort to get information under the Freedom of Information Act on the planned 1986 plutonium-fueled space probe shots. They had been postponed, as Butler suspected, and the editorial said, "That suspension should be made permanent."[36]

Another *Nation* editorial followed three weeks later, also running on the front page, entitled "Plutonium Cover-Up." It told of how "if anything happened to the shuttle or the Centaur" on the two planned plutonium shuttle flights "the plutonium would be broadcast to do its deadly damage." And it noted the hearings that had just begun on the plutonium-fueled shuttle missions by a House Subcommittee on Oversight and Investigations chaired by Congressman Edward Markey of Massachusetts. "So far the agencies involved have been stalling, if not stonewalling," stated the editorial. The DOE "won't declassify" a study for the subcommittee detailing the consequences expected from the dispersion of plutonium in an accident on the missions. "One official said the study was being kept secret because it discussed the potential worldwide distribution of plutonium particles and their effect on unnamed countries. Markey is pressing for declassification, which some officials say may come by the end of the month. Whether it does or not, Congress should conduct a full-scale investigation."[37]

Congress never did conduct a full investigation into the dangers of the Galileo and Ulysses missions, and has balked, as well, at conducting probes into the Cassini nuclear space flight or other nuclear space missions.

The pieces in the *Nation* also sparked a touch of media interest, just a touch, primarily the alternative media. Listener-supported New York City radio station WBAI was the most active in following the issue. (And that's also the situation today.) I was beginning to encounter the marked disinterest of most of mainstream media in doing reporting on the issue of nuclear power in space, which continues to this day.

There was no way of avoiding a major governmental inquiry, of course, of the Challenger disaster—an accident that stunned the nation, indeed the world. It became an icon for technological failure and cast a pall on the U.S. space program.

A presidential commission was promptly empaneled to examine the causes of the Challenger accident. Headed by former U.S. Secretary of State William P. Rogers, its vice chairman was Neil Armstrong. Astronaut Sally Ride, the first

U.S. woman to go into space, was another member, and also on the commission was a Nobel Prize-winning physicist, Dr. Richard P. Feynman.

It was Feynman who, at a commission hearing in front of TV cameras, showed with visible simplicity what NASA had done wrong by launching Challenger on a cold morning.

Into a glass of ice water, Dr. Feynman dropped a piece of rubber from the O-rings, the seals between sections of the space shuttle's solid rocket boosters. The O-rings had to stay flexible to work, otherwise fuel could leak out and an explosion result. He demonstrated that cold caused the rubber to lose resiliency, thus the Challenger disaster. "It was a simple demonstration that cut directly through jargon and obfuscation to the heart of the matter," wrote James Gleick, the author of *Genius: The Life and Science of Richard Feynman*.[38]

Gleick went on:

> But Mr. Feynman's more profound contribution to our understanding of the disaster was even subtler: his independent investigation of how the space agency calculates risk. He ridiculed the agency's estimates that the chances of disaster on each flight were about 1 in 100,000—a number that its engineers knew was a product of wishful thinking and fraudulent arithmetic. NASA now more honestly estimates the chances of catastrophe on any shuttle flight to be 1 in 78. That's not much less than the chance of dealing the queen of spades off the top of a deck of cards—a staggeringly high risk for a disaster that would cost billions of dollars and the lives of the crew. But where it matters most, Mr. Feynman's legacy has turned to dust: The agency launches shuttles anyway, bending its own rules. This is surely the gambler's self-deception.[39]

Feynman wrote his own book, *What Do You Care What Other People Think?*, covering his experiences on the commission investigating the Challenger accident. A major emphasis in it: faulty NASA oddsmaking, and the California Institute of

Technology physics professor tied that into plutonium-fueled space missions.

"Fantastic Figures" is the chapter in which Feynman, a former Manhattan Project scientist, tells of challenging NASA on its claim prior to the Challenger disaster that the chances of a catastrophic shuttle accident were one-in-100,000. He related confronting a NASA range safety officer at its Kennedy Space Center. "That means you could fly the shuttle *every day* for an average of *300 years* between accidents—every day, one flight, for 300 years—which is absolutely crazy!"[40]

"Yes I know," he said the officer, a Mr. Ullian, replied, and then added, "I moved my number up to 1 in 1,000." Meanwhile, wrote Feynman, "a new problem came up: the Jupiter probe, Galileo, was going to use a power supply that runs on heat generated by radioactivity. If the shuttle carrying Galileo failed, radioactivity could be spread over a large area. So the argument continued: NASA kept saying 1 in 100,000 and Mr. Ullian kept saying 1 in 1,000, at best." Also, Ullian said he "never could get through" to a NASA higher-up to "find out how NASA got its figure of 1 in 100,000."[41]

A *Science* magazine article on Feynman as a commission member jousting with NASA on its oddsmaking began with his declaration that "'when playing Russian roulette, the fact that the first shot got off safely is little comfort for the next'....Feynman was stunned to learn that NASA rejects the historical data and claims the actual risk of a crash is only 1 in 100,000. This is the official figure as published in *Space Shuttle Data for Planetary Mission RTG Safety Analysis* on 15 February 1985. It means NASA thinks it could launch the shuttle, as is, every day for the next 280 years and expect not one equipment-based disaster. Feynman concluded that NASA 'for whatever purpose...exaggerates the reliability of its product to the point of fantasy.'"[42]

The Odd Man Out vs.
Public Relations by the Numbers

Science pursued the NASA odds issue itself, interviewing NASA Chief Engineer Morton Silveira on the one-in-100,000 likelihood estimate. He said the "figure was hatched for the Department of Energy...for use in a risk analysis DOE puts together on radioactive hazards on some devices carried aboard the shuttle. These are plutonium-driven power units for deep space probes, such as Galileo and Ulysses. To reassure the public, the government must certify that the shuttle can take off from Cape Canaveral without dumping plutonium on the beaches and orange groves of Florida. DOE and General Electric, supplier of the power units, write up a detailed risk analysis before launch."[43]

As to how NASA derived such a figure, *Science*, the leading journal of the U.S. science and technology establishment, the publication of the American Association for the Advancement of Science, quoted a "NASA official" as saying: "'They get all the top engineers together down at Marshall Space Flight Center and ask them to give their best judgement of the reliability of all the components involved.' The engineers' adjectival descriptions are then converted to numbers. For example, [NASA Chief Engineer] Silveira says, 'frequent' equals 1 in 100; 'reasonably probable' equals 1 in 1,000; 'occasional' equals 1 in 10,000; and 'remote' equals 1 in 100,000. When all the judgements are summed up and averaged, the risk of a shuttle booster explosion was found to be 1 in 100,000. That number was then handed over to DOE for further processing. To no one's surprise, the overall risk of a plutonium disaster was found to be terribly, almost inexpressibly low. That is, 1 in 10,000,000, give or take a syllable. 'The process,' says one [Rogers Commission] consultant who clashed with NASA, 'is positively medieval.' He thinks Feynman hit the nail exactly on the head."[44]

The commission, in the end, issued a report that was soft on NASA. "Missing from the final version, for example," noted the *New York Times*, "are recommendations about such critical issues as whether the space agency should limit the crews of shuttle flights to...professional astronauts, how much time the agency should take in preparing and inspecting space shuttles between launchings and where blame should lie for the creation of an atmosphere that engineers say made them afraid to delay any liftoff."[45] Rogers rebuffed suggestions that criminal charges be considered "against officials of NASA and its contractors who knew of the life-threatening flaws in the space shuttle's solid rocket boosters," noted *Newsday*. Rogers said this would "not be in the national interest."[46]

Dr. Feynman issued his own minority-of-one report. The shuttle, he wrote, "flies in a relatively unsafe condition, with a chance of failure on the order of a percent. (It is difficult to be more accurate.) Official [NASA] management, on the other hand, claims to believe the probability of failure is a thousand times less. One reason for this may be an attempt to assure the government of NASA's perfection and success in order to ensure the supply of funds."[47]

"Let us make recommendations to ensure that NASA officials deal in a world of reality," Feynman continued. "NASA owes it to the citizens from whom it asks support to be frank, honest, and informative, so that these citizens can make the wisest decisions for the use of their limited resources. For a successful technology, reality must take precedence over public relations, for Nature cannot be fooled."[48]

Feynman died of cancer in 1988. Meanwhile, in 1987, NASA rescheduled its Galileo and Ulysses missions.

And it was back to PR over reality and risky operations which NASA, and DOE, hoped would continue to beat the true odds, and continue to fool nature.

NASA Withholds the *Right* Stuff
(Information)—Again

With the rescheduling of the Galileo and Ulysses launches, my FOIA quest began anew. I wrote to the DOE and NASA, cited my prior FOIA request, the successful appeal, having finally obtained the information and then the Challenger accident. "We presume that since that accident," I wrote, "DOE and NASA as well as DOE and NASA contractors have done more intense analysis of the possibilities and consequences of an accident involving the dispersal of plutonium from the plutonium-fueled space probes to be sent up aboard shuttles on the Ulysses and Galileo missions because projections in the earlier documents of a shuttle explosion were that it was an extremely unlikely event."[49]

I asked for "all reports and data on the possibilities and consequences of release and dispersal of plutonium if there is an accident involving the plutonium-fueled space probes," and this time I also called for "any information available on your studies about power source alternatives to the plutonium-fueled generating system which is to be used on the Ulysses and Galileo missions."[50]

The trouble I had before in getting information was a prelude to the new difficulties. DOE this time turned to lying. I received a letter from DOE's Chief of FOI and Privacy Acts citing the documents I eventually received in 1985 and flatly stating that "since that time no further studies/reports have been completed on the subject."[51] Proof that this was bogus came in a NASA letter-to-the-editor the following year to the *Nation* complaining about my stories and claiming that the government had been busy studying the issue of using nuclear power in space in the wake of the Challenger accident and listing new safety studies including two completed in 1986 in which DOE was involved.[52]

NASA replied to my new FOIA request after four months—although FOIA specifies that the government agency approached must respond within ten days. "It is taking us longer than 10 working days to respond to the FOIA request received in this office," declared NASA. "Please be assured that your request will be answered in turn."

Well, years went by—with me all along objecting strenuously to the lack of response.

The new FOIA stonewall I was hitting with the federal government while trying to get information about the use of nuclear power in space and specifically about the Galileo and Ulysses plutonium-fueled missions appeared insurmountable. I was getting a "Nuclear Shuffle," to use the headline for a story I wrote about the situation for *Our Right To Know*, the publication of the Fund for Open Information and Accountability.[53] Both DOE and NASA weren't providing a thing under FOIA.

Instead, NASA made a public mailing in November 1987 of a *Supplemental Draft Environmental Impact Statement for the Galileo and Ulysses Missions* and the following month held a press conference to announce that Galileo would be launched in 1989 and Ulysses in 1990.

Meanwhile, NASA had added a new wrinkle to the Galileo flight. It had eliminated the Centaur rocket after concerns were raised by astronauts about carrying the volatile liquid-fueled rocket in the cargo bay of the shuttle. The shuttle astronauts "began to shy away from riding" with the volatile Centaur "in the cargo compartment," relates former Jet Propulsion Laboratory director Bruce Murray.[54] Indeed, NASA, in one internal document Markey obtained in his Congressional inquiry, described the Centaur as a "veritable bomb" on a shuttle flight. In its place, NASA planned to use a solid-fueled Inertial Upper Stage rocket, acronymed IUS.

The problem with this, however, was that the IUS did not have the power to get the Galileo space probe to its final destination of Jupiter. On the Galileo mission as originally planned, the Centaur was to take the space probe directly from Earth to Jupiter. So NASA devised, for the first time for one of its spacecraft, a plan to use the Earth as a target of a "slingshot maneuver"—a risky set of maneuvers in which the Galileo probe and its 49.25 pounds of plutonium were to conduct two "flybys" of Earth, one in 1990 and the other in 1992.

NASA PR representatives stressed to reporters that planetary "flybys" had been done before—but they did not make clear that this was the *first* time the Earth was the planet at which a NASA space device would be hurtling, and this space device, the Galileo, had more plutonium than had ever been used in a space device, up until that point. What was to be the first Earth "flyby" was still to come: one done by the non-nuclear Giotto space probe of the European Space Agency. Giotto was to do a "flyby" of Earth in July 1990 but at a healthy distance of 14,375 miles above the planet.[55]

Meanwhile, NASA was arranging Galileo's first "flyby," for December 1990, at an altitude of 600 miles and a 1992 pass at just 185 miles high.[56]

The *Supplemental Draft Environmental Impact Statement for the Galileo and Ulysses Missions* admitted: "During the second Earth flyby...there is a remote but finite chance that the spacecraft may re-enter the Earth's atmosphere. Based on preliminary analysis, the Galileo project expects that this accident scenario will be deemed not credible...Therefore, the project estimates the chance of inadvertent reentry to be less than one chance in one million."[57]

Here we went again...NASA in its wisdom deeming an accident scenario "not credible" and again offering high numbers—one-in-a-million—to claim all would be safe.

But as for the real basis for what it planned, the unvarnished documents I was seeking through FOIA, it was no dice.

Meanwhile, a citizens movement was emerging to challenge the use of nuclear power in space. In 1986, right after the first *Nation* articles had appeared, I had gotten a telephone call from Bruce Gagnon, coordinator of the Florida Coalition for Peace & Justice. Being in Florida, on the front line of the U.S. nuclear-in-space program, he and his members wanted to begin organizing against it. He and the Florida Coalition for Peace & Justice did just that, subsequently joining in with other organizations in the U.S., especially Citizens for Peace in Space, a group based in Colorado Springs, Colorado, the headquarters of the U.S. Space Command, which was challenging the use of weaponry in space. Later the effort would become international with the founding of the Global Network Against Weapons & Nuclear Power in Space.

Gagnon and the Florida Coalition began demonstrations against the Galileo and Ulysses missions at the Kennedy Space Center. They also applied political pressure and sought legal redress in the form of a federal lawsuit seeking to stop the Galileo flight brought on behalf of the Florida Coalition by the Christic Institute of Washington, D.C.

The Galileo launch was set for October 1989. And lo and behold, in April 1989, I received a letter from NASA stating: "We are sorry for the long delay in responding to your Freedom of Information request dated February 7, 1987. If you would still like this office to process your request, please notify us."[58] Now that was nerve, I thought, considering my protests during the period.

I sent a blunt reply citing "your more than two-year cover-up of information relating to NASA's plan to launch space probes carrying the deadly dangerous substance plutonium later this year and in 1990....Of course, I am still interested. As you are aware, I'm sure, I have been complaining publicly about the suppression of this information by NASA for the two-year-plus period. What is involved here is a rape of the

Freedom of Information Act. Under the act, requests are to be handled promptly. Two years-plus is not prompt. Further, this request concerns an issue which can involve life and death for thousands or tens of thousands or even more human beings. And most importantly, the Galileo mission is scheduled for launch in just five months. Obviously, your aim was to stonewall my request and make it moot. At your rate of inaction, if material ever gets to me, it will be *after* the Galileo launch." I reiterated what I sought and elaborated on details "so there is no confusion."[60]

I also sent a copy of the letter to then NASA Administrator Richard Truly with a note about how "the enclosed relates to an outrageous cover-up by your agency."[61] I wanted to make sure that the very top of the agency was aware of the stonewall I had been forced to overcome to obtain information from NASA through FOIA.

And again, I sought more Congressional help—letters to NASA calling for release of the information I had been seeking under FOIA.

In August 1989, I was leaving for California to receive an award from Project Censored, the media monitoring group, (my articles on nuclear power in space had made its list of the most "under-reported," "best-censored" stories for the third year running), when I received a packet from NASA with a group of documents. "This is a partial response to your letter," said NASA.[61] It sure was partial. There were none of the documents I had sought about alternatives to plutonium on the Galileo mission.

Still some of what I did receive was damning. I read the documents on the airplane heading to the Project Censored event, which included the first "Project Censored Press Conference"—an opportunity, I felt, to speak about the nuclear-in-space story before other journalists and maybe get it more widely reported. The *Final Safety Analysis Report for the*

Galileo Mission, for example, prepared by the NUS Corporation for NASA, spoke of an explosion at launch involving the massive amounts of liquid fuel that would be present. "Analysis of these accident environments and their probabilities indicate that given an accident, a release of RTG fuel [plutonium] could occur about 8.3 times in 100."[62] This was a far cry from what the NASA PR people had been claiming: that there was virtually no chance of plutonium being released in an accident on launch.

Another important piece of information, which revealed the scale of what was at stake, came in a GE report prepared for NASA, also titled *Final Safety Analysis Report for the Galileo Mission*. It said that only after the Galileo probe flew past Earth on its second "flyby" and attained an "escape trajectory" would the threat to "the Earth's population" from the 49.25 pounds of plutonium be over. "At this point," said the report, "with a successful and correct burn of the IUS [Inertial Upper Stage rocket], escape of the spacecraft from the Earth's gravitational pull will be effected, and the RTG's will no longer present a potential risk to the Earth's population."[64]

I also received, from NASA's Jet Propulsion Laboratory, a thick document called *Earth Avoidance Study Report*. This was a real beaut reflecting the concern, at least of some NASA scientists, about using the Earth as a target of a "flyby" for a nuclear-fueled space device.

The scientists struggled with the notion that having Galileo do the "flyby" at a higher altitude than 600 miles and then 185 miles over the Earth might be safer.

"The idea is that presumably there is an inverse relationship between the altitude of the Earth flyby and the probability of reentry," they wrote. However, having Galileo fly at a higher, safer altitude above the Earth and still get the "gravity assist" to make it to Jupiter could not be. "With these alterations, the mission would not be possible," said the report. "The spacecraft cannot carry enough propellant to make up for the energy shortfall from raising the Earth flyby altitudes."[64]

They also said that the "flyby" of Earth, although new, would be "identical in both concept and implementation to that used in previous JPL missions" involving other planets. "The fact that the Earth is a 'target' for this mission doesn't introduce any different issues other than the safety issues addressed in this report."[65]

Reading these documents on the airplane flight west, it was so clear why NASA had not wanted me to obtain them through FOIA. These were the kind of things NASA and DOE did not want people to know.

Challenging Galileo

Still, where was the data about alternatives to plutonium? Where was the information about the alternatives to using a deadly nuclear substance on a space mission?

That was a key issue in the lawsuit of the Florida Coalition for Peace & Justice and the Christic Institute, joined by the Foundation on Economic Trends of Washington, D.C. A restraining order was sought to stop the Galileo mission, charging that NASA had not fully considered the alternatives to its plan to use a plutonium-fueled power system, as required under the National Environmental Policy Act.

The mission was also challenged for constituting a huge threat to the environment and public health because of the possibility of an accident dispersing plutonium.

Dr. Morgan filed an affidavit opposing the nuclear-powered mission. He stressed that "I enthusiastically support efforts to study all bodies in our solar system and of our nearest stars," but said there must be an understanding of the great risks involved in using nuclear power in space. Dr. Morgan noted that his years of working in the nuclear field—including the Manhattan Project— did not give him faith in the government or nuclear industry when it came to assessing the real dangers of radioactivity. "During the 58 years I have worked with ionizing radiation, I have seen so many mistakes, misstatements, coverups and untrue statements by members of our government agencies (e.g. AEC, DOE, NRC, NASA, etc.) and by representatives of the nuclear industry that I seek independent evaluations of radiation risks before I trust their accuracy."[66]

Morgan recalled how "the day before the U.S. space rocket carrying...2.1 pounds of Plutonium-238"—the mission involving the SNAP-9A—"was scheduled to blast off, some of my AEC [U.S. Atomic Energy Commission] friends assured me the risk of an abortive mission and Earth reentry was one chance in 10 million. I laughed at them because this was essentially a zero risk of reentry. As it turned out, the risk was one [in one]—for the rocket and its cargo of 2.1 pounds of Plutonium-238 was incinerated over the Indian Ocean in April 1964."[67]

Dr. Morgan went on:

> We, of course, do not know how much of this Plutonium-238 resides in persons now living or dead and in children to be born...By comparison, if Galileo incinerated its 50 pounds of Plutonium-238, the risk to the world population would be over 20 times greater. To make matters especially bad, Plutonium-238 deposited in some body organs is essentially permanent...Further, there are more radiation-induced cancers induced per rem at low doses (especially for alpha emitters) than at high doses. The causes of a cancer at low doses may 'hide' but this cannot remove the guilt of those responsible.[68]

Michio Kaku, in an affidavit, spoke of the two planned "fly-bys" which "by NASA's own admission pose by far the greatest danger of a serious radiological accident"[69] and stated:

> Because the Galileo needs to attain a velocity of 33,000 miles per hour, it must execute a highly unorthodox and potentially dangerous flight path: it must fly all the way past Venus, and

then whip around the Earth, and then whip around the Earth a second time, even before it begins its voyage to Jupiter…If the space probe misses by even a factor of one part in a trillion, it may hit the Earth's atmosphere and disintegrate. Some of the craft will disintegrate in the atmosphere; and some will impact on the ground. By most scientific accounts, nothing known to science can withstand a direct impact at 33,000 miles per hour on solid rock.[70]

And he criticized NASA's claim of there being little chance of an accident happening. "As the insurance companies are well aware, the probability of a booster rocket failure is routinely 1%," stated Dr. Kaku. The estimate by NASA of there being only a one-in-10 million chance of a "flyby" accident "is not credible and is probably a carry-over from the pre-Challenger methodology."[71]

"The bureaucrats at NASA," charged Kaku, "have made scientists into gamblers, a role for which they have little experience."[72]

Bill McInnis, former NASA manager of risk assessment, senior staff engineer and assistant to the chief engineer at NASA, was deeply involved in assisting the Christic Institute with the lawsuit. He had become extremely concerned over the way space shuttle safety was being handled—particularly engine testing—and came to the conclusion that "we were going to kill people and we were going to kill the space program."[73] So after twenty-two years he resigned from NASA and became a whistleblower, speaking out on what he described as a continuing disregard for safety—even after the Challenger disaster. He moved to Washington and served as consultant to the Christic Institute in the litigation. In an affidavit he filed in the suit, he said technical problems with the shuttle and a disinterest in safety at NASA could easily result in catastrophe.

NASA, on the other hand, insisted that it was highly unlikely that the environment or the health of people on

Earth would be impacted by the Galileo mission. As John R. Casani, the project manager for Galileo at JPL, stated in an affidavit for the government, "considerable attention has always been given to the packaging of the plutonium in the RTGs to insure safety. The RTGs are designed to have the maximum chance to survive mission aborts, reentry and ground impact, without release of the plutonium."[74]

And as for the lawsuit's claim that NASA had not considered the alternatives for plutonium power on Galileo, he and other witnesses for the government insisted at length that there was no substitute.

Casani stated:

> Batteries and fuel cells were considered as a possible power source but were rejected because then no known form—or indeed presently no known form—of stored chemical energy could provide the sustained power requirement for a long-duration mission to Jupiter...Solar options, such as photovoltaic cells and a wide range of other solar types of power sources, were also considered in these studies. The solar options were all found to have serious deficiencies, specifically their excessive weight, their susceptibility to radiation damage in Jupiter's magnetosphere, and their poor performance in the low sunlight intensity and low temperatures at Jupiter's distance from the sun.[75]

Also in his sworn testimony, Casani declared: "Early in the Galileo project, a solar-power option for the Galileo spacecraft was examined by JPL. Even though solar-cell and solar-array technologies had continued to evolve, these power sources could not satisfy the Galileo mission requirements. Since that time, the solar power option for the Galileo spacecraft has been reexamined on two occasions with the same conclusion: solar power was not a viable option for the Galileo mission."[76]

The judge, Oliver Gasch, discounted the concerns about the environment and public health posed by the Galileo mission. As to an alternative to its plutonium-fueled system, he took

NASA at its word that there was no alternative to plutonium for producing the 560 watts of electricity needed to run instruments on the Galileo probe. "In fact, currently there is no known alternative power source which is feasible for the mission," the judge declared in his October 10, 1989 decision.[77]

An appeal was brought. Forty-three members of the Green Party in the German Parliament filed a support brief in the appeal. Their "motion to intervene" stated that "as members of the Bundestag we are concerned that the Galileo mission...constitutes both potential and actual violations of the Treaty on Principles Governing the Activities of States in the Exploration and Use of Outer Space" of which their country and the U.S. were signatories.[78]

They declared:

> The potential violation of the Outer Space Treaty is the harmful contamination of the environment of Germany by the release of plutonium from the Galileo mission...As graphically demonstrated to the people of Germany by the Chernobyl accident, such releases can drastically affect people far from the site of the accident. The amount of plutonium on the Galileo mission exceeds the inventory of radioactivity in the Chernobyl reactor at the time of the accident by orders of magnitude.[79]

An affidavit was filed on behalf of the Greens by Dr. Ted Taylor, a former nuclear weapons designer at Los Alamos National Laboratory who worked on nuclear space propulsion in the 1950s and 60s, and a professor of mechanical and aerospace engineering at Princeton University.

Dr. Taylor said that "if accidentally dispersed in the atmosphere, the Plutonium-238 in the power supply for the Galileo spacecraft could render uninhabitable an area several times the area of Germany for more than 100 years...Though the chances of such an accident may be small, the consequences could be cataclysmic...Proceeding with the launch of the Galileo...is highly irresponsible."[80]

The appeal was denied on October 16, 1989.

Two days later, while Christic Institute lawyers were delivering an emergency petition to the U.S. Supreme Court, the Galileo space probe was launched on the space shuttle Atlantis. Meanwhile, in the months up to the launch, The Florida Coalition for Peace & Justice had conducted protests including civil disobedience actions resulting in arrests at the launch site at Cape Canaveral.

Here Comes the Sun

And then, two weeks later, in my post office box in Sag Harbor, New York, I received the response to the other part of my long-pending Freedom of Information Act request: documents telling how solar energy *could have* substituted for plutonium power on Galileo.

I will never forget opening up the envelope and seeing the first page of the 1981 NASA-funded JPL report which began: "Study results indicate that a Galileo Jupiter orbiting mission could be performed with a concentrated solar array power source." There was no question about it. As the introduction to the research began: "Based on the current study, it appears that a Galileo orbiting mission could be performed with a concentrated photovoltaic solar array power source without changing the mission sequence or impacting science objectives."[81]

After pages describing in words and pictures the solar equipment that could be used and how, the report noted that on the Galileo mission there would be "lengthy periods of spacecraft shadowing as it passes behind Jupiter" and "modifications" would be "required in the altitude control, propulsion, and power conditioning systems. However, these modifications neither significantly change the mission sequence nor compromise the mission science objectives." The summary reiterated: "It appears that the Galileo mission could be successfully performed with a concentrated solar array power source."[82]

I must say, nothing that had happened up to then was more outrageous to me than opening up this packet and reading the documents. The tremendous risk of using plutonium power on Galileo, I kept thinking, was never necessary.

Then there was the series of charts with an "Interoffice Memo" from Jet Propulsion Laboratory as a cover page. "The attached charts were presented to," said the memo, but then the details of who they were presented to were deleted. "The impetus for the presentation grew from NASA's interest and concern over the ability to use RTG's in the Post-Challenger era." The series of charts was titled: "Galileo Power Subsystem Solar Array Power Option." They were dated July 1986. One was headed: "Rough Estimates Of Power Subsystem Schedule" and for "Solar Array" said "2-3 Years." For "Battery" it said "3-4 years." In other words, in 1986 NASA's Jet Propulsion Laboratory was saying that in two to three years it would have a solar system ready to substitute for plutonium power on Galileo. It could have a solar system ready—in sufficient time for Galileo's 1989 launch. "The presentation was extremely well received," said the memo. But by whom it was "well received" was censored, whited out.[83]

Then there was a report urging the use of solar photovoltaic systems for deep space probes to save taxpayer money. "Radioisotope Thermoelectric Generators (RTGs) have served as the power source for missions beyond the orbit of Mars. Recent government costing practices have indicated the cost to the user of these power sources will significantly increase. Solar arrays can provide a low cost alternative," said *Interplanetary Exploration—A Challenge For Photovoltaics*. "Budgetary constraints and increased mission complexity...has strained the nation's ability to conduct an effective interplanetary effort."[84]

The report stated:

Within the past few years the cost of RTGs has come under examination. Historically, the cost of the fuel for an RTG power source has been 'subsidized' by DOE, resulting in a relatively low RTG cost to NASA. This policy is presently under review and not yet resolved. Existing estimates of the RTG fuel costs range up to $3,500 per thermal watt. If NASA is required to assume these costs or a significant portion of them, the RTG cost per mission could be prohibitive within the context of a constrained budget.[85]

This NASA-funded report actually concluded that seeking to continue the use of plutonium-fueled RTGs could "jeopardize" the future of space missions. "The need to provide for stability in the U.S. planetary exploration program has been addressed by NASA. The means for achieving this relies on the use of less complex, yet scientifically high priority, low cost missions. The potentially high cost of RTG power sources may jeopardize the viability of this approach," it said. "Photovoltaic solar arrays offer a low cost solution for powering a number of far earth missions."[86]

A 1988 memo from Dudley McConnell, then director of NASA's Propulsion Power and Energy Division, to a variety of NASA and JPL officials said that "there are uncertainties in the supply of Plutonium-238 for civil programs. There is also the specter of a three-fold increase in the price NASA may be charged for Plutonium-238. These are significant threats to NASA's outer planet research program. On the other hand, I understand there have been significant advances in solar-electric conversion capabilities. There may be ways to combine solar-electric and electrochemical systems [fuel cells or batteries] in ways to provide power systems competitive to RTG's in power-to-weight ratio."[87]

After coming home from the post office, I called Lanny Sinkin, the lead attorney for the Christic Institute in the legal challenge to Galileo, and told him about the reports. He was equally outraged. The JPL reports "stand in direct conflict" with the NASA testimony, he noted. "NASA has again been exposed for lying to the public and here it also lied to federal courts," said Sinkin. "We would have won this case if the other side had been honest. We're talking about the central issue in the litigation." Sinkin declared, "If we just had these reports when we needed them."[88]

But clearly, that wasn't the way it was supposed to be.

"It sort of comes as no surprise," said Gagnon, "that all along they knew that solar was a possibility. It's as we've said all along: this was an icebreaker for more and more nuclear space shots. It's obvious that NASA misled everybody by claiming there was no other alternative and that we can't trust anything they're telling us. And, ultimately, we can't trust their safety claims."[89]

"It's fascinating," said Kaku. "All these years and all these claims that they can't use any alternative. This amounts to scientific censorship. We're talking about the fact that NASA deliberately concealed information from the American people. NASA has been deceiving the American people and in a democracy, this is impermissible. They have a hidden agenda."

Bill McInnis, meanwhile, committed suicide. "The October launch of the Galileo mission was extremely demoralizing to Bill," Sinkin wrote in the Christic's Institute newsletter, *Convergence*. "A man of great personal and professional integrity, Bill worked ceaselessly to reform the space program and to protect the planet from disaster. For his efforts, he was blacklisted by NASA and derided as a troublemaker and a boat rocker by many of his former colleagues in the government."[90]

"He had lost almost everything—including his career and many friendships—because he refused to keep silent on government negligence," wrote Sinkin. "A particularly appropriate memorial to Bill would be a letter to your representatives in Congress demanding the end to the use of plutonium in space. This action will advance the work to which Bill was so selflessly dedicated."[91]

Earth to Galileo, Come in, Please

Galileo was on what became a very rocky voyage. "Stray Signal Shuts Down Jupiter Craft," headlined *Newsday* in March 1991. "The United States' complex Galileo spacecraft, en route to Jupiter, unexpectedly shut down all but its essential functions this week, in reaction to a stray electronic signal of an unknown origin in its circuitry," said the article, going on about how "controllers are working to return Galileo to normal operations."[92] In fact, though Galileo was on its way to Jupiter, it was not mentioned by *Newsday* that at the time it was heading back for a second Earth "flyby." And, of course, no mention was made of plutonium being on Galileo nor was there any reference to nuclear power. It took thirteen days for NASA to get the "essential functions" of Galileo back. And they were lost again, in May 1991.

Further, NASA was unable to get Galileo's main antenna to unfurl. "Move Seeks to Salvage Space Mission," was the *New York Times* headline in August 1991. The story told of how Galileo was "crippled by a malfunctioning antenna" and "failure to repair the antenna, a project official said, would be 'devastating' to the most advanced planetary mission now underway."[93] "Galileo Failure May Devastate NASA," was the headline in the *Tampa Tribune*.[94] "Galileo is the most expensive and sophisticated machine ever sent to another world...The problem is Galileo doesn't work," said the story.

"Stuck Antenna Limits Jupiter Probe," headlined *Newsday* in December 1991. "After repeated failures to fix the crippled main antenna aboard the Galileo spacecraft, its handlers are confronting the possibility that the device may be lost for good."[95]

By the following year, NASA was still trying to unfurl the antenna. "Galileo's Tangled Mission," headlined *Newsday* in

June 1992. "Like a ballerina dancing with one toe caught in her tutu, America's talented Galileo space craft is heading for an inelegant *pas de deux* with Jupiter."[96]

In fact, it was coming back for a "flyby" of Earth in just six months—and at only 185 miles in altitude. Fortunately, in this second round of spaceborne nuclear Russian roulette, Galileo did the second "flyby" successfully. And with a burn of its Inertial Upper Stage rocket it headed for Jupiter and finally the 49.25 pounds of plutonium on it "no longer presented a potential threat to the Earth's population," as the GE *Final Safety Analysis Report* had earlier put it.

But mechanical problems with Galileo were to continue. "NASA Will 'Hammer' Probe's Stuck Antenna," headlined *The New York Times* as Galileo was *really* heading for Jupiter. It was a "last ditch effort."[97] It was 1993 and "Scientists Set to Give Up on Galileo's Antenna," reported the *Times*.[98] "Galileo Antenna Resists Latest Repair Attempt," headlined *Space News*.[99] The saga of screw-ups continued through to 1995—just as Galileo was to arrive at Jupiter—its "reel-to-reel tape recorder...stuck in reverse," reported *Space News*.[100]

Galileo eventually did get to Jupiter and did send back signals using a small antenna—amid great ballyhoo by NASA PR. Media joined in the ballyhoo. "Jupiter Rendezvous Is A Marvel of Perfection," headlined the *New York Times*.[101]

Meanwhile, Ulysses—the nuclear-powered space probe with 24.2 pounds of plutonium that Challenger was supposed to loft—was launched on its mission to the Sun in October 1990. NASA conceded in its *Final Environmental Impact Statement for the Ulysses Mission (Tier 2)* that solar energy could produce the mere 284 watts that plutonium power was to generate on Ulysses. Although claiming in a first version of the *Final Environmental Impact Statement, (Tier 1)*, that solar wouldn't do, the *Tier 2* report reversed that. Not only did it say that solar energy was a practicable alternative power source but it contained a chart with a column telling of the "Technology Readiness/Subsystem Application" for each solar system that could be used. For a "Rigid Array" solar system, the time indicated for it to be ready was "Now." For a "Solar Array Flight Experiment" the time was "Now." For an "Advanced Photovoltaic Solar Array" the time was "1995/2000." For an "advanced Solar Dynamics" system the readiness time would be the year 2000. For a "Concentrated Solar Array" it would be 2010.[102]

There was a lawsuit challenging Ulysses brought by the Florida Coalition for Peace & Justice and the Foundation on Economic Trends, an organization headed by Jeremy Rifkin. (The Christic Institute was suffering from financial problems connected, in part, to the cost of the first lawsuit.) Throughout 1990 NASA had been shaken by a series of fiascos—including a flawed mirror on the Hubble space telescope and fuel leaks causing shuttle flights to be scrubbed. "We have an extraordinary risk here from an agency whose competency in the last year has been abysmal," declared Andrew C. Kimbrell, lead lawyer for the Foundation on Economic Trends.[103]

And now the solar alternative was admitted. Said an *amici curiae* (friend of the court) brief filed by the Committee to Bridge the Gap, Los Angeles Physicians for Social Responsibility and the Southern California Federation of American Scientists: "From the very inception of the Ulysses project, NASA has committed itself irretrievably to use of the RTG plutonium power source." Now NASA had made the "startling admission that at least *five* non-plutonium power sources will work and that at least two are 'now' available." NASA, said the brief, "will undoubtedly claim" that it would mean a "3 to 5 year delay" of the mission. But NASA "has previously delayed this mission on four occasions over nine years from its original launch date due to budgetary constraints and modifications to the spacecraft and launch vehicle which had nothing to do with environmental concerns. Second, this mission is designed to take measurements of the sun." The brief quoted from a response to NASA by the Committee to Bridge the Gap, an exhibit in the case, to its *Tier 1 Final Environmental Impact Statement:* "The sun has been here a long time, and will be here a long time more. Measurements of the sun can be made in other years besides 1990. It will still be there a few years from now."[104] The brief declared that NASA "has finally admitted" that solar energy is an alternative to plutonium power and "the returns in improved safety are worth delay." But NASA wasn't moving to use the solar alternative[105] and it is "therefore, unquestionable, that NASA has violated the NEPA [National Environmental Policy Act] and CEQ [Council on Environmental Quality] mandates."[106]

NASA tried to deny that solar energy could be used on Ulysses. The PR campaign was conducted nervously and with a big bungle. NASA sent a form letter reply to every member of Congress who forwarded a constituent's complaint about the use of plutonium on the Ulysses mission which said: "Ulysses will be using RTGs because it will be operating too close to the Sun for solar panels to function properly."[107] After the *Nation* published an article by Judith Long and myself about the phony claim—"NASA Nonsense"—NASA admitted that this was a big misstatement.[108]

And there were citizen protests. "No More Plutonium In Space," called out the banner carried by one of the protesters in a demonstration at the Kennedy Space Center. "There are alternatives to putting nuclear power into space," declared Gagnon.[109]

Dan Hirsch, president of the Committee to Bridge the Gap. addressed the protestors. "The choice is not between launching this with this risk or not launching. The choice is whether we are going to start following a different set of values, where the environment is placed No. 1 and dollars and expediency are ranked No. 2 and 3."[110]

Ulysses took off on October 6, lofted into space on the shuttle Discovery, and "started gyrating on November 6," reported the Associated Press. "The Ulysses spacecraft is wobbling like an off-balance washing machine, threatening to cripple the $750 million...mission to study the sun's poles," noted AP.[111]

At least Ulysses wasn't coming back with its deadly plutonium to do a "flyby" of Earth.

CHAPTER FOUR

"ULTIMATE HIGH GROUND"

Why, I kept asking, such an intense push to use nuclear power in space?

There were—and are—the obvious elements:

- There is the Department of Energy, which took over the U.S. government's promotional role for atomic power from the U.S. Atomic Energy Commission when the AEC was disbanded in 1974. The AEC was eliminated when Congress—after years of citizen complaints—finally acknowledged that the AEC's dual roles of promoting and at the same time somehow regulating nuclear power was a conflict of interest. A U.S. Nuclear Regulatory Commission was set up to supposedly monitor nuclear power in the U.S. The DOE got the AEC's promotional function. Indeed, the Division of Special Applications of the DOE, which I ended up fencing with in my FOIA pursuits, was essentially an old AEC operation promoting "special applications" of nuclear power, like its use in space. Thus DOE is following its promotional role and, of course, the DOE bureaucrats doing that promotion have a personal interest—their jobs—in seeing that nuclear power continues and expands. The DOE works with NASA, as did the AEC for decades before it, in developing power systems for spacecraft.

- There are the national nuclear laboratories, like Oak Ridge and Los Alamos, facilities which grew out of the Manhattan Project. With the end of World War II, the Atomic Energy Commission replaced the Manhattan Project, taking over its facilities. Then, with the end of the AEC, the labs came under the DOE. During the Cold War, they made nuclear weapons—50,000 of them. Nuclear power for space, along with other ways nuclear technology could be used, has represented more reason to perpetuate the national nuclear labs. Former AEC Chairman David Lilienthal, who ended up critical of the field in which he was once deeply involved, has written about the "elaborate and even luxurious laboratories that have grown up at Oak Ridge, Argonne, Brookhaven,"[1] and of atomic scientists pushing the most dubious and dangerous of schemes for vested interest. "The classic picture of the scientist as a *creative* individual...this has changed. Now scientists are ranked in platoons. They are organization men" working to "justify expenditures and see that next year's budget is bigger than last's...The vested interest in a project and its funds has more and more dominated the scientists' life and motivation."[2] (The U.S. space program, he charged, was on a similar road. "The space program happens, at the moment, to be the most extensive illustration of what has happened to science through its absorption into a fast-building and gargantuan establishment," he also wrote in 1963. "Here the goals of the program are not scientific goals; they are political."[3])

- There are the corporations that have been involved in the manufacture of space nuclear systems, General Electric and, more recently, Lockheed Martin with its absorption of what had been the GE Aerospace Division, and Westinghouse. The motive here: money. As John W. Simpson, former president of Westinghouse Power Systems relates in his 1994 book, *Nuclear Power from*

Underseas to Outer Space, the basic question for Westinghouse when it considered moving to manufacturing nuclear space systems was: "What was our market for nuclear power in space?"[4] GE and Westinghouse are the Coke and Pepsi of nuclear power worldwide. Some 85% of commercial nuclear plants are of GE or Westinghouse design. And with no new nuclear plant being ordered in the United States since before the 1979 Three Mile Island accident, space has represented an especially attractive market in recent years. Moreover, the power of GE and Westinghouse over the federal government has been enormous. During the presidency of Ronald Reagan, the U.S. had a leader who for eight years had been a GE spokesman, what the company called its "general good will ambassador," traveling the nation promoting GE's line—including its nuclear products.

- There are, too, those in NASA and its Jet Propulsion Laboratory who sincerely believe in nuclear power for use in space, consider it essential for space travel. They concede there might be danger involved—but they stress that there is always danger attached to exploration— Columbus, after all, had to take risks. As to the risks to the billions of human beings who inhabit the planet but who are not professionally involved in space activity, the NASA nuclear advocates join in minimizing their danger. They tell themselves—and seek to tell the world—that the risks, relative to other dangers, are acceptable and there is a low probability of harm.

Still, this push for using nuclear power in space has been—and is—so extremely heavy. I asked: is there even more behind it?

Here we have had NASA, even with the option of safe and cheaper solar energy staring it in the face, so stubbornly insisting on going nuclear.

Then slowly, another piece of the puzzle became clear: the military connection.

"High Ground Has Always Been a Superior and Defensible Platform"

"If you can grab the high ground in a battle, you have the advantage—a very distinct advantage," Colonel Mike Heil, commander of the U. S. Air Force Phillips Laboratory declared in a 1997 interview in *Focus*, the newspaper of Phillips Lab, the New Mexico-based research and development facility for space weaponry.

Focus noted: "Heil knows his history. He understands its lessons. From the ramparts of ancient Masada to the sheer cliffs at Normandy, high ground has always been a superior and defensible platform from which which to wage war."[5]

Then it was back to Colonel Heil: "But for us here at Phillips Lab, yesterday's high ground of remote ridge lines and distant hilltops has a modern corollary: Space."[6]

"Our technologies are the ladder that enable military commanders, now and in the future, to reach that ultimate high ground," said Colonel Heil.[7]

"The Air Force," Colonel Heil went on, "is in the midst of a shift in emphasis from an 'air and space' force to a 'space and air force' which is the essence of Chief of Staff General Ronald Fogelman's new vision for global awareness and engagement...Phillips' role will be to inject new technologies into systems the military will use...As a result, from its position in space, the Air Force will eventually 'see' every potential target on the face of the earth and, if need be, engage them militarily. That is what we do here: develop technologies to take the high ground."[8]

This is not just the view of one U.S. Air Force colonel or one Air Force facility. And Phillips Laboratory, located on the grounds of Kirtland Air Force Base in Albuquerque, is quite explicit on its role. As Phillips' current, slick multi-colored brochure describing its activities declares: "Phillips Laboratory supports the war fighter...Phillips Laboratory is helping **control space** for the United States." (Boldface is that of the Phillips Laboratory.) [9]

The view of space being the "ultimate high ground" and how, from space, war can be waged and the Earth below controlled, is now the U.S. military's accepted policy, what it calls its "doctrine."

It is called "space control" and "space force application."

As General Joseph W. Ashy, commander-in-chief of the U.S. Space Command, stated in 1996: "We'll expand into these two missions because they will become increasingly important. We will engage terrestrial targets someday—ships, airplanes, land targets—from space." [10]

"It's politically sensitive, but it's going to happen," General Ashy continued in an article entitled "USSC Prepares for Future Combat Missions in Space" in *Aviation Week & Space Technology*, a trade magazine of the aviation and space industries. [11]

"Some people don't want to hear this, and it sure isn't in vogue," the general continued, "but—absolutely—we're going to fight *in* space. We're going to fight *from* space and we're going to fight *into* space when [orbital assets] become so precious that it's in our national interests....That's why the U.S. has development programs in directed energy and hit-to-kill mechanisms. We are developing direct-force applications." (Italics in *Aviation Week & Space Technology*.)

"Space-based Weapons of Devastating Effectiveness"

And nuclear power is seen as an important, perhaps critical element in the U.S. applying force from the "ultimate high ground."

"In the next two decades, new technologies will allow the fielding of space-based weapons of devastating effectiveness to be used to deliver energy and mass as force projection in tactical and stategic conflict," declares the 1966 fifteen-volume U.S. Air Force report *New World Vistas: Air and Space Power for the 21st Century.* "These advances will enable lasers with reasonable mass and cost to effect very many kills." But, says the report, "All current spacecraft are either power limited or restricted in some measure by inadequate electric power. Power limitations impose restrictions on the communications and propulsion subsystems and currently make large space-based radar and space-based weapons relatively unfeasible. A revolutionary change in capabilities will result from power technologies capable of providing large amounts of power on board satellites."[12]

"A natural technology to enable high power is nuclear power in space," concludes *New World Vistas* in its "Space Technology Volume."[13]

It goes on to acknowledge the "political and environmental" opposition to nuclear power. But "setting the emotional issues of nuclear power aside, this technology offers a viable alternative for large amounts of power in space."[14]

Solar power just cannot produce the necessary amount of energy needed for military purposes in space, stresses *New World Vistas'* "Space Technology Volume," prepared by a sixteen-member Air Force Space Technology Board. "All solar collection systems in Earth orbit are limited by the solar constant of 1.4 kilowatts per square meter," it says, and "large powers from solar collectors require large collection areas."[15]

Lots of power is needed for "space-based radars, space-based directed energy weapons, and the use of high performance electrically driven maneuvering technologies." "Over the years, there have been several programs in nuclear powered spacecraft. NASA has been using Radioisotope Thermoelectric

Generators (RTGs) for the interplanetary missions that generate a few tens of watts of power. Russia has flown nuclear reactors in space," states *New World Vistas*.[16]

Nuclear power "remains one of the attractive alternatives in generating large amounts of power in space," says the report, declaring that "the Air Force should continue efforts toward making a safe nuclear reactor in space."[17]

The End of the Civilian Space Program?

The turning point for combining space military activities and nuclear power was the Strategic Defense Initiative or Star Wars program. As conceived in the administrations of Ronald Reagan and George Bush, it had a huge nuclear component. As the first head of the Strategic Defense Initiative Organization, Lt. General James Abrahamson, declared at the Fifth Annual Symposium on Space Nuclear Power and Propulsion in 1988: "Without reactors in orbit [there is] going to be a long, long light cord that goes down to the surface of the Earth" bringing up power. Abrahamson said: "Failure to develop nuclear power in space could cripple efforts to deploy anti-missile sensors and weapons in orbit."[18]

The central figure in the formation and operation over the decades of Lawrence Livermore National Laboratory, Dr. Edward Teller, and his associates, especially his "main protégé,"[19] Lowell L. Wood, Jr., devised the initial plan to use orbiting hydrogen bombs as a power source for X-ray lasers. The concept: "Around the H-bomb at its core are long, thin metal rods which, when struck by radiation, emit powerful bursts of X-rays," as *New York Times* reporter William J. Broad explained in his book *Star Warriors*.[20] "As the bomb at the core of an X-ray battle station exploded, multiple beams would flash out to strike multiple targets before the entire station consumed itself in a ball of nuclear fire. That is the vision."[21]

Battle platforms with hypervelocity guns and particle beams—also needing nuclear power as a source of their energy—were quickly added into the "layers" of armaments in the system. They would not be "bomb-driven." Instead, they would receive their power from nuclear reactors affixed to the orbiting platforms. And also part of the plan was a nuclear-propelled rocket using a "particle bed reactor" as an energy source, a design developed at Brookhaven National Laboratory. Code-named "Timberwind," the nuclear-powered rocket would loft Star Wars weaponry and other heavy equipment into space.

With Star Wars, the deployment of nuclear-powered weaponry in space was embraced by two U.S. administrations: the Reagan and then Bush administrations. Space nuclear power, something which for years had greatly interested the AEC then DOE, the national laboratories, GE and Westinghouse and the military—but did not receive strong backing by a national administration—suddenly got a giant military mission and enormous funding.

NASA, seeing its budgets shrink with the end of the "man-on-the-moon" Apollo missions of the 1960s and 70s, was keenly aware of what was going on. It had been created in 1958 as a civilian agency. "The Air Force, Army, Navy, and CIA all had space programs under development by the mid-fifties," relates Jack Manno in *Arming The Heavens*.[22] He traces much inspiration for the U.S. military space programs to scientists who had worked building rockets for Nazi Germany during World War II who, with their rockets "and ideas," were brought to the U.S. after the war. The 1957 Soviet launch of Sputnik—the world's first satellite—projected the Soviet Union as a country leading the world in space prowess. And the Eisenhower administration saw the need for a great effort not only to develop ways to counter the Soviets militarily in space, but also to answer the Sputnik challenge, to "maintain the image of an America dedicated to the peaceful, scientific exploration of space. A dual national space program divided into military and civilian sides resulted."[23]

President Dwight Eisenhower, as he wrote in his papers, "decided that nonmilitary research in outer space could best be conducted by a new civilian agency....The highest priority should go to space research with a military application, but for national morale, and to some extent national prestige, this should likewise be pushed through a separate agency."[24]

The National Aeronautics and Space Act of 1958 was passed, creating NASA and stating that "the Congress declares that it is the policy of the United States that activities in space should be devoted to peaceful purposes for the benefit of mankind." But, Manno points out, pressure from "space hawks," including then presidential hopeful Lyndon Johnson, made sure military space "perogatives" were also stressed in the bill. So there is also a provision that "activities peculiar to or primarily associated with the development of weapons systems, military operations, or the defense of the United States shall be the responsibility of and be directed by the Department of Defense."[25]

NASA got its manned space program going, while "providing a suitable cover for military space activities and giving a boost to the fledgling aerospace industry." With Apollo, "the marriage of big money and a reachable, if dramatic goal had created a huge government program of space activity," writes Manno, and "in that way Apollo was a success. But its work had been done before its goal was reached, and that imparted a strange aura of anticlimax."[26]

In 1970, President Richard Nixon rejected NASA's bid for a manned mission to Mars. "At the same time Nixon cut NASA's overall budget for fiscal year 1971 to the lowest level in ten years," notes Manno. But he did increase the budget for NASA to build a space station and a space shuttle, both of which the military was interested in, indeed had been "pushing for over ten years." NASA and the military became partners in the space shuttle.[27]

NASA was getting cozier and cozier with the Pentagon. By the 80s, with the advent of Star Wars, to keep its budget up and its operations bustling, NASA was in bed with the Pentagon. Half the shuttle missions and other NASA activities were shared with the military. NASA was coordinating its approach to space with military needs and desires. Star Wars became where the action and money were. The shuttle could be used for Star Wars experiments and, with Star Wars' implementation, as a service vehicle for orbiting battle stations. The military and the Reagan and Bush administrations wanted a nuclear-powered Star Wars system in space, so NASA had a powerful additional incentive to promote nuclear power in space. The military connection gave it yet more of a motive to integrate nuclear power into its operations.

"Many people don't realize the close connection that NASA has with the Department of Defense," explains Dr. Michio Kaku. "Specifically look at the shuttle. About 50% of the early funding for the space shuttle was paid for by the United States Pentagon [which] wanted a very large platform that could be used in outer space for Star Wars experiments."[28]

"We have to realize that NASA, because it has been short on funding, has taken money from the Pentagon," relates Kaku. "But when you cut a deal with the devil, there's a price you have to pay. And the price you have to pay is that NASA did become, in the 1980s, increasingly military-oriented, making allowances for its space shuttle missions, many of which are totally classified" and—to keep a nuclear space-oriented Pentagon happy—ever more insistent on the "the nuclearization of the space program."[29]

And this continues in the Clinton administration. Candidate Bill Clinton claimed to want to put an end to the Reagan/Bush administrations' vision of Star Wars. Yet the

Clinton administration has continued to budget between $3 and $4 billion annually for what has been renamed Ballistic Missile Defense.

Many elements have continued, like the "Stars" program, a Star Wars endeavor rather crudely renamed. It has been challenged in recent years by protests and civil disobedience resulting in arrests. "Stars" involves the launching of Polaris missiles from Kauii in Hawaii to fly down a range that ends at Kwajalein Atoll 2,200 miles to the west. Ancient Hawaiian burial grounds and important natural habitats on the island are in the "evacuation zone" set up by the military in case launches go bad. Suzanne Marinelli of the Sierra Club of Hawaii, one of those arrested in the protests, warns that an accident on launch could be "catastrophic, raining burning debris and hazardous waste."[30] "We are enslaving our own people for the empowerment of particular individuals and programs, and it's a sin."[31]

A similar program is supposed to soon come to Florida. "'Star Wars' Over Florida, Pentagon Ponders Missile-Testing Program," was the front-page headline of the *Gainesville Sun* with the announcement of the plan in 1995. "Tourists at Disney World or surfers in Florida beaches may get the opportunity to witness Pentagon tests of the 'Star Wars' anti-missile system," the paper reported. The plan is to "launch rockets from the Florida Keys and then try to knock them down with anti-missile rockets fired from the Florida Panhandle....Airplane traffic at the busy Key West airport would be shut down during rocket launches. U.S. 1, the lifeblood of the Keys, would be closed for up to 70 minutes for each launch—a worry for residents and tourists alike."[32]

As hearings were getting scheduled in early 1997, Mike Collins, president of the Florida Keys Fishing Guide Association, was telling the *Palm Beach Post,* "It's massive federal stupidity all over again." Dennis Henize of Cudjo Key, said, "There's no way they're going to convince us that launching twelve tons of missile less than a mile away is not a safety concern."[33]

Meanwhile, the Republican majority in Congress, both in its "Contract With America" and its "Defend America Act," has been demanding a revival of even more of the original Stars Wars program. The "Defend America Act" calls for deploying national "missile defense" with space-based components, a "layered defense" including "space-based kinetic energy interceptors" and "space-based energy systems."[34]

Explained House Speaker Newt Gingrich in justifying what has been termed "Star Wars II" after $36 billion had already been spent on Star Wars: "One day, mathematically, something bad can happen and you ought to have a minimum screen on a continentwide basis and that's doable. And I think compared to the loss of one city, is is clearly a very small investment, although it's a lot of money over time." [35]

The Republican majority would like a "completion of the Reagan revolution," comments Dr. Kaku, whose books also include *To Win A Nuclear War*.[36] "They see Star Wars as an incomplete revolution. And they would like to complete that by hoisting into outer space laser battle stations."[37]

As to the Clinton administration and the use of nuclear power in space, some people who were involved in the opposition to the Galileo and Ulysses plutonium-fueled missions in the late 1980s hoped that with Clinton's election, there might be a major change in U.S. policy.

That was not to happen.

The Democrats in Nuclear Lockstep

The White House, a year after the Clinton administration took office and after conducting what it termed a study of the issue, declared its support for nuclear power in space—for civilian and military uses. As the Clinton White House announced in a document entitled "National Policy on Space Nuclear Power and Propulsion" issued August 17, 1993:

> The United States already has a *de facto* national policy regarding the use of space nuclear power and propulsion, which has developed as a result of the fact that the Nation has been launching space nuclear power supplies for over 30 years, has an established safety review process including Presidential approval of such launches, and continues to fund, although in a limited way, the study and development of space nuclear power and propulsion. This policy has resulted in the highly successful use of several national security applications. The development of nuclear technology for space missions has historically been the responsibility of the Department of Energy, based on existing legislation.[38]

Thus, said the "National Policy on Space Nuclear Power and Propulsion," the Clinton administration recognizes that "space nuclear power and propulsion systems can contribute to scientific, commercial and national security space missions."[39]

There was a caveat: "Correspondingly, this policy suggests that space nuclear power and propulsion systems should not be used unless they enable missions that would otherwise not be reasonably possible, or which would be significantly enhanced by the use of nuclear power or propulsion. The use of radioisotope power sources on long range space probes, such as the Galileo mission to Jupiter and the Cassini mission to Saturn, where reliable long term alternative power sources are not available, is an example of the appropriate use of space nuclear power."[40]

Later in 1993, the Department of Energy placed a notice in the *Federal Register* announcing that it sought to "fund research and development studies directed at...identifying innovative approaches using nuclear reactor power and propulsion systems for potential future NASA, DoD [Department of Defense] and commercial space activities."

Continuing the Reagan and Bush administrations' development of nuclear power for civilian and military purposes in space, in September 1996 the Clinton administration moved to develop nuclear-propelled rockets. The policy statement "of the administration of U.S. President Bill Clinton...mandates maintaining space nuclear power capability to support future missions," reported *Space News*. Under the Clinton program, the Pentagon's Defense Special Weapons Agency "is to issue...solicitations for research and development of thermoionic technologies to support long-duration space missions," while NASA's Marshall Space Flight Center's Advanced Concept Division along with Los Alamos National Laboratory will develop nuclear propulsion for civilian uses. [41]

The military effort "will culminate in the manufacture and electrical thermal testing of multiple nuclear propulsion concepts. DSWA [Defense Special Weapons Agency] will then select one or more competitors to demonstrate the systems' reliability in missions lasting longer than five years and requiring 40 kilowatts to 100 kilowatts of power."[42]

That's nuclear propulsion for rockets, not simply RTGs to generate electricity. And not RTGs producing 25 watts (as on SNAP-9A) or 560 watts (as on Galileo) or 745 watts (as on Cassini) but *40 to 100 thousand watts* of nuclear-generated power on spacecraft.

Nuclear Propulsion: A History Leading Nowhere

There was no lack of trying, before Star Wars and the commitment by national administrations to nuclear-powered military activity in space, to develop nuclear-powered space and aviation capabilities.

Nukespeak, The Selling of Nuclear Technology in America, an incisive look at the history of nuclear power in the U.S., tells of the programs for nuclear-powered rockets as well as nuclear-powered airplanes between the 1950s and early 1970s.[43]

"The nuclear rocket program began at Los Alamos [National Laboratory] in 1955 with the development of Kiwi nuclear reactors, inauspiciously named after the flightless New Zealand bird," relates *Nukespeak*.[44] Out of the Kiwi effort came NERVA—for Nuclear Engine for Rocket Vehicle Application—program. There were also Projects Pluto, Rover and Poodle to build nuclear-powered rockets.

Westinghouse was a major contractor for the nuclear rocket program. With the Manhattan Project, a pattern was set that continues to this day, of the U.S. government contracting out much of its nuclear work to corporations. Thus early on, an additional, private money-making factor was added to the momentum for governmental nuclear programs. It was through contracts given to them by the Manhattan Project that GE and Westinghouse got their starts in nuclear manufacturing. Recounting "winning the NERVA contract" in *Nuclear Power from Underseas to Outer Space*, former Westinghouse Power Systems Co. President John W. Simpson comments that "my staff and I took a real deep breath after the cheering stopped. Our careers would have been seriously set back if we had not won the contract." He relates how Westinghouse was up against GE, Pratt & Whitney, North American Aviation, Aerojet General and Thiokol, but in "nuclear technology...Westinghouse was number one. Believe me, we pulled out all the stops—not only technical effort but also marketing and political savvy. This was, after all, a government contract."[45]

A 1961 editorial in *Nucleonics*, a nuclear industry trade publication, declared that the U.S. was "on the threshold of an era which some are already calling 'The Nuclear Space Age'—the joining in inevitable matrimony of two of contemporary man's most exciting frontiers, nuclear energy and outer space." *Nucleonics* said nuclear rockets offered "the only realistic possibility for overcoming the space payload lead of the Soviet

Union....In short, the nuclear rocket gives this country its only chance to catch up with—indeed to surpass—the USSR."[46]

However, by 1961 the Pentagon was still not ordering nuclear rockets, a situation which *Nucleonics* deplored, saying there surely would be an "easier flow of development dollars" if there were "a clear-cut military requirement."[47] In 1972, after $2 billion was spent on developing nuclear-propelled rockets, the AEC cancelled the program. No nuclear rocket ever got off the ground.

"The major problem was that we had no mission," recounted Norman Gerstein who headed the engine project office for NERVA as a NASA engineer. In ground-testing, said Gerstein, "we were generating a lot of thrust" with the rocket engines. "But nothing ever flew. We had no specific mission." Gerstein said one hope was that a Mars mission might happen, but it didn't. "We wound up just doing ground-testing. There were twenty successful tests of a thousand to 42,000 megawatts," he recalled. Gerstein said he began working on nuclear rockets for NASA with the AEC in 1960, a job that ended with the end of the program a dozen years later when "I was a NASA employee working in the AEC building...The office was disbanded."[48]

"The U.S. government," recounts *Nukespeak*, "also funded a radically different nuclear-powered rocket program in the late 1950s and early 1960s. This wild scheme, known as Project Orion, called for propelling a spacecraft into orbit and out into the solar system with a series of nuclear bomb explosions."[49]

Nukespeak describes the truly wild Project Orion:

Using an apparatus modeled on coin-operated Coke machines to move the bombs from storage to the launch position, the craft would use bursts of compressed air to whisk the bombs to about 100 feet from the ship. The shock wave from each successive blast would slam into a giant pusher plate, sending the ship lurching through the cosmos at a top speed of 100,000 miles per hour. NASA called Orion's bombs "pulse units," while the Air Force referred to them as "charge propellant systems."[50]

And then there were the efforts at building a nuclear-propelled airplane, for which GE was a major government contractor. "Atomic-powered airplanes would make long-distance bombing easier, since the planes were expected to be able to circle the globe without refueling," notes *Nukespeak*. As late as 1959, the U.S. Joint Chiefs of Staff were assuring Congress of the military potential of nuclear-powered airplanes and urging that they be built. But nixing the program in 1961—after more than $1 billion (in 1950s dollars) had been spent—then Secretary of Defense Robert S. McNamara told Congress that an atomic plane would "expel some fraction of radioactive fission products into the atmosphere, creating an important public relations problem if not an actual physical hazard."[51]

The military side of the nuclear rocket and airplane program story is told in an obscure 1960 work edited by an Air Force colonel: *Nuclear Flight: The United States Air Force Program for Atomic Jets, Missiles, and Rockets.*[52]

It opens with then Air Force Chief of Staff General Thomas D. White asserting: "Pre-eminence in air power has been the goal of American airmen since the military potential of air operations was first recognized....Today, however, as air power evolves into aerospace power, our position is being seriously challenged....We must always be on the alert for new and radical methods to break through barriers which impose limitations on the employment of our aerospace forces. One major step in this direction would be the successful achievement of airborne nuclear propulsion."[53]

General White further stated:

The military exploitation of airborne nuclear propulsion will provide a significant increase in our future deterrent capability—an increase which must be realized if this capability is to remain effective. Thus the support of this effort by the United

States Air Force is in keeping with our constant goal—the preservation of peace through the unquestioned pre-eminence of this nation's aerospace power.[54]

The Air Force's Deputy Chief of Staff for Development, Lt. General Roscoe C. Wilson, writing on "The Payoff in Nuclear Propulsion," stated:

Today we stand at the threshold of nuclear propulsion in the air and in space, an advance in technology which will immeasurably extend the strategic and tactical potentials of aircraft and missiles as we know them....We are now at a stage in technology where our gains in the energy of chemical fuels are...approaching the maximum limit as governed by the physical laws of nature....The taming of the atom...now brings atomic-powered aircraft and missiles within our grasp. Atomic-powered boosters can have enormous, controlled thrust; atomic-powered aircraft can have whatever endurance we care to give them.[55]

General Wilson spoke of nuclear bombers with "unlimited range" being on "missions of several days duration" and capable of "low-altitude penetration...Chemically powered aircraft are extremely limited in range at low altitude because of the tremendous increase in fuel consumption, even at moderate speeds. The nuclear engine will operate at low altitude by increasing slightly the power level of the reactor, causing only a negligible increase in fuel consumption."[56]

And as for nuclear-powered rockets:

Nuclear propulsion looks extremely attractive in rockets....In the ballistic missile, the ratio of payload weight to gross weight...serves as an index of mission capability. For rocket vehicles relying on chemical combustion, progressively smaller improvements in this ratio can be expected....A new, more powerful source of energy that yields a breakout beyond those limits would mean a major advance....Nuclear rocket propulsion offers our best hope for future high-payload rocket missions in orbit or beyond in space.[57]

Also "because nuclear energy can be converted into electrical energy in sufficient amounts and for extended periods of time, it offers advantages for use in meeting the internal power requirements of space vehicles," Lt. General Wilson stressed. "Satellites depend on power sources of light weight and long duration to operate the instrumentation designed to collect and transmit data back to earth. Radioisotope devices and small nuclear reactors offer successful answers."[58]

The general pointed to the early SNAP plutonium-fueled radioisotope thermoelectric generators and said "potentially such lightweight power packages, unencumbered by enormous quantities of chemical fuel or by storage batteries, can offer sustained, dependable service not only in satellites but in space platforms and space probes."[59]

Nuclear Flight: The United States Air Force Programs for Atomic Jets, Missiles, and Rockets also considered some safety and health issues. There is a chapter covering the effects on the members of a crew flying an airplane powered by a nuclear reactor. The authors, the director of medical research and the chief of radiobiology at the Air Force's School of Aviation Medicine, say it is important that "the biological hazard of dose-effect and the response to various radiation sources be well understood" and they ask: "How often can an individual be exposed to this amount of radiation without significant detrimental effects?" Nearly forty years ago, they noted how the impacts of large doses of radiation are known "from data on the people of Hiroshima and Nagasaki" and residents of the Marshall Islands where atmospheric nuclear weapons tests were conducted and from victims of "accidental exposures at Argonne, Los Alamos, and Oak Ridge laboratories." But, they say—hinting then of the concerns over low-level radiation of later years—"attention must be given also to the smaller doses of radiation exposure received...over relatively long periods of time (months to years). Experimental data show a marked difference between acute and delayed responses to radiation exposure."[60]

As to "public hazards" if "a nuclear-powered aircraft crashes, it is likely that some fission products will be released," says this chapter's authors, the chief of nuclear research and development at the Convair aircraft company and an Air Force lieutenant colonel. They say "military and civilian records show that a high percentage of flight accidents occur during take-off or landing and that in these accidents the airplane will almost certainly come to rest inside an area two miles wide by nine miles long, centered on the runway." So "the predicted chance of people being affected in a nearby town is about 1 in 10,000,000. It should be remembered that being 'affected' means receiving a maximum permissible exposure but not a large dose enough to cause mild radiation sickness."[61]

A big political advocate for the use of nuclear power in space during this period was U.S. Senator Albert Gore of Tennessee, the father of the current U.S. vice president .

In a 1962 Senate speech, Gore declared:

> In 1958, I introduced a bill authorizing $1 billion for an accelerated atomic power program, including the first substantial funds for nuclear rocket propulsion. At that time I indicated what I believed was the path to space leadership when I said: "If we are to succeed in the race to place into operation a space vehicle subject to control and direction by man, we must proceed with all possible speed in the development of nuclear propulsion." Today, four years later, I hold firm in my belief that another great stride in space leadership lies in the union of space and the atom.[62]

Senator Gore, in whose home state lies Oak Ridge National Laboratory, which he staunchly supported—as did the present vice president when he was a representative and senator—

went on to say that "it is true that chemically fueled rockets provide adequate power for the immediate foreseeable missions." But longer space "voyages require large amounts of power. At the same time, the package delivering this power must have a high-energy output at a low weight. Moreover, it must have a long-term reliability. Perhaps only nuclear energy can fill the bill."[63]

> There are two principal areas in which nuclear energy can be used to supply power for space exploration. First, it can be used to boost vehicles into space and then provide necessary sustained power for voyages over vast distances. Second, it can serve as a source of auxiliary power for a wide variety of miscellaneous functions such as navigation, communications, environmental conditions, and guidance...We have been told that if the United States fails to develop nuclear rocket engines, it will be left a second-class space power. Leading space scientists have emphasized that "space will be conquered only by manned nuclear-powered vehicles." I have been impressed that nuclear energy is essential for leadership in space.[64]

Senator Gore concluded: "The president of the United States has described outer space as an 'ocean we must sail'...I submit that the success of our voyage, in large measure, depends upon the common destiny of space and the atom."

The Joint Congressional Committee on Atomic Energy held a three-day session on "Space Nuclear Power Applications" in 1962. The lead-off speaker was Leland Haworth, an AEC commissioner, who declared: "Nuclear power not only will enhance space exploration. Its use, both for propulsion and for auxiliary power, is the key to extensive outer space exploration."[65]

In 1961, the year before, General Electric's RTGs began being put into use for space satellites.[66] But then there was the 1964 fall to Earth of SNAP-9A—dimming prospects for nuclear-powered satellites.

Space nuclear development proceeded—but without a mission.

And then came Star Wars.

A Thousand Beams of Light

"My fellow Americans, tonight we are launching an effort which holds the promise of changing the course of human history," said President Reagan in a nationally-televised address on March 23, 1983 announcing the Strategic Defense Initiative (SDI) soon to be known as Star Wars. [67]

War In Space by Nigel Flynn is among the books that probe how that came about, how in 1967 Reagan, then governor of California, visited Lawrence Livermore Laboratory east of San Francisco. Dr. Teller told Reagan of his plan for a space-based nuclear-powered X-ray laser code-named "Excalibur... In theory, the weapon is simple enough. It consists of an orbiting nuclear bomb which, when detonated, releases multiple laser beams. Directed at incoming Soviet ICBMs it would destroy everything in its path before it was itself consumed in a nuclear fire-ball. This device, Dr. Teller believed, would provide the United States with the defense against nuclear missiles that he had always claimed was possible, despite the fact that the use of such a weapon in space is banned by treaty."[68]

When Reagan became president, Teller continued to push his scheme and, further, got another follower, nuclear physicist George A. Keyworth from Los Alamos National Laboratory, appointed as Reagan's science advisor. "Bluntly, the reason I was in that office is because Edward first proposed me, and the president very much admires Edward," Keyworth later admitted.[69]

Then "Teller, already a force in the formal process of advising the White House, penetrated an even more important center of power—a highly organized group of Reagan friends, most of them millionaires," relates *New York Times* reporter William J. Broad in his book *Teller's War, The Top-Secret Story Behind The Star Wars Deception.*[70] This was a group "formed in May 1981 by Karl R. Bendetsen, undersecretary of the army for President Truman" and subsequently a corporate executive. Bendetsen had heard retired Lt. General Daniel O. Graham, former head of the Defense Intelligence Agency and a Reagan campaign adviser, give a speech about the need for an "antimissile defense" against the Soviet Union. He offered "to help raise money for the founding of a lobbying group."[71]

It was to be called High Frontier and include such arch-conservatives as brewer Joseph Coor. The "sole scientist," according to Broad, was Teller. Teller and Bendetsen were also connected through Teller's role as a fellow at the conservative Hoover Institution of which Bendetsen was an overseer, notes Broad. "The official White House liaison to the panel was science adviser Keyworth."[72]

Thus at the White House, the "idea of a space-based strategic policy began to take shape in the president's mind...assisted in 1981 by the formation" of the High Frontier group, states *War In Space*.[73] *War In Space* tells of High Frontier growing out of the Heritage Foundation, a group (with some of the same players) which earlier "set up business in Washington, D.C. with generous funding from a number of undisclosed, private sources. The group's deputy director was an ex-Army Lt. General, Daniel O. Graham...advisor to Ronald Reagan in the 1976 and 1980 campaigns. The aim of the group was to publicize the growing danger of Soviet nuclear aggression, and bring public pressure to bear upon the White House to increase America's defense spending in order to reassert American nuclear superiority. The group included Dr. Edward Teller, and it was not long before the Heritage Foundation was advocating that the United States abandon the concept of 'Mutual Assured Destruction' (known by the appropriate acronym MAD), which had guided America's strategic nuclear thinking since the 1960s."[74]

Teller, working closely with protégé Lowell Wood, Jr., was getting his way—even after Lt. General Graham balked at his concept of using hydrogen bomb-powered X-ray lasers at the base of an anti-missile system. Graham held that the scheme was flawed because "while other weapons could protect themselves, an X-ray laser waiting in orbit for an enemy attack would have to destroy itself in order to fire a beam at the attacker" and also the U.S. "public would never accept the placing of nuclear weapons in space," reported Broad.[75]

Nevertheless, the plan which Teller pushed became a key element of Reagan's Star Wars. Overall, according to Broad, Star Wars became "basically a scientific free-for-all, a license to spend tens of billions of dollars...Nearly any idea that seemed to show a hint of antimissile promise was praised by Pentagon planners and often lavishly funded. No concept seemed too wild."[76]

Because placement of nuclear weapons in space would be "in direct contravention" of the 1967 Outer Space Treaty committing signatories to the peaceful uses of space and in violation of the 1974 Anti-Ballistic Missile or ABM Treaty between the U.S. and the Soviet Union, the Pentagon would claim that with Star Wars "the emphasis is being given to non-nuclear weapons," noted Flynn in *War In Space*. But massive amounts of money were being spent on what the Pentagon called "nuclear-driven systems." Between 1984 and 1989 alone, $900 million went for development of the Teller X-ray laser element.[77]

And it was becoming clear—despite the Pentagon spin— that Star Wars was shaping up to be a program based on nuclear-powered weapons systems in space. As General Abramson testified at a Congressional hearing in 1985: "Success of nearly all elements of SDI is dependent on major advancements in space power...Power level, life cycle, and survivability requirements for continuous baseload power for many SDI payloads to beyond the capabilities of conventional or even advanced solar and isotope systems."[78]

Thus, said Abramson, "We are examining nuclear power generation in space. Research on nuclear systems technologies for both base load and potential weapons power is being conducted in conjunction with the Department of Energy."[79]

"At the same time," the general stressed, "the results of NASA projects are of great interest to us...Conversely, many developments in our program can be of great benefit to NASA in many of their future applications. The potential for a synergistic relationship exists, and we will do our utmost to nurture the potential."[80]

Indeed, "NASA is cofunding the SP-100 space reactor project with the SDI and the Department of Energy," Abramson told the House Subcommittee on Energy Research and Production of the Committee on Science and Technology at its hearings on "Space Nuclear Power, Conversion and Energy Storage for the Nineties and Beyond."[81]

The message of General Abramson at the Annual Symposium on Space Nuclear Power and Propulsion in 1988 that "without reactors in orbit [there is] going to be a long, long light cord that goes down to the surface of the Earth" to power Star Wars weaponry, further brought home what was happening. In that presentation, too, General Abramson declared that there was "a 100-kilowatt space reactor being developed jointly" by his Star Wars office, DOE "and the National Aeronautics and Space Administration."[82]

"There is broad consensus among the Strategic Defense Initiative Organization, the Department of Energy, the American Physical Society Study Group on Directed Energy Weapons, and the [Congressional] Office of Technology Assessment that nuclear power reactors in space are likely to be an essential component of the later phases of SDI—those that would employ directed energy weapons," Steven

Aftergood, then executive director of the Committee to Bridge the Gap, wrote in the premiere issue of the magazine *Science and Global Security* in 1989.[83] The Committee to Bridge the Gap was deeply involved in challenging Star Wars —especially its nuclear component.

Aftergood quoted from a report of the American Physical Society Study Group on Directed Energy Weapons that even "a few tens of kilowatts of electrical power necessitates nuclear power reactors for two reasons. First is survivability: The large area needed for solar cells would make a satellite very vulnerable to actions of the offense. Second is reliability. The long expected stay in orbit could reduce the availability of power [from solar cells] because of the radiation damage that occurs over 10-year time scales."[84]

Meanwhile, as a result of Star Wars, "the applications of current and proposed space nuclear power supplies, particularly in earth orbit," said Aftergood, had become "predominantly military."[85]

And NASA was, as General Abrahamson said, in a "synergistic relationship" with the Star Wars operation—working closely with NASA. Indeed, NASA admittedly decided to "redirect" its approach based on the relationship. Robert Rosen, NASA's deputy associate administrator for aeronautics and space technology, told a Congressional panel in 1992 that NASA was involved with DOE and the Pentagon on a "tri-agency steering committee" to develop a space nuclear reactor which ultimately became the SP-100. "Initially NASA did not provide direct funding for the program but provided support in the form of manpower and requirements for civil applications. We also redirected an ongoing power technology development program associated with longer term technologies so that it would be fully compatible with the SP-100 program."[86]

A brochure issued by the DOE declared: "The SP-100 space reactor power system is being developed to meet the large electrical power requirements of civilian and military missions planned for the 1990s and beyond."[87] It was designed, notes the publication, so it could be carried on "either a reusable space shuttle or an unmanned expendable launch vehicle."[88]

And despite its SP-100 name, the publication said that the SP-100 power could range beyond 100 kilowatts—to 1,000 kilowatts[89] (a thousand-thousand or a million watts).

"A successfully developed SP-100 reactor power system will facilitate exciting new space exploration and exploitation opportunities and will support national defense objectives," the publication, *SP-100 Space Reactor Safety* declared.[90]

Some $2 billion was spent on development of the SP-100.[91] GE was the contractor.

Then there was work on a super-RTG, one generating 10 kilowatts.

"In the wake of the Cosmos 954 disaster, then Energy Secretary James R. Schlesinger declared, 'I regard it as inappropriate to have nuclear reactors orbiting the Earth,'" defense columnist David Morris noted in the *National Journal* in 1988. "And President Carter sought a ban on orbital nukes. But, after a long hiatus, motivated primarily by 'Star Wars,' the United States is now back in the space reactor business. The latest Pentagon report on the Strategic Defense Initiative thus calls space reactors the 'cornerstone' of the SDI power program."[92]

The Afterglow of Timberwind

The "Timberwind" nuclear-powered rocket project was in the "black" until "somebody gave me a stack of classified program documents," recounted Aftergood, then of the Federation of American Scientists. "The source thought the ["Timberwind"] program was crazy and was happy to blow its cover. There had been no indication that such a thing was underway. I had the documentary evidence and I was able to release it to the media. It became front-page news of the

Washington Post and the *New York Times*. April 3, 1991, it was probably the busiest day in my life."[93]

And on this nuclear power-in-space story, the media did move. "U.S. Developing Atom-Powered Rocket," headlined the *Washington Post*.[94] "The Department of Defense has begun secretly developing an extraordinarily nuclear reactor-powered rocket capable of lifting immense weapons or satellites into space on short notice," began the story. "Rocket Run by Nuclear Power Being Developed for 'Star Wars,' Secret Pentagon Program Revealed in Documents," was the front-page headline of the *New York Times*. Its story began: "In great secrecy, the Pentagon is developing a nuclear-powered rocket for hauling giant weapons and other military payloads into space as part of the Star Wars program....The program was disclosed by the Federation of American Scientists, a private group based in Washington that has opposed the Star Wars anti-missile program and some uses of space reactors."[95]

The documents provided to Aftergood not only revealed a program that had been going on for years and on which hundreds of millions of dollars had been spent but also revealed a plan to flight-test a prototype "Timberwind" rocket around Antarctica. The object was to avoid a heavily populated part of the planet for testing the nuclear-propelled rocket. However, the Timberwind rocket would pass over New Zealand in its flight-test and an analysis from Sandia National Laboratory obtained by Aftergood projected the risk of the nuclear rocket crashing on New Zealand at one-in-2,325.[96]

The manufacturer of the rocket engine for "Timberwind" was Babcock and Wilcox, builder of the ill-fated Three Mile Island nuclear plant. "The design is based on research done by Brookhaven National Laboratory, on New York's Long Island, beginning in 1982," reported the *Wall Street Journal*. Sandia National Laboratories conducted a ground-test, the newspaper noted, of a "one-twentieth scale" model of the reactor. "The test produced poor results."[97]

Dr. Henry Kendall, chairman of the Union of Concerned Scientists and a Nobel laureate, speaking of the "Timberwind" rocket, said that for such a vehicle "the needle just goes up to the end of the [danger] scale and stays there." He said that the rocket would "release a stream of radiation" as it flew and if it underwent an accident and broke up, "you've got radioactive material spraying all over the place...the risks are extremely great."[98]

Star Wars Goes Global

With the end of the Cold War, the U.S. began acquiring Topaz II space reactors from the Soviet Union for Star Wars. Ironically, of course, Star Wars was advanced by Reagan, Teller and other conservatives to deal with a Soviet threat. Any Soviet threat had disappeared, but Star Wars was to continue anyway—with nuclear hardware from the former enemy.

The deal to buy the Topaz IIs for Star Wars was announced in January 1991 at the Eighth Annual Symposium on Space Nuclear Power and Propulsion in Albuquerque, New Mexico. (The annual symposia continue to the present time. It is organized by the Institute for Space and Nuclear Power Studies at the School of Engineering, University of New Mexico in Albuquerque and is co-sponsored by the Pentagon's Defense Special Weapons Agency, DOE and NASA.)

Nikolai Ponomarev-Stepnoi, first deputy of the Kurtchatovis Institute of Atomic Power in Moscow, explained at the 1991 symposium: "Our institution got its budget cut 50% and...we need to look for finances from different sources."[99]

At the United Nations soon afterward, Russian President Boris Yeltsin provided another angle: "The time has come to consider creating a global system for protection of the world community. It could be based on a reorientation of the U.S.

Strategic Defense Initiative to make use of high technologies developed in Russia's defense complex."[100]

Six Topaz IIs were purchased and underwent ground-testing at Phillips Laboratory. A flight test had been scheduled for 1995 but was postponed after complaints from U.S. astronomers. The members of the governing council of the American Astronomical Society "emphasized that they were not opposing the mission or the use of nuclear reactors in space...Instead, they wanted to put pressure on" the government to use a "more powerful rocket" that would put the reactor into a higher orbit "to avoid any interference with current or planned astronomy missions," according to a *New York Times* story on the postponement of the Topaz II flight test.[101] Topaz II, noted *Space News*, "would leave a trail of nuclear particles."[102]

In fact, the Topaz II reactor could do even more damage than that. According to a Sandia National Laboratories' safety report, if an accident occurred on a Topaz II launch and the reactor fell into the water, it could undergo "inadvertent criticality," a runaway nuclear reaction; if it fell from orbit it "may break up on reentry."[103] Physicist Ned S. Rasor, who has worked on U.S. space reactor development, pointed out that because Topaz II "will go critical—meaning an uncontrolled nuclear reactor—if immersed in water; [it] is therefore unsafe for launch according to both U.S. and Russian safety standards." Also, he explained that "no Topaz II system has been operated in space."[104]

Proponents of the Topaz II and nuclear power in space pushed for a flight test. "John Stevens of Martin Marietta Astronautics Group, Denver, praised the planned Topaz flight test, which has been championed by Air Force Col. Pete Worden, SDIO's deputy for technology," *Space News* reported in 1995. The space trade newspaper said that Stevens "predicted" that "the Topaz flight test will break down political barriers for use of nuclear power in space."[105]

As American as Nuclear Power

Interestingly, there is a question of whether nuclear power was ever even necessary for Star Wars. In the wake of what had been the expected fall of the Soviet nuclear-powered Cosmos 1900 in 1988 (the Soviets were able to finally loft their reactor to a higher orbit averting another nuclear space disaster), a U.S. Senate committee held a hearing on "Cosmos 1900 and the Future of Nuclear Power."

The chairman of the Senate Committee on Energy and Natural Resources, J. Bennett Johnston of Louisiana, was questioning Colonel George Hess of the Strategic Defense Initiative Organization.

From the transcript of the hearing:

The Chairman: Colonel Hess, you have got a difficult problem here in terms of stating the position because my belief is that SDI certainly for [weapons] requiring tens of megawatts and certain weapons platforms, if they are based upon beams are going to require nuclear power. I think it is possible, properly structured, to have those reasonably safe. But there is a lot of opposition to that, nuclear power in space. But if you tell this Committee that you do not need nuclear power, I am telling you, it is going to be hard to get SP-100 and the follow-ons funded up here because if there is an option of choice other than that, the Congress is going to go for it. I would submit to you it is very clear that you have got to have nuclear power in space for all those platforms, that solar is out of the question. I mean that is out of the question...You have got this big huge array up there which could be shot down with the most rudimentary space weapon, whereas you can harden a nuclear power system. Now, am I misstating that?

Colonel Hess: No, sir. We need the option to pursue nuclear power systems. They will be, for certain applications, the system of choice...

The Chairman: And anything else is really out of the question?

Colonel Hess: I believe in the inventiveness of the American engineer, sir, that if we were restricted to have no nuclear power that we would address other options. [106]

Well, the "inventiveness of the American engineer" was not allowed to look for an alternative to nuclear power for Star Wars—which, though, no matter how it might be powered, whether it be "Star Wars I" or "Star Wars II" or the Clinton/Gore versions, is wholly unnecessary and unworkable.

It is "folly," explains Dr. Kaku. There can be no "impenetrable shield around the United States. First of all, any enemy nation can simply put decoys inside the nose cones of their missiles. Even with Scuds you can put literally tens of thousands...of balloons that will simply inflate" and "confuse" spaceborne laser systems rendering them "essentially useless." Further, cruise missiles "can fly underneath any Star Wars system. So even [with] a Star Wars laser-based system in outer space, small nations are going to get interested in cruise missiles, which will simply fly underneath any Star Wars system."

But Star Wars did seal the union between NASA and the Pentagon. In 1991, NASA established a Nuclear Propulsion Systems Office at Lewis Research Center in Cleveland "to serve as the focal point for a renewed effort to develop nuclear propulsion for spacecraft" with NASA working with the Defense and Energy departments, which have been pursuing space-based nuclear power systems for the Strategic Defense Initiative."[107]

We have been getting used to military shuttle missions. Indeed, in 1991 the first one was held in which NASA did not even feel a need to downplay what was happening to the shuttle program, for which there was "no veil of secrecy. Flying 161 miles above the Earth, the crew of seven astronauts is to test anti-missile sensors for the Strategic Defense Initiative," reported the *New York Times*. "'This is the grand slam of all shuttle missions,' Discovery's pilot, Lieut. Col. L. Blaine Hammond Jr. of the Air Force, told reporters today."[108]

The militarization of the U.S. space program irked a few, a very few, federal officials. Congressman Harold Hollenbeck was among those bothered. As the book *Prescription for Disaster: From the Glory of Apollo to the Betrayal of the Shuttle* by Joseph Trento related, as the marriage blossomed Hollenbeck began "complaining openly about concessions from NASA to the Pentagon."[109]

In a 1982 "Space Day" speech back in his home district in New Jersey, Hollenbeck declared:

> On next week's flight a secret military cargo aboard Columbia will limit the use of live television....The question of the decade may be whether we use the shuttle for peace or for war. Now that the shuttle works, the military has climbed aboard the bandwagon. The gauntlet is down. The battle will be to save the civilian agency that brought us to the moon and beyond. I promise you that there are fights ahead and unless we Americans are vigilant, the civilian space program could be swallowed up in the giant whale called the Pentagon.[110]

"The tragedy is the American people are not aware of the politicizing and militarizing of the civilian space agency," Hollenbeck also declared in 1982, during a House committee hearing. "The Congress and the press have failed to do their jobs. How depressing it is to know that America's space policy for the 1990s is classified 'Top Secret'...The arrogance of this administration, of the military, and of some of the contractors toward a civilian agency that accomplished so much does not go unnoticed...I speak for a strong civilian space program not simply to annoy those that now run NASA, but because it was a civilian-run team that put us on the moon, that did it in budget...I, for one, do not want a gold-plated space program that is part of some Star Wars Pentagon."[111]

But that is exactly what much of the U.S. space program became: tied into the activities of the Pentagon, including its push for space nuclear power.

A Permanent Military Program

This move continues unabated. A *Space News* headline further announced the marriage in the spring of 1997: "Air Force, NASA Will Consolidate Space Efforts."

Washington—The NASA administrator and the commander of Air Force Space Command agreed...to coordinate and consolidate Pentagon and space agency efforts ranging from transatmospheric vehicles to studies of solar variability. In a two-page memorandum obtained by *Space News*, NASA Administrator Daniel Golden and Gen. Howell Estes, commander in chief of the Air Force Space Command in Colorado Springs, Colo., agreed to establish a Partnership Council to oversee consolidation of long-range planning, joint technology development programs and consolidation of rendundant assets.[112]

The story went on that "Air Force Space Command officials expect NASA's planned $1 billion investment in reusable launch vehicle technology will benefit the Pentagon's nascent military space plane development effort." It also quoted Goldin saying a few weeks before that "it would be foolhardy to have a separate budget in (the Defense Department) and a separate budget in NASA" for reusable launch vehicles. Also, "NASA and the Pentagon share a facility at Patrick Air Force Base and Kennedy Space Center, Fla," the article continued, again quoting Goldin as saying: "We want to make sure we are getting the most productive use out of those facilities."[113]

The article concluded with a quote from Lt. Colonel Don Miles of the U.S. Space Command saying that "the partnership" was "a great thing for America."[114] Really now? Whatever happened to the civilian U.S. space program? Clearly it is dying, if not dead.

CHAPTER FIVE

"NUKES FOREVER!"

There are many projects to use nuclear power in space that are underway, planned or being considered in addition to the Cassini plutonium-powered space probe and the Pentagon's schemes to use nuclear power for space weaponry and rocket propulsion.

Here are the ones we know about:

The New Evil Empire in Space: Killer Asteroids

A big campaign is being mounted for the use of rockets with nuclear weapons on them to deflect asteroids that might hit the Earth. With the Soviet Union, of Ronald Reagan's "Evil Empire" fame, no longer a threat for which a nuclear-powered Star Wars system would supposedly be needed, asteroids are seen as a perfect justification for NASA, DOE, the national nuclear laboratories, the Pentagon—the whole nuclear-in-space gang—to keep busy.

"There's a big surge of PR," Dr. Robert Park, professor of physics at the University of Maryland, was saying in early 1997 about the "flap" to field nuclear-armed rockets to fend off asteroids that might have their sights on Earth.[1]

In the spring of 1997 General Electric's NBC TV network broadcast a set of programs, one a two-part, four-hour miniseries called *Asteroid*. Headlined the review in the *New York Times:* "Will the Asteroids Destroy Kansas City? Guess."[2] The following week, NBC aired *Asteroids: Deadly Impact*, a *National*

Geographic hour on "the likelihood of asteroid annihilation,"[3] as *Newsday* described it. The message of the shows: Preparations must be made to fight off asteroids to defend the Earth as we know it—and fast.

To further pound the point home, geologist Eugene Shoemaker was on NBC's *Today* show the day *Asteroids: Deadly Impact* was to appear, stressing: "We know how to do it but we'd have to use nuclear devices."[4] Shoemaker and his wife Carolyn, who appeared with him on *Today*, were among the discoverers of a comet named Shoemaker-Levy that crashed into Jupiter in 1994.

The same week, Discovery Channel was airing a two-hour documentary on asteroids: *Three Minutes to Impact*. The following month, TBS TV was to enter the asteroid arena with *Fire From the Sky*. "And we haven't even mentioned the three big screen flicks on the subject in development," *Newsday* noted.[5]

Print media also jumped into the asteroid fray. "Chicken Little Was Right...The Sky *Is* Falling" was the line used during this same period on the cover page of the National Weekly edition of the *Washington Post* to promote a story inside headlined "The Sky *Is* Falling."[6] And the *New York Times* had an article, too, beginning with: "Astronomers who scan the sky for big rocks on a collision course with Earth are getting new support for their pet nightmares from once-secret military data."[7]

Just coincidentally, at Los Alamos National Laboratory, physicist Gregory Canavan was busy developing a plan that would cost $50 to $100 million a year—to use nuclear-tipped missiles to deflect asteroids.[8] "If you have a very short period of time and you have an object that's a couple of kilometers in diameter coming at you, then the main thing you have to work with is energy to knock the thing out of the way. Nuclear explosives produce the highest energy density of anything we now have available," Canavan told the space magazine *Final Frontier* for an article entitled "Killer Asteroids, Can Science Prevent Doomsday?"[9]

The push to develop rockets armed with nuclear weaponry to do battle with asteroids, meteors and comets has, in fact, been going on for several years. Dr. Park explained what the hoopla is really about in a 1992 op-ed piece in the *New York Times* and shot holes in the call for nuclear-armed rockets to beat off such space objects. His article was headlined "Star Warriors on Sky Patrol, Edward Teller Wants to Nuke Asteroids."[10]

"The cold war had ended, governments on both sides of what had once been an iron curtain were making plans to convert nuclear weapons laboratories to civilian purposes and to begin dismantling their huge arsenals of nuclear missiles. But on a bitterly cold January morning in New Mexico, a hundred scientists gathered at the Los Alamos National Laboratory to discuss new weapons armaments," noted Dr. Park. "Many of the nation's top experts on nuclear weapons and 'Star Wars' were there, including legendary father of the H-bomb, Edward Teller. The press was barred from the meeting."[11]

It was "a call to arms," Dr. Park said. "One speaker called for a fleet of 1,200 powerful new missiles to be made ready and armed with...nuclear warheads. Dr. Teller himself urged the development of a new superbomb—ten thousand times more powerful than any bomb ever built, a bomb so powerful it could never be detonated on Earth. It was Dr. Teller's 84th birthday...but he had lost none of his fervor."[12]

"As calls for more and bigger bombs continued, Lowell Wood, Dr. Teller's protégé at the Lawrence Livermore National Laboratory, could not contain his excitement," Dr. Park related. "From the back of the auditorium he shouted, 'Nukes forever!'"[13]

"The enemy? A killer comet. One might be discovered any day, headed for a collision with Earth. The handful of non-weapons scientists at the meeting, including experts on comets and asteroids, were horrified. The reduced threat of self-annihilation by an all-out nuclear war between super-powers had driven the weapons scientists to concoct a new justification for their work. Those who had defended the free world from the evil empire, far from becoming irrelevant, would now save Earth from cosmic disaster. How real is their fantasy?"[14]

There is the issue, of course, of how dinosaurs and other life forms became extinct on Earth 65 million years ago, with most scientists thinking that this occurred, explained Dr. Park, because of the "impact of an enormous asteroid in the Caribbean basin near present-day Mexico. Perhaps 10 miles in diameter and traveling 30,000 miles per hour," it is believed that "the killer rock kicked up a cloud of debris that plunged the entire world into cold and darkness lasting for months."[15]

Small asteroids, "packing a wallop equivalent to a thousand tons of TNT, slam into Earth every year or so. You rarely hear about them because they disintegrate on impact with the atmosphere," wrote Dr. Park. Pieces of asteroids—meteorites— "sometimes reach earth traveling only at the terminal velocity of a falling stone, occasionally punching a hole in someone's roof. The remarkable fact is that in all of recorded history, there is not a single account of anyone being killed by a meteorite."[16]

In 1991, what was described in some press accounts as a "'near miss' with a small asteroid...helped feed public apprehension. 'Near' is a relative term," Dr. Park pointed out.

"In this case, it meant the asteroid, about 30 feet in diameter, passed inside the moon's orbit. It was as though you stepped off a curb one day and declared that you had narrowly missed being run down by a truck that went by six hours earlier—on a different street. And it wasn't much of a truck anyway."[17]

The "greatest concern" involves large objects—a mile or more in diameter at least—but "fortunately, on the scale of human life, encounters with such large earth-crossing objects are extremely rare. Indeed, impacts of objects a mile or more in diameter seem to occur only about once every million years or so—or about as long as humans have existed. But when will the next one hit?"[18]

The Low-Tech Solution Ignored—Again

In fact, "scientists know the answer to that question," explained Park. Asteroids larger than a few hundred feet in diameter "can be detected and tracked with relatively modest telescopes," and once located, their orbits can be easily plotted. "The laws of celestial mechanics are rigid; if an orbit is accurately known, any collision with Earth can be foreseen far into the future."[19]

Researchers have been "cataloguing" asteroids and "none of the large asteroids" found "poses any threat to Earth." Still, Congress directed NASA in 1991 "to conduct two workshops on earth-crossing asteroids." The first was on what else might be done to look for asteroids and other objects that might hit the Earth. "The second workshop was charged with recommending ways to intercept and destroy or deflect such objects. It was that Los Alamos workshop that turned into a revival meeting for Strategic Defense Initiative true believers. The Star Warriors proposed to defend Earth at stupendous cost against an imagined menace that, if it exists at all, might not threaten Earth for millenniums—or thousands of millenniums."[20]

"By that time," declared Dr. Park, "civilization, if we haven't destroyed it, will presumably be better equipped to deal with the problem. In defending Earth against this miniscule threat, the Star Warriors would create a vastly greater hazard of nuclear missiles at the ready. Who will protect us from the 'nukes forever' mentality?"[21]

Five years later, Dr. Park was commenting that the asteroid frenzy was "starting up all over again. It's as crazy now as it was then." And the motive was the same: "This is employment for dislocated weapons scientists."[22]

Dr. Park repeated that "the frequency is so slight that to start making preparations now makes no sense at all. What does make sense is to track the asteroids. Once you have the asteroids tracked we know where they are going to go for the next couple of hundred years" and that would provide adequate time to "mount a defense against an asteroid."[23]

The Costly High-Tech Solution Doesn't Even Work...

A nuclear defense is not the answer. "Blowing the thing apart with a nuclear device may not be the best thing to do," said Dr. Park. For one thing, said the physicist, "setting off a hydrogen bomb next to it will not necessarily blow an asteroid up." Secondly, fragments of the asteroid could just keep flying in the same direction. Also, said Dr. Park, a non-nuclear approach should be considered. If "we really want to do something," launching a weaponless rocket that would intercept an asteroid "far enough away" could deflect it from its course in the friction-less void of space. "You would not have to push very hard," said Dr. Park. "And that would certainly be more effective than trying to blow it apart."[24]

Moreover, the non-nuclear approach is far preferable, said Dr. Park, than the "insane risk" of proliferating nuclear weaponry all over the Earth for the ostensible use of fighting off asteroids—but available for terrestial nuclear strife. "Having such weapons at the ready is so much a greater risk than the potential threat of asteroids that there is no comparison. And these people are talking about nuclear weapons mounted on missiles ready to go."[25]

An investigative article by Fran Smith on using nuclear power in space to fend off asteroids—and the gathering Dr. Park wrote about—came in *West*, the magazine of the *San Jose Mercury News*. The title: "Killer Asteroid Dooms Earth! And

If You Believe That, Edward Teller and Friends Have Several Billion Dollars Worth of Space Weaponry To Sell You."[26]

This piece emphasized that Dr. Wood, of the cry "Nukes forever!" was not just some mad scientist yelling from the back of the room, but a principal architect of the Star Wars program, a chief lieutenant of Teller's at Lawrence Livermore Laboratory. "His record is pretty good for having influence, even when his ideas are crazy," Louis Friedman, executive director of the Planetary Society, was quoted as saying about Wood. Indeed, according to Smith, the abrupt departure of NASA Administrator Richard Truly in that year was seen by "some people in the space community" as involving "Wood's hand....Wood had drafted a plan for a sweeping NASA reorganization, and sent it to the National Space Council, headed by [then Vice President Dan] Quayle," who then "engineered the ouster" of Truly.[27] (*Aviation Week & Space Technology* also described Wood as having a major role in Quayle forcing Truly out as NASA chief.[28])

Smith reported that the meeting at which Wood cried out "Nukes forever!" and Teller spoke, figured in this leadership change at NASA. "Scores of interviews, and private memos and letters obtained by *West* show that scientists are deeply split over what to do about asteroids. In one camp: astronomers who want to study rocks in space. In the other camp: Edward Teller and the Star Wars brain trust, post-Cold War. 'They want to introduce weapons in space,' says Louis Friedman...of the Planetary Society. 'And they'll come up with any justification they can to do that.'....The questions have taken on new urgency in recent weeks with the nomination of Daniel Goldin to head NASA. Goldin—an executive of TRW, a leading Star Wars contractor—was unknown among space scientists but a familiar figure in defense circles. Some asteroid astronomers now recognize that they inadvertently walked into a battle over NASA's fate."[29]

Journalist Smith added: "Truly's departure sparked fears of a growing military influence in the civil space program." Goldin, vice president and general manager of TRW Space and Technology Group, a prime Star Wars contractor, was appointed in 1992 to replace Truly as NASA administrator. And despite the departure the following year of President Bush and Vice President Quayle, under whom he received his position, Goldin was reappointed by President Clinton and remains NASA administrator today.

The *West* article quoted planetary scientist Dr. Clark Chapman as saying, after attending the meeting, that plans to use nuclear-armed rockets against asteroids were "outrageous projects...because they're so radically more expensive and elaborate and potentially dangerous than the modest threat they would address."[30]

But, noted Smith, "The asteroid threat might provide a new justification for SDI, which had been sold as a missile shield against the Soviet Union, an enemy that fell apart like a microasteroid hitting the atmosphere. 'We have a large technological community in the United States that has a large mission to play: protecting us from missiles raining down from the Evil Empire,' Clark Chapman says. 'Well, the Evil Empire has disintegrated. But the technological community hasn't.'"[31]

An exhaustive legal analysis on using nuclear power against asteroids and comets, *Asteroids and Comets: U.S. and International Law and the Lowest-Probability, Highest-Consequence Risk*, by attorneys Michael B. Gerrard, a specialist in environmental law, and Anna W. Barber,[32] was presented in 1997 at the New York University Law School Colloquium on Outer Space Law.

In it they stated:

It strikes us that the development, fabrication and launch of a device to carry out the experiments proposed by Dr. Teller and others is fraught with risk. A release of dangerous quantities of radioactive material (whether or not through detonation)

could occur through manufacturing error, launch failure, terror-
ist action, or several other plausible scenarios. The probabilities
of a radioactive release with locally adverse effects, or even a
catastrophic detonation, seem to exceed the chances of a long-
period comet sneaking up on us[33]

They saw numerous legal problems under U.S. and international law and treaties, although also pointing out that Star
Wars itself, with its design based on using nuclear weaponry in
space, was in violation of international law that forbids orbiting
nuclear weaponry.[34]

The late astronomer Carl Sagan was strongly opposed to the
notion of using nuclear rockets to try to fend off asteroids and
comets. He termed it "premature and dangerous...This is a case
where the cure might be worse than the disease." With the
push, coming at the end of the nuclear arms race, by the
national laboratories, for rockets to be used against space
objects, the timing was more than a coincidence, said Sagan,
and seemed like "an attempt to hitch nuclear weapons" to a
new and dubious rationale. He supported a program of inven-
torying large asteroids which might threaten the Earth, an
effort now going on internationally, named Spaceguard.[35]

Building nuclear rockets to do battle with asteroids might
sound nutty, but is it any more nutty than the plans to build
nuclear-powered airplanes or nutty (and illegal) as Star Wars
itself?

Nuclear-Powered Satellites
for High Definition TV

"High-definition, multichannel television beamed from
nuclear-powered communications satellites is being pursued by
scientists and engineers at Sandia National Laboratories in
Albuquerque," heralded the *Albuquerque Tribune* in 1994.[36]

Described as the pathway to making the United States a global telecommunications superpower, the Sandia proposal would pair controversial space nuclear power with entertainment and communications on demand. It has tantalizing economic potential and market implications, and it's being promoted as an opportunity for an alliance of U.S. companies, government agencies and the national laboratories to dominate the entertainment communications industry from space.[37]

The project was unveiled at the 11th Annual Symposium on Space Nuclear Power and Propulsion. "It's a window of opportunity," Roger X. Lenard of Sandia was quoted as saying. Dr. Lenard dismissed any concerns about the use of nuclear-powered devices in space. "Look, space already is highly radioactive," he exclaimed.[38]

Lenard said a "constellation of five such satellites, powered by high-energy reactors and strategically located in orbit around the Earth, could provide complete coverage of global markets," according to *Space News*." It would make the reception of so-called next generation HDTV available anywhere, anytime." Lenard said the first of the five nuclear-powered satellites "could be in orbit by the year 2000."[39]

High definition television or HDTV involves a high resolution television image that is to become the new standard for television broadcasts in coming years.

Nuclear-Powered Trips to Mars

This scheme was first outlined in 1991 to provide an additional, civilian use for the "Timberwind" rocket being developed for Star Wars. The military "Timberwind" endeavor was renamed the Space Nuclear Thermal Propulsion Program. It was cancelled in 1993[40] but the push continues to use a nuclear-propelled rocket to go to Mars. Advocates hope that the new Clinton administration national space policy announced in September 1996, under which the U.S. would develop nuclear-powered rockets for military and civilian use, will resurrect a program of building nuclear rockets to go to Mars.

"Nuclear thermal rockets are the choice propulsion technology for the interplanetary phase of the Mars mission," declared the report of the White House-created Synthesis Group on America's Space Exploration Initiative in 1991.[41]

That call is more relevant now than ever, insists Dr. Stanley K. Borowski, senior research engineer at the Advanced Space Analysis Office at the NASA Lewis Research Center. Nuclear power for rockets constitutes "the only technology that can satisfy all of NASA's future mission needs—from robotic science missions to piloted missions to the Moon and Mars." Further, he stated in 1996, the years of work on NERVA and related nuclear rocket projects during the 1960s and early 1970s established a foundation for rapid development today of nuclear-powered rockets. "A total of 20 rocket reactors" were "built and tested" then, he noted. Thus nuclear rockets have "already been demonstrated and could be readied for flight in less than a decade!"[42]

Borowski sees nuclear rockets having "early use on lunar missions, for exploration initially, and then to support "commercialization and settlement" and ultimately being utilized to open "the entire solar system to human exploration and settlement."[43]

Dr. Robert Zubrin, chairman of the National Space Society's executive committee and author of the 1996 book *The Case For Mars*,[44] also argues that nuclear power is necessary for a trip to Mars—and for all of space travel. "What could be worse than to be powerless? Wood, wind, water, coal, oil, gas and nuclear: these are the powers that have turned, and continue to turn, our wheels," says Zubrin. "Of these seven major sources of humanity's power, only one, nuclear, can work in space."[45]

"In order to provide a flight-qualified nuclear thermal rocket for the [then proposed] 2014 Mars mission, an aggressive development program must be initiated," said *America At The Threshold*, the 1991 report of The Synthesis Group, which was chaired by Air Force Lt. General Thomas P. Stafford, a former NASA astronaut.[46]

"Testing of an integrated nuclear thermal rocket presents a challenging engineering and political problem," acknowledged the 180-page report. "The safety issues regarding operation are principally concerned with accidental release of radioactive material." However, "location of potential Department of Energy ground test sites are very isolated and the amount of radioactive material in the engines assures that even if an accident releases 100% of the fuel, radiation levels outside the test site boundary would be below accepted national nuclear safety standards."[47]

"The issue of using a nuclear rocket in a flight test is more complex," The Synthesis Group went on. "Social and political perceptions, not just technical realities, are involved."[48]

But because a nuclear reactor would be involved, producing radioactive fission products only after a chain reaction begins, "the amount of radioactive material in the rocket engine prior to the nuclear engine's start would be orders of magnitude less than radioisotope thermoelectric generators which have already been safely launched (most recently, Ulysses)."[49]

Among those listed as "senior members" of The Synthesis Group in its report were former Strategic Defense Initiative Organization head Lt. General Abrahamson, who at that point had gone on to become executive vice president for corporate development of the Hughes Aircraft Company; Dr. Michael D. Griffin, then the current deputy for technology of the SDIO; former NASA Flight Director Christopher C. Kraft, Jr.; Lt. General Donald L. Cromer, former commander of the Air Force's Space and Missile Test Organization at Vandenberg Air Force Base; and Lt. General Thomas S. Moorman, Jr., commander of the U.S. Space Command.

The Synthesis Group reported to the National Space Council chaired by then Vice President Quayle, who staunchly endorsed its call for nuclear rocket propulsion. Quayle commented that "we're going to have to sell" the public "on the idea."[50]

The report said that a "particle bed reactor" design would be particularly promising to use on a nuclear-powered rocket for a Mars trip.[51] That, of course, was the nuclear system to propel the Star Wars "Timberwind" rocket. Soon after publication of the report, the move began to apply the "Timberwind" rocket to a Mars trip.

"Astronauts May Rocket to Mars, Trips Will Be Powered With Nuclear Energy," was a front-page headline of the *Albuquerque Tribune* in 1992. The story told of how Phillips Laboratory "will begin testing components of a powerful experimental nuclear rocket intended to take astronauts to Mars in the next century. The rocket technology grew out of secret Star Wars research already under way at Philips, the U.S. Air Force's space-research superlab."[52]

"The heart of the rocket engine will be 100 pounds of radioactive Uranium-235 made into black BBs," the article went on. "The tiny pellets, about one-half millimeter in diameter, will be encapsulated in ceramic. When the pellet bed is allowed to get hot during a launch, it will heat the hydrogen propellant to 5,000 degrees Fahrenheit, which will then roar out the back of the rocket and provide thrust. Phillips officials said an environmental impact statement has been completed, but not yet cleared for release to the public."[53]

A *Final Environmental Impact Statement for the Space Nuclear Thermal Propulsion Program*—as distinct from the earlier codename "Timberwind" program—was issued on May 1993. It did not deal with the impacts of the proposed nuclear-propelled rocket undergoing an accident on launch, crashing back to Earth or any other aspect of flight-testing or actual operation. Instead, the document concerned the "potential environmental consequences" of construction and ground-testing of the nuclear-propelled rocket "at two candidate test locations," DOE's Nevada Test Site or its Idaho National Engineering Laboratory.[54]

The Air Force found that in either location, the building and testing of the nuclear rocket would cause "less than 1 percent of the environmental radiation" in surrounding areas up to 50 miles away, "well below...EPA emission standards." It added that its analysis found "potential impacts of the test program on cancer fatalities and genetic defect rates were found to be extremely low relative to the normally expected occurrences in the exposed population."[55]

There was hot resistance in Nevada and Idaho.

The Environmental Defense Institute of Idaho complained that "for Idahoans this project is a resuscitation of the old" NERVA program "tests conducted at INEL [Idaho National Engineering Laboratory which], according to DOE's own studies, released over 781,300 curies of long-lived radiation to Idaho's air." Indeed, said Chuck Broscious of the organization, "DOE plans to reuse the same test facility and underground control room bunker" for the new nuclear rocket program. "The 2,000 megawatt nuclear rocket will use highly enriched (93%) Uranium-235 fuel particles. This is the equivalent of two or three conventional nuclear electrical power reactors being run to meltdown in an 850 second burst. The nuclear alchemists have clearly gone off the deep end. They must realize that Idahoans will not tolerate additional radiation in their environment. Getting the military's needless Star Wars hardware into orbit around Earth simply is not worth it."[56]

"This is folly, just sheer folly," said Chris Brown, Las Vegas director of Citizen Alert. "The military just never stops thinking up some new nuclear nightmare that they want to foist on the desert West."[57]

The U.S. Air Force tried desperately to sell the project. "Air Force officers are traveling the countryside of Nevada, Utah and Idaho, telling anybody who will listen that they have a great idea that poses no danger to civilians," reported the *Chicago Tribune*. "All the Air Force wants to do is test a radioactive machine in the deserts near their homes. The government was going to do it in secret anyway, the officers admit, but after the Soviet military threat eased, the cat got out of the bag and, well, by law they have to ask permission....The National Environmental Policy Act requires that an environmental impact statement be prepared for every contemplated major federal action. That was done in secret when 'Timberwind' was carried in the so-called 'black budget.' Now that it is declassified, the Air Force must prepare an environmental impact statement for the public. The act also requires a round of public meetings, called 'scoping sessions.'...They started last Tuesday in Las Vegas. Environmental groups and several lawmakers used the occasion to lodge angry objections and to voice dark suspicions."[58]

The military was doing rhetorical somersaults to try to gain support in this trip out into the world of public opinion. Lt. Colonel Roger X. Lenard—the same Roger X. Lenard who would be employed, the following year, at Sandia National Laboratories and unveiled the plan for nuclear-powered satellites for high definition television—wrote to the Institute for Security and Cooperation in Outer Space and insisted that a new approach was being taken: telling the truth.

"As you will find if you take the time to read through this document, the realities of public safety and potential environmental impact are truly inconsequential," Lenard, then chief of the Air Force's Concepts/Exploration Division, wrote the organization in 1993 as he sent it a copy of the environmental impact statement on the nuclear-powered rocket program. "The seminal issue is to ensure the public accepts the veracity of our statements. Unfortunately, in the past, we have assumed that we can be somewhat less than completely 'up-front' with the public regarding nuclear technologies: it has always led to problems."[59]

Lt. Colonel Lenard went on:

> My initial meetings with the environmental contractors on this program were quite revealing. There was substantial discussion as to how we were going to present an "acceptable" story to the public so we wouldn't have to explain the thorny issues. I quipped: "Why don't we just tell the truth?" This seemed to be an amazing revelation, but it worked so far.[60]

But the Space Nuclear Thermal Propulsion Program itself didn't work—so far. It was "cancelled after the U.S. Department of Energy declined an offer from the Pentagon that [the Department of] Energy assume responsibility for the project," reported *Space News*. The paper said it had "obtained a copy of the letter" that DOE Secretary Hazel O'Leary sent to the Pentagon advising that "current funding constraints and the lack of an identified mission require that we decline your offer. If the Department of Defense identifies a future application for either space nuclear propulsion or power, we would consider supporting those applications by sponsoring the development of the required nuclear technology." (The article, in its list of "key contractors," noted that Babcock and Wilcox was to manufacture the reactor for the nuclear rocket—the same company that produced the Three Mile Island nuclear plant.)[61]

Alternatives Dismissed, as Ever

Meanwhile, the Soviets and now the Russians have been offering the U.S. an extremely powerful non-nuclear rocket they make, the Energia, to use for a Mars mission.

"There would be no need for nuclear-powered rockets as assumed in some NASA interplanetary exploration studies," declared a group of four Stanford University professors, five Soviet space engineers and a team of 25 Stanford graduate engineering students which conducted a joint six-month study in 1991 on use of the Energia for a Mars mission.[62]

"It has a very feasible and very reasonable budget. It is the most direct and economical route," said Bruce Lusigan, a professor of electrical engineering at Stanford and director of the study group.[63]

The research concluded that "an international Mars mission, sharing costs and technologies, would be well within the present space budgets of the major space-faring nations [and] all but one of the technologies for human exploration of Mars is currently available to NASA. The exception—because of the abandonment [by NASA] of the Saturn V rocket—is a heavy launch vehicle capable of lifting the 100-ton spacecraft into Earth orbit. The Soviet rocket Energia would be a suitable substitute."[64]

Space News stated that in the Stanford-Soviet plan "Energia boosters first would deliver exploration vehicles and other supplies to an orbit around Mars. A crew of three men and three women would arrive two years later...The crew then would descend to the surface of Mars in a region known as Candor Chasma. After a year of exploration, they would return to Earth, leaving behind a base ready for subsequent visits."[65]

"The Stanford study," said *Space News*, "suggests that each Energia could be launched at a cost of $300 million, versus estimates of $12 billion by NASA and the U.S. Air Force to build the basis of a new family of rocket boosters."[66]

Professor Lusigan said: "We were urged by U.S. engineers and scientists of the international Mars exploration community to evaluate and document an efficient approach to manned exploration of Mars." And his group found the best way to Mars, he said, was using the Energia.[67]

The Energia, the most powerful rocket booster in the world, is still around and ready for expeditions to Mars. "The Russians lost the cold war, but they are starting to win the international race to fire hundreds of new satellites and spacecraft into the heavens, challenging Western rocket scientists and companies for launching jobs worth billions of dollars," William J. Broad wrote in the *New York Times* in 1996 in a story about Russian rockets. It was accompanied by a photo of the engine of the Energia with a caption noting how "it is so powerful that a weaker model is being developed for Western use."[68]

The *Times* story continued: "During the cold war Moscow perfected possibly 10 times as many kinds of liquid-fuel rocket engines as Washington did, analysts estimate. It clearly tried harder and refined a host of rocketry tricks that ended up giving its engines leads in performance and reliability."[69]

The *Times* said that Aerojet of California "is marketing one Russian rocket engine, the NK-33, that at least two American rocket makers are vying to use for commercial launchings....As companies race to exploit the Russian prizes, Western experts are probing, admiring and sometimes imitating the secrets."[70-]

> Over all, the Russian fleet of liquid fuel rockets was far more diverse than the West's and its rockets were far more powerful....Significantly, the Russians excelled without pushing technological limits—the opposite of the West's approach. Moscow often relied on kerosene, an inexpensive fuel....In their hunt for high performance, the Russians avoided hydrogen but sought to perfect higher combustion-chamber pressures, achieving ones for kerosene twice as high as those in the West, boosting the fiery push. They also managed to take advantage of every ounce of energy....The strides by the Russians made their engines robust, cheap and powerful.[71]

The article quoted Ted Casner, a Pratt & Whitney program director, as saying "as knowledge of the Russian expertise becomes more public, everyone is trying to arrange the appropriate partner that has access" to Russian rocket technology.[72]

But the chemically-fueled Energia is being shunned by the U.S. while the push goes on for trips to Mars by nuclear-propelled rockets.

On To Pluto

NASA plans to launch two plutonium-fueled space probes to Pluto in 1999. And despite the Energia not being actively considered for trips to Mars, NASA is considering another conventionally-powered Russian rocket, the Proton, to launch the probes.[73]

The Pluto probes will be smaller and cheaper than Galileo or Cassini. "Four years ago," the *New York Times* reported in 1995, NASA "engineers came up with a concept patterned on the big Galileo and Cassini spacecraft and costing as much as $4 billion. They were sent back to the drawing boards several times. Finally, they have developed a mission, called Pluto Express, at an estimated cost of $400 million, which NASA officials say may be an affordable level....Instead of packing many instruments in a single craft weighing several tons, engineers have designed two lightweight craft weighing as little as 300 pounds."[74]

Still, both probes to Pluto would use plutonium-fueled RTGs. The amount of plutonium in each has not been announced. NASA is considering the use of "flybys" on the Pluto Express mission.

A "Bi-Modal" Reactor for Military Satellites

The U.S. Air Force embarked on a $2 million study in 1994 of the use of "a space reactor that would provide power and propulsion for military satellites." The reactor is being called "bi-modal," said *Space News*, because of "the two modes [it] would operate in: as a propulsion system and for electric power."[75]

The "bi-modal" reactor is seen as necessary because "if a problem developed and managers wanted to reposition a satellite to another part of the world, current systems require weeks to make the shift," said *Space News*. "With bi-modal power, a satellite might be moved in a few days."[76]

Air Force Lieutenant Fred Kennedy, the "bi-modal power and propulsion program manager" at Phillips Laboratory, said, "the interest of [the U.S.] Space Command is clearly crucial in the development of the system."[77]

Space News added that David Buden, "bi-modal program systems engineering team leader" at Phillips, "said that the bi-modal system has several features that make it safe for use in space. It will not operate in low Earth orbit for 'appreciable times' and if it failed" the reactor could be boosted "to a higher orbit." Also, "if a launch accident landed it in the water, the design would prevent it from going critical. The reactor would be smaller than the nuclear power source required for the controversial 'Timberwind' project."

Sending Nuclear Waste Into Space

For many years, the U.S. planned to use rockets to send nuclear waste into space—but no such scheme was actually pursued because of a concern over the Earth getting doused with radioactive waste in the event that a rocket full of it blew up.

But at the Fourteenth Annual Symposium on Space Nuclear Power and Propulsion in Albuquerque, New Mexico in 1997, scientists from Brookhaven National Laboratory were back with a new plan. Doctors Hiroshi Takahashi and An Yu gave a presentation and submitted "an alternative plan to dispose of long-lived fission products (LLFPs)" by sending nuclear waste up on a space shuttle and then having it shot from the shuttle to the sun with an "electrostatic accelerator." "There is much concern about the possibility of a failure when launching LLFPs from the Earth," they noted. But the scientists didn't see a problem with their plan because "to protect the astronauts, NASA extensively studied the shielding of the rad-wastes which will be loaded into the space shuttle. Experiments were performed by dropping the capsule with its heavy shield material on to hard and soft ground surface; damage to the payload was examined to evaluate its impact in a launching failure." In any event, the radioactivity from all the radioactive waste "generated by running one nuclear power plant for one year...is less than the radioactive material Pu-238 [Plutonium-238] which is planned for use for the Cassini mission...The radioactivity of this Pu-238 is about 1000 curies compared to about 500 curies of our LLFPs."[78]

They also had an alternative to their "alternative plan"— bringing the nuclear waste to "the moon's surface" and from the moon, again using an "electrostatic accelerator" to send it off to the sun.[79] In this presentation, they did not spell out how the nuclear garbage would get to the moon.

In an earlier presentation of the plan by Dr. Takahashi and another Brookhaven National Laboratory scientist, Xinyi Chen, at a 1995 conference of the American Institute of Physics, they stated that through the years "it has been proposed to isolate HLW [high-level nuclear waste] in outer space using a rocket. However, this approach might disturb astronomical observations because the HLW would be a local source of radiation. Further, injection of HLW into the sun requires a rocket with more than about 30 km/sec velocity to carry the HLW, and even if the best chemical rocket fuel were used [the] mass of payload becomes very high [and] not economical unless a nuclear propulsion rocket can be developed."[80]

They said NASA has "studied the possibility of disposing of HLW waste using the space shuttle" and considered "several options for the potential space destinations for HLW, such as Earth orbits, solar orbits, solar system escape, and solar impact."[81]

Again, the idea of "ejecting" nuclear waste "using an accelerator" is proposed and they spoke of launch safeguards. For launches, the "shielding" of the radioactive material "should be considered, especially when a possible abort of the launching is considered. The package of LLFPs will have to be able to withstand the shock of crashing into the Earth."[82]

And they had an additional suggestion: "We might use a machine such as a rail gun or a large gun for sending [up] small LLFP projectiles; then the probability of a launching abort...can be substantially reduced compared to a large package of LLFPs. In this approach, a spacecraft could catch the LLFP's projectile while it is circulating in Earth orbit, and transport it to another spacecraft which is loaded with the electrostatic accelerator...needed to propel the LLFPs into outer space."[83]

At the end of both written versions of the presentations, the Brookhaven National Laboratory scientists noted that the research on nuclear garbage-dumping in space was paid for by Department of Energy contracts.

Nuclear-Powered Communications Satellite

An "aerospace industry alliance" was working on developing an "advanced communications satellite, *Space News* reported in 1994. "The satellite would need high power, perhaps as much as 100 kilowatts, and would use a nuclear fuel source in any version with power higher than about 25 kilowatts."[84]

A "consortium of seven firms including a Russian company" were involved in the scheme. Sterling Bailey, general manager of space power for Martin Marietta (now Lockheed Martin), said, according to *Space News*, that "the nuclear aspect of the project should not hinder it, although some opposition to a launch might occur." *Space News* said "the staff of U.S. Vice President Al Gore and the White House science office" had been "briefed" on the plan.[85]

Mining The Sky

"Lunar Mining Could Provide Future Energy Source For The Earth" was the heading of the NASA press release. "What will the 21st Century power plants look like?" it began. "Will they derive their energy from the burning of fossil fuels like 90 percent of their 20th Century predecessors? Or will they operate on a new, cleaner, more efficient fuel source?"[86]

"Researchers at the University of Wisconsin's Center for Space Automation and Robotics, one of 16 NASA Centers for Commercial Development of Space, are betting on the latter," the release went on. "They believe the future lies with helium-3, a rare element on Earth that potentially exists in large amounts on the Moon. One ton of this so-called Astrofuel could supply the electrical needs of a city of 10 million people when combined in a fusion reactor with a form of hydrogen."[87]

The scheme for mining the moon for helium-3 as fuel for fusion nuclear reactors has been expanded substantially since that 1990 release. Indeed, John Lewis, codirector of the NASA/University of Arizona Space Engineering Research Center, broadened the concept beyond the moon and beyond helium-3 in his 1996 book: *Mining The Sky: Untold Riches from the Asteroids, Comets, and Planets*.

Nuclear power figures centrally in the scheme to mine the moon. Further, in Lewis' plan, nuclear power would be the energy of choice for broader space exploitation.

Lawrence E. Joseph, a proponent of mining the moon for helium-3, stressed in an op-ed article in the *New York Times* in 1995, that through helium-3, a relatively safer and cleaner form of nuclear fusion could be done.

Fusion has been promoted by nuclear scientists as relatively safer and cleaner than nuclear fission. Fission is atom-splitting, the process that causes an atomic bomb to explode or a nuclear reactor or nuclear plant to work. Fusion involves fusing together atoms and is how a hydrogen bomb works. Is fusion less radioactive than fission? A fusion device generates somewhat less radioactivity than a fission system. But there's still plenty of radioactivity involved. Consider the hydrogen bomb and how "clean" it is.

(If you have been confused about fission and fusion, that is, in fact, the way it is supposed to be. As a classified Atomic Energy Commission document which surfaced during 1979 Congressional hearings on governmental responsibility for cancers caused by U.S. atomic weapons testing disclosed, Gordon Dean, chairman of the AEC, stated in a May 17, 1953 memo after speaking to President Eisenhower: "The President says 'keep them confused about fission and fusion.'"[88] That way, people would be further in the dark about the consequences of nuclear technology.)

Joseph, in his *Times* op-ed piece, agreed that fusion is not clean. "There's a dirty little secret to nuclear fusion: it can be very dirty. Somehow the myth has sprung up that unlike fission, the atom-splitting process that powers nuclear plants, fusion burns clean," he wrote.[89]

The "standard method of creating nuclear fusion," he related, has involved hydrogen and having it heated "to more than 100 million degrees centigrade while squeezing it so tightly that the nuclei of its atoms are forced to merge, releasing energy. Right now this process yields about 25 percent less energy than it takes to achieve and sustain fusion."[90] The hydrogen which gets squeezed is not normal hydrogen but radioactive isotopes of hydrogen—tritium and deuterium—the reason that fusion is plenty radioactive.

Despite the claims of fusion promoters, it is a process laden with radiation, Joseph admitted. "In fact, deuterium-tritium fusion, the hydrogen-based process on which the U.S. government has gambled nearly all its research funds, produces 80 percent of its energy in the form of lethal neutron radiation. At best, this means enormous problems with high-level radioactive waste. At worst, the neutron fallout could weaken the reactor walls and cause a meltdown."[91]

The Persian Gulf of the 21st Century

"But there's an alternative, helium-3, an isotope of the gas that makes balloons float," said Joseph. "Fusion based on helium is much cleaner and more efficient than hydrogen fusion."[92]

Again, as in the case of fission as compared to fusion of hydrogen, the difference is relative: "much cleaner" is not radiation-free by any means—helium-3 is also radioactive.

Still, pointing to this relative improvement, Joseph and other helium-3 fusion advocates argue for its use. The problem: there's very little helium-3 on Earth. But "there are vast amounts of helium-3—perhaps a million metric tons or the energy equivalent of 10 times all the recoverable fossil fuel that ever existed on this planet—lying ready to be extracted from the surface gravel of the moon," said Joseph.[93]

So the premise is that we should be off to the moon to mine helium-3.

And, it would not only be for power on Earth. "Harrison Schmitt, the former Apollo 17 astronaut who also served a term as U.S. senator from New Mexico, has taken up the cause," Joseph related. "He believes that compact helium-3 fusion reactors will one day extend the range of space vehicles much the way that fission reactors have enabled nuclear submarines to spend months at a time underwater."[94]

Joseph concluded his article by stressing that "NASA's case for financing space programs will be a lot stronger if the objective is profit as well as prestige. If we ignore the potential of this remarkable fuel, the nation could slip behind in the race for control of the global economy, and our destiny beyond."[95]

Joseph warned that the Russians may be coming—to the moon—for the helium-3 there, and the Japanese, too. So the U.S. had better get going. "Will the moon become the Persian Gulf of the 21st Century?" he asked.[96]

There, indeed, has been interest in Japan in mining helium-3 on the moon, working with Russia and also with a U.S. company on a "commercial robotic mission to the moon"—with the robots being nuclear-powered. *Space News* reported in 1996 that the U.S. company, LunaCorp, and the Mitsubishi Corp. of Japan is considering having a Japanese rocket send "a pair of rovers" to the moon. Each robotic rover would be powered by a "large, nuclear-powered radioisotope thermal generator—like those used on NASA planetary missions." As to what the moon robots would do, *Space News* said that LunaCorp Executive Vice President James Dunston told it: "One of the concepts behind the remote-controlled moon rover idea is for high-definition, live television images of the moon to be fed back to theme parks and other venues here on Earth where people could pay to be a part of the adventure."[97]

John Lewis, in *Mining The Sky*, calls not only for mining the moon for helium-3 but mining planets for helium-3 as well—Uranus is "the target of choice for helium-3 retrieval"[98]—and mining asteroids, and comets, too. "Asteroids contain a variety of rare radioactive isotopes of potassium, uranium, thorium, rubidium, and so on. Of these, uranium and thorium can be used to generate power in nuclear reactors."[99]

Nuclear power—in terms of material to be mined and the use of nuclear power—permeates the Lewis approach. In his plan for mining on Mars, for example, he says "a small reactor or radioisotope thermoelectric generator makes electrical power available 24.5 hours per day on Mars. The size of the power plant is fixed by the need to provide all the processing plant power needs, both electrical and thermal, from its electrical output."[100]

Even mining on far-off and inhospitable Uranus would involve nuclear power.

> We would begin by launching a Uranus entry probe from a space station in orbit around Earth. The probe would perhaps be 'slingshot' through Jupiter's or Saturn's gravity well to cut

down the trip time to Uranus. After about six years of flight, the probe enters the upper atmosphere of Uranus at high speed. A heat shield, very similar to that carried by the Galileo entry probe, protects the probe mechanism during entry and deceleration to below the speed of sound. Once the probe drops to subsonic speed, it deploys a small parachute to drag out a larger chute, which in turn slows the probe down to low speeds. Then a balloon, looking like a bundle of long cylinders, is unreeled from the probe and inflated with atmospheric gases. The heat shield and parachutes, no longer needed, are dropped off, and a megawatt nuclear reactor starts up and begins heating air and flushing the balloon cluster with heated air. The probe slows in its descent as it passes through ever denser layers of atmosphere until, at a pressure of a few atmospheres, it finally reaches neutral buoyancy and stops falling. Pumps and refrigeration equipment, powered by the reactor, turn on and start liquefying the atmosphere.

Part of that liquefied Uranus atmosphere would be helium and of this, helium-3 would be "separated from" the rest of the helium and "stored for return to Earth." The helium-3 will be "worth $16,000,000 a kilogram (about $7,400,000 per pound)," emphasizes Lewis.[101]

And, in addition to being used back on Earth, the helium-3 would be widely used "in spacecraft propulsion."[102] Lewis envisions fleets of fusion rockets.

This fusion rocket has such a high exhaust velocity that it can outperform the best chemical propulsion systems, like hydrogen/oxygen rockets, by enormous factors. The fusion rocket could, for example, lift heavy payloads out of the atmospheres of Jupiter and Saturn—such as big tanks of helium-3. Thus, helium-3/deuterium fusion is not simply an end in itself but also an extraordinarily useful tool...Fusion-powered outbound trips to Mars can be flown in eight months...Comparable trips to the heart of the asteroid belt would take about eighteen months. Cargo deliveries from

Uranus and Neptune could be speeded up from six years to about two...Manned flights to any planet, asteroid, satellite, or comet in the solar system is within our reach if we master helium-3/deuterium fusion. *The solar system is ours to take*.[103] (His italics.)

Exploring space for profit—and before the Japanese or the Russians beat us to the nuclear gold way yonder—is seen as a major new strategy by those pushing the U.S. space program.

The National Space Society held a "Space Summit" in Washington in November 1996 "to discuss Mars and the future of the U.S. space program," as *Ad Astra*, the magazine of the National Space Society put it. NASA officials were there, as were former Senator Harrison Schmitt, now a member of the National Space Society's board of governors, Dr. Zubrin, and the ubiquitous Teller protégé, Dr. Lowell Wood, among others, said *Ad Astra*. The "final speaker" for the "Space Summit" was S. Pete Worden, who formerly was an Air Force colonel with the Star Wars program and then went on to become director of advanced concepts, science and technology for the National Space Council.[104]

Worden told the "Space Summit" that it won't likely be scientific inquiry that will get money flowing for a Mars mission, said *Ad Astra*. Reported the magazine: "Curiosity, he suggested, is a long shot for getting funding for a human to Mars mission. The qualities that will drive such a mission forward are greed and fear—fear that somebody else will beat us to the prize and the possibility that riches could result."[105]

New principles for the U.S. space program: "greed and fear?" Or are they so new?

CHAPTER SIX

CENSORED

Why is it most likely that you, reading this book, are learning for the first time about the use of nuclear power in space? Or, if you had some idea about what was going on, why is it until now you never had the details about an activity that could so severely impact all of us?

Project Censored, a media research project based at Sonoma State University in California, has repeatedly cited my journalism on the use of nuclear power in space as among the most "under-reported" or "best-censored" stories in its annual judging. Indeed, this year, 1997, the Project Censored panel of judges determined it was the top "under-reported" or "best-censored" story of the prior year. The panel includes such figures as Ben H. Bagdikian, professor of journalism emeritus, Graduate School of Journalism, University of California at Berkeley; Herbert I. Schiller, professor of communications emeritus, University of California, San Diego; George Gerbner, dean emeritus Annenberg School of Communications, University of Pennsylvania; Pulitzer Prize-winning journalist and author Susan Faludi; Citizens Union President Rhoda H. Karpatkin; author and Center for Living Democracy co-director Frances Moore Lappé; former Federal Communications Commission member Nicholas Johnson; Donna Allen, founding editor of *Media Report to Women*; author Holly Sklar; Judith Krug, director of the Office for Intellectual Freedom of the American Library Association; Barbara Seaman, co-founder of the National Women's Health Network; and Charles Klotz, editor of the *St. Louis Journalism Review*.

My journalism on nuclear power in space has made the Project Censored list in three previous years: 1987, 1988 and 1989. Mark Lowenthal, associate director of Project Censored, says that is more times than any single issue has been cited "in the top ten other than the general issue of nuclear safety, which has been cited seven years over the twenty-one years of Project Censored. However, the issues clearly dove-tail."[1]

Why the dearth of coverage on nuclear power in space?

First, there has been little critical press coverage overall, throughout the years of NASA's space program. This media deficiency—the result of "boosterism" by space reporters and the view of much of the U.S. media that the space program is a kind of "motherhood" issue, not to be criticized—has been a subject of examination by media reviews in the wake of the Challenger disaster and, nearly two decades before that, the fire on a Saturn rocket which killed three astronauts preparing for the Apollo missions.

Second, add in nuclear power and the situation becomes even more of a hot potato for media. Most of the U.S. press historically has been soft, some in fact outright derelict, in reporting on nuclear technology. This has been a result of the nuclear establishment's well-orchestrated public relations effort to manipulate the media—right from the start of the nuclear enterprise—and the nature of who owns U.S. media. Much of the corporate media have either indirect or direct connections to the nuclear industry. General Electric and Westinghouse, the two biggest nuclear hardware manufacturers in the world, own two of the three major U.S. TV networks: GE owns NBC and Westinghouse owns CBS and their associated media operations. Before acquiring the two networks, both controlled a good chunk of U.S. media.

In the U.S., censorship does not happen like it does in other nations, where powerful forces, usually governments, dictate what is to be reported in the "official" or "semi-official" media.

In the U.S. the censorship function typically involves the sin of omission.

Certain subjects just don't get reported.

The Space Con Job

Long-time media analyst William Boot's article, "NASA and the Spellbound Press"[2] was published in the *Columbia Journalism Review* after the Challenger accident. In this strong analysis of the poor reporting on the U.S. space program, Boot claims there is a breakdown in the supposed watchdog role of the U.S. media.

"Dazzled by the space agency's image of technological brilliance, space reporters spared NASA the thorough scrutiny that might have improved chances of averting tragedy— through hard-hitting investigations drawing Congress's wandering attention to the issue of shuttle safety," wrote former *Columbia Journalism Review* editor Boot.[3]

He found "gullibility" in the press. "The shuttle seems, in retrospect, to have been one of the biggest con jobs in recent memory—a craft without a clear purpose sold by NASA on the basis of wildly optimistic cost and performance projections. The press, infatuated by man-in-space adventures, was an easy mark."[4]

Even if a few reporters had concerns, editors did not, Boot found. "ABC national correspondent Lynn Scherr told me she could not convince editors that shuttle launches were much more dangerous than 747 takeoffs. The prevailing complacency was epitomized by *Chicago Tribune* columnist Bob Greene, who wrote during Sally Ride's flight as the first American woman in space: 'Although she's all that way out there, we feel we can talk candidly about her because there's no doubt that she's coming home safely.'"[5]

"News organizations, which tended to assume that the spacecraft was relatively safe, nagged NASA about launch delays while paying little heed to a growing list of danger signs,

from fuel leaks to failing brakes to engine accidents," wrote
Boot. "They tended to assume that NASA was reasonably well
run, despite much evidence to the contrary."[6]

And also:

> Journalists who did try to assess dangers associated with shuttle
> equipment prior to the accident speak of a layman's frustration
> in matching wits with experts. For instance, *Houston Chronicle*
> reporter Carlos Byars says he once tried to check out a claim of
> some astronauts that the danger of shuttle-tire blow-outs
> (potentially fatal) was heightened because the Kennedy Space
> Center runway was too rough. He quizzed NASA engineers
> who had designed the runway. These experts insisted that it
> was not too rough. Byars was not entirely convinced, but felt
> he had to drop the matter. "I'm not equipped to debate the
> engineering of such a system," he told me.[7]

"Jim Askers of the *Houston Post* also admits that the glamour
of space travel helped to divert reporters' attention from the
safety issue," said Boot. "What most space journalists wanted to
write about, and what their readers presumably wanted to read
about, was the derring-do of dauntless astronauts ('looking like
a modern knight-errant in shining space suit, [he] sallies forth
into the darkness, powered by a Buck Rogers backpack,' *Time*,
November 26, 1984) and the sheer, untechnical marvelousness
of the shuttle itself ('magnificent on the pad, a space age Taj
Mahal that leapt into the sky on twin pillars of impossible
bright yellow and blue flame,' *Newsweek*, April 27, 1981)."[8]

And "beyond space reporters' technical insecurity and
preference for glamour lay another impediment to criticism
of NASA: the agency's powerful positive image. It had been
polished by the triumphs of Project Mercury and the moon
landings and by the accolades of reporters themselves. *U.S.
News & World Report*, for instance, once described NASA as
a 'concentration of mechanical and human genius.'"[9]

All in all, "U.S. journalists have long had a love affair with the space program," wrote Boot. "In the pre-[Challenger] explosion days, many space reporters appeared to regard themselves as participants, along with NASA, in a great cosmic quest. Transcripts of NASA press conferences reveal that it was not unusual for reporters to use the first person plural. ('When are *we* going to launch?') Howard Benedict, the AP's veteran Cape Canaveral Bureau chief, said in a lecture on the shuttle in 1984: 'One had a feeling of...participating in the beginning of a truly great adventure' ('Writer Lauds Space Shuttle Flights,' *Salt Lake Tribune*, October 18, 1984)."[10]

"And, of course, there was NASA's Journalist In Space competition, which, prior to the Challenger accident, had drawn 1,705 applicants (including me)," Boot continued, "eager, as the NASA form stipulated, to 'share the experience of space travel.' The contest elicited responses such as the following from former ABC correspondent Geraldo Rivera: 'To beat through the air and clouds and sail through the vast ocean of vacuum, what must that be like?' Not much like investigative reporting, I wouldn't think."[11]

"That contest notwithstanding, reporters' self-interest was perhaps only a drop in the bucket of pro-NASA bias," related Boot. "Journalists, after all, comprised a cheering section for the space program long before there was any hope that one of them could bag the great cosmic assignment. In Project Mercury days, as Tom Wolfe observed, journalists lionized U.S. astronauts as single-combat cold warriors, airbrushed the physical imperfections from news photos of their wives, and refused to quote Chuck Yeager, the man who broke the sound barrier, when he derided the pilot skills required of Mercury astronauts ('A monkey's gonna make the first flight')."[12]

One driving force in space reporting has long been a kind of techno-patriotism, as Wayne Biddle, a former *New York Times* technology reporter puts it, "In our society, technological optimism is clearly a kind of religion, a matter of faith." So it was on the space beat when the shuttle made its first flight. For the news media, the craft became a symbol of U.S. technological redemption following an era of American malaise....It is difficult to knock a powerful symbol of what is "right" with America; most reporters were not pre-disposed to try, and those who were skeptical of the shuttle, such as Biddle, encountered editorial resistance. Biddle, who resigned from *The New York Times* in September 1985, out of frustration, he says, with his editors, recalls that "it was always an uphill battle to get articles critical of the shuttle into the paper. There was a great deal of resistance—a sort of corporate culture where you knew you were swimming upstream."[13]

The More Things Change...

There was "some new blood" brought in to report on the U.S. space program after the Challenger catastrophe, indicating, said Boot, that "the days of NASA as a journalist's sacred cow are presumably gone forever. It is sad that it took the deaths of seven astronauts to goad journalists into assuming the thoroughly skeptical role they should have been playing all along."[14]

There were a few switches in reporters covering the U.S. space program in 1986—but that ended up meaning nothing. Boot's hope of NASA no longer being a "journalists' sacred cow" has, in fact, not become reality.

Indeed, a few years afterwards, *New York Times* space reporter John Noble Wilford was giving a lecture to scientists at Brookhaven National Laboratory on "Science and the Media."

"I am a great admirer of science, of scientists," Wilford, twice the winner of the Pulitzer Prize for science reporting, told the national lab scientists. "Why else would I be doing what I'm doing? I'm particularly intrigued by science and scientists because I believe they are the very heart and soul of exploration in our century...My favorite subject is planetary science."[15]

I was able to get in to witness the 1990 presentation and from the audience asked Wilford about the earlier *Columbia Journalism Review* article which found that space reporters did not challenge NASA, were too cozy with the agency.

"This is one of the problems in journalism, particularly reporters who cover a specific beat," Wilford replied. "You get to know people, you get to be friendly with some and not so friendly with others. But you get to know them and you get to respect them, and maybe you trust what they say and maybe you do let your guard down and not ask the tough questions."[16]

"However," insisted Wilford, "I think Challenger would have happened anyway." This is because, he said, no "whistle-blower" had come to the press to tell of the problem with the O-rings on the shuttles. Wilford went on: "What if reporters had then gone out and sort of brow-beat NASA to make fixes...would this have prevented it? Well, yes," he ventured. Yet, he then went on, "No reporter could have gone through every system in the shuttle to review its reliability. You have to have whistleblowers."[17]

After his talk, I walked down from the audience, introduced myself as a journalist, and asked Wilford whether he thought a lack of vigor among space reporters continued. He said: "Yup, there's still a lot of space reporters who are groupies. Some [of them] are turned on by rockets and science fiction and they got into it because of that, and they tend to be the least critical. They go along because it's fun. But I think the mainline reporters are more critical and more skeptical when NASA says this, this and this. We are more apt to ask some tough questions, tougher questions than we used to [before the Challenger accident]."

Still, he said, "some of the things that NASA does are so great, so marvelous, so it's easy to forget to be critical. You go in and watch pictures of the back of Neptune and stand in awe, but then you read about some of the management snafus" and wonder "how did we ever do what we did?"

Later that year, when the Galileo space probe with 49.25 pounds of plutonium on board made its first Earth "flyby" 600 miles above the planet, Wilford didn't use the words plutonium or nuclear at all, or give any indication of the concerns— including those in the NASA safety reports—about the Galileo "flybys." His story began, "A spacecraft bound for Jupiter was back in the neighborhood yesterday..."[18]

Then, two years later, when Galileo was back for its second "flyby" 185 miles overhead, Wilford again didn't discuss the nuclear issues, nor write about the series of serious Galileo problems between "flybys." Instead, Wilford's story reported: "Flight controllers at NASA's Jet Propulsion Laboratory in Pasadena, Calif. said Galileo's course was true, with no chance of an errant plunge into Earth's atmosphere."[19] And he quoted Galileo project manager William J. O'Neil as likening the "slingshot maneuvers to a 'multi-cushion planetary billiard shot.'"[20]

In his then recently-published book, *Mars Beckons, The Mysteries, The Challenges, The Expectations of Our Next Great Adventure in Space,* newsman Wilford waxed poetic on how "a fleet of cargo ships, possibly powered by a new kind of rocket using nuclear-electric propulsion" would provide supplies for a base on the moon. "Experiments would be carried out in all aspects of long-duration human planetary habitation: life sciences, psychological effects and group dynamics, exploration of natural resources, and scientific exploration." From there, on a nuclear-powered rocket, Wilford related, "people would be ready to take the greater stride, to Mars."[21]

"Could the Media Have Prevented Shuttle Disaster?" was the headline of the lead article by M.L. Stein in *Editor & Publisher,* the press trade journal, after the Challenger accident. It began: "Reporters knew about the problems plaguing the shuttle Challenger but the story was never fully told because of their complacency, NASA publicity hype and a dwindling interest in space achievements by the public and editors."[22]

CBS reporter Bruce Hall, who covered the space program, was quoted in the article saying: "We now know that NASA was playing space-age Russian roulette and lost....We had become lackadaisical. We were being spoonfed by a very good NASA public affairs office. And when we did turn up something, editors and show producers had no interest."

Also, "when reporters did get wind about NASA's problems, its PR apparatus was excellent at refuting and defusing the story."[23]

Los Angeles Times reporter Gaylord Shaw also said in the article, "We know that NASA is like any other government agency. We now know plenty about what happened [and] didn't do a very good job pre-Challenger. We missed the story. But the media has done quite a good post-Challenger job," he claimed, insisting that "the good old boy network is gone—and the public should be the winner."[24]

In fact, "the good old boy network" of reporters covering NASA is not gone at all—it remains the prime characteristic of the corps of space reporters. And the public still stands to be the loser—and with nuclear power involved, a big, big loser.

"A lot of these space reporters see themselves as privileged spectators, space boosters, cheerleaders," says Bruce Gagnon, co-coordinator of the Global Network Against Weapons & Nuclear Power in Space and coordinator of the Florida Coalition for Peace & Justice, who has had dealings with space reporters for many years.[25]

He was speaking after the Russian Mars space probe had fallen on Chile and Bolivia in November 1996 and he had just sought to hold a press conference in front of NASA's Kennedy Space Center to warn that the Russian space probe accident was, at the least, an important wake-up call in the face of an expanding U.S. program to use nuclear power in space. In faxes to media, as well as notices he distributed to "tons of media" arriving for a shuttle launch, Gagnon noted that NASA intended to launch the Cassini space probe in October 1997 with 72.3 pounds of plutonium, 150 times more than the Russian space probe carried. The press kit contained information on the danger NASA was acknowledging in its *Final Environmental Impact Statement for the Cassini Mission*, both with the Cassini launch and NASA's plan to have it come hurtling back at Earth for a "flyby" in 1999. Gagnon suspected that few reporters might be coming to the press conference because "you could just see the look on their faces when I gave them the material: that this was a space controversy and 'I don't want to touch that.'" Only two reporters showed up.[26]

Three months later, Gagnon was pointing out that "some of the space reporters are still reporting that the Russian Mars space probe fell 'harmlessly' into the ocean."[27]

"These reporters don't know very much or are firmly in the pocket of NASA," said Gagnon. "Either way, it doesn't say much for the media."[28]

Gagnon said he has found the reporters who cover space for television "the worst. They are the biggest boosters of all." But print reporters are not far behind, including those near the launch site in Florida. "One of the big issues in Brevard County" where both the Kennedy Space Center and Cape Canaveral Air Station are located "is the toxic problem from launches. It's endemic. I recently received a letter from a woman suffering from serious lung problems. There have been wildlife and fish kills but you can't get that into print. The press doesn't want to touch that in Brevard County. It might end up being critical of the space program."[29]

Space reporters in general approach the space program like "it's a game and they report launches like baseball box scores," said Gagnon. "They won't do any real investigative work.

They see themselves as part of the space program. They view anyone critical of it as unfriendly."[30]

"But we can't just blame the space beat reporters," said Gagnon. "We've also got to look at the editors and the people who own the media. They see themselves as part of the system, a system that promotes nuclear power and weapons in space."[31]

Dan Hirsch, president of Committee to Bridge the Gap, who, because of the group's years of challenge to Star Wars—especially its nuclear component—has also had long experience dealing with space reporters, comments, "I have just been stunned about the way they genuflect to NASA."[32]

There is "a combination of factors here: an identification of mainstream reporters with the establishment, thus their allegiance to government agencies they consider respectable and a tradition going back" to the early years of the space program when boosterism in space reporting became a tradition, said Hirsch. "Journalists are supposed to keep an arm's length from what they cover but I've found space reporters to be cheerleaders for NASA."[33]

The Circus of History

The situation, in fact, goes way back, well before the Challenger disaster.

Nineteen years before the Challenger blew up, the *Columbia Journalism Review* did an extensive, two-part series on the lack of vigilant press coverage of the U.S. space program. That came a few months after the fire on a Saturn rocket to be used for an Apollo mission which killed astronauts Virgil "Gus" Grissom, Edward White and Roger Chaffee.

"Of the questions raised by the Apollo fire of January 27, 1967, one of the most important, yet least discussed, is whether the American press, print and electronic, performed its traditional 'watchdog' role in covering the space program before the fire," wrote James A. Skardon. "Did the press demonstrate that it can monitor effectively such a powerful and virtually autonomous multi-billion-dollar governmental complex as the National Aeronautics and Space Administration?"[34]

"The money, the risks, the national prestige, and the scope of scientific and military research involved add up to a public stake great enough to demand full and continuous information about NASA projects," he went on.[35]

Skardon declared: "NASA is required by law to keep the public informed. Yet one of the revelations of the Apollo tragedy was that the public not only knew relatively little about NASA and the true state of Apollo before the fire, but much of what it did know was distorted."[36]

Skardon quoted from a piece in the *Nation* earlier that year by William Hines, science editor of the *Evening Star* of Washington, "one of the handful of newsmen who have looked at NASA with a critical eye" who commented "that NASA's initials are jokingly said to stand for 'Never A Straight Answer.'"

Hines also contended that "in these flack-ridden times it is perhaps not surprising that the taxpaying public should be hoodwinked, falsely propagandized, deliberately misled and, on occasion, even lied to by its servants. It is deplorable, however, and dangerous in the bargain, that NASA has deluded itself into believing the reality of its own Image."[37]

Skardon continued: "The show-business approach of the [TV] networks to the launchings and the accompanying ratings battles characterized the early phases of the space program. The print media also contributed their share toward turning the space shots into circuses."[38]

Starting the second article in the series, Skardon wrote: "If there was one aspect of the space program in which it was incumbent on the press to serve as watchdog, it was in the matter of safety. Yet the record shows a superficial and incomplete performance—despite the frightening precedent of the Mercury project, which logically should have served to a much greater degree to alert the press."[39]

As far as the public was concerned—on the basis of what it read, heard, and watched—the Mercury flights were by and large marvels of success. Yet the report of manufacturing performance that NASA finally released in October, 1963, revealed such a shocking record of defective parts, carelessness, and ineptitude, that, in the last analysis, only good fortune and the skill of the astronauts prevented a disaster. Through 1966—and up to the time of the Apollo fire—there was a series of accidents which, if viewed as a pattern, could have alerted the press to a need for a thorough re-examination of the Apollo program. These mishaps were reported as individual events...No space writer or publication considered them as a pattern nor did any extensive looking into the quality and safety aspects of Apollo. Instead there were stories such as the one in the December 26, 1966 issue of *Aviation Week* which reported, "Apollo System Maturing Despite Problems [less than 30 days prior to the fire that killed the three astronauts]."[40]

"Why did the press fail to provide the public with adequate information on...the evidence of shoddy workmanship and the accident record, and the circumstances touching on the Apollo fire itself?" The reason, concluded Skardon, "is that many of the journalists covering NASA were so caught up with the rest of the country in the challenge, drama, and excitement of the race to beat the Russians to the moon that they came to regard themselves as part of the space 'team.'"[41]

"Two factors may have contributed to the drift that brought some members of the press to close to the Establishment. The first was the scientific-technical language that the press and the space people used in common. This had the effect of drawing the press into the NASA 'family.' The second factor," said Skardon, "involved the 'hostile' outsiders, who came to be identified primarily as Congressmen and their supporters who would cut the NASA budget. All hands, consciously or unconsciously, seem to have made a common bond that they would do nothing to endanger appropriations."[42]

Even a veteran of the space program, Dr. Bruce Murray, former director of NASA's Jet Propulsion Laboratory, a space scientist, has spoken out on the uncritical way media have approached the program.

As Murray wrote in *Journey Into Space: The First Thirty Years of Space Exploration:*

> Prior to the Challenger accident the Space Shuttle received uncritical and unduly supportive treatment by nearly all journalists and reporters....The fantasy of the Shuttle as a safe, cheap, and effective means for Americans to enter the new frontier of space was so appealing to most audiences that there was simply no journalistic market for naysayers. Most serious for informed American opinion, the media were not committed enough to the public interest. The print media and, especially, television did little more than tell the public what it wanted to hear....Until the Challenger, there was rarely any incisive reporting about NASA's shortcomings.[43]

The Nuclear Con

If the press hasn't done its job when it comes to the space program, its dysfunction on the issue of nuclear power has been of even longer and broader duration.

Those involved in atomic power began manipulating the media at the birth of the technology—with the rationale, at the time, that war necessitated deception.

In 1945 The Manhattan Project, getting ready to test and deploy the atomic bombs it had built, hired *New York Times* reporter William L. Laurence as a public relations consultant. Laurence remained on the *Times'* payroll.[44] The *Times* managing editor had "approached" Laurence that spring and said, "I have a letter here from General Leslie R. Groves. He wants to see you," according to a history of nuclear technology, *Time Bomb.* Laurence "met with General Groves," the head of the Manhattan Project, and thereafter "went 'on loan'" working out of the laboratory in Los Alamos, New Mexico (now Los Alamos National Laboratory) where the earliest bombs were built.[45]

A first major assignment for Laurence: figuring out how to mislead the press—and public—when the first atomic bomb test, code-named Trinity, took place at the government's Alamogordo bombing range in the New Mexico desert on July 16, 1945. The scientists of the Manhattan Project were unsure what would happen. "Anything might go wrong. They had gambled three years and two billion taxpayers' dollars on the project; the time had come to see if it would work," related *Time Bomb*. "Would the bomb produce a mighty explosion or a fizzle?"[46]

"Safety was a second concern," according to *City of Fire*, a history of Los Alamos and the Manhattan Project. "What if radioactive dust drifted over nearby towns?" An army major was "stationed north of the test area with 160 enlisted men on horses and in jeeps [and] instructed to evacuate ranches and towns at the last moment if necessary."[47]

In any case, the press and public were not to know what was happening. They were to be kept in the dark—as a matter of wartime censorship. The test was scheduled for the middle of the night. The bomb would likely light up the night sky.

Laurence prepared "four different press releases" based on a lie to keep the story of the first atomic explosion out of the press, notes *Nukespeak*.[48] The release would claim that an ammunition dump explosion had occurred. Laurence's four press releases only differed "on the size of the explosion they described."[49]

The Manhattan Project sent an intelligence officer, Phil Belcher, to the Associated Press office in Albuquerque with the press release, recounts *City of Fire*.[50]

The atomic bomb was exploded. When the fireball rose and the desert was bathed in eerie, blinding white light with an ominous mushroom cloud billowing, the scientific director of the Manhattan Project, Dr. Robert Oppenheimer, was struck, he later recalled, by the words of the sacred Hindu book, the *Bhagavad-Gita:* "I am become death. The shatterer of worlds."[51]

The light of the explosion was seen all over the southwest. "The first flash of light was seen in Albuquerque, Santa Fe, Silver City and El Paso," notes *City of Fire*. "Windows had been broken in nearby buildings and had been rattled in Silver City and Gallup. A rancher sleeping near Alamagordo was awakened suddenly with what seemed like a plane crashing in his yard...A forest ranger in Silver City reported an earthquake to the Associated Press....The Associated Press office in Albuquerque soon had a number of queries and reports on a strange explosion in southern New Mexico."[52]

It was then that Belcher gave the AP the "news release," says *City of Fire*.[53] The AP obediently moved this phony account written by newsman William Laurence:

Alamogordo, July 16—The Commanding Office of the Alamogordo Army Air Base made the following statement today: "Several inquiries have been received concerning a heavy explosion which occurred on the Alamogordo Base reservation this morning.

"A remotely located ammunition magazine containing a con-siderable amount of high explosives and pyrotechnics exploded.

"There was no loss of life or injury to anyone, and the property damage outside of the explosives magazine itself was negligible.

"Weather conditions affecting the content of the gas shells exploded by the blast made it desirable for the Army to evacuate temporarily a few civilians from their homes."

"New Mexico newspapers ran the story in different versions, and the story appeared in a number of radio shows," notes *City of Fire*. "No further word was issued by the Alamogordo Base."

The first atomic bomb was detonated in a blast stirring cities and towns through the southwest of the U.S., and there was no difficulty in "managing" the news about it.

That has continued in the story of nuclear technology to the present day. Behind the management of information to minimize the dangers, health impacts and cost of nuclear technology has been an army of public relations practitioners—often using deceptive information in the tradition of Laurence's press release, although no longer is there a war going on for which to rationalize the cover-up.

John Stauber and Sheldon Rampton, watchdogs of PR practitioners as editors of the magazine *PR Watch*,[54] are among those who have explored the story of public relations and nuclear technology. It is the subject of a chapter ("Spinning the Atom") in their book *Toxic Sludge Is Good For You! Lies, Damn Lies and the Public Relations Industry*. They describe the "public relations campaign to transform the image of nuclear technology" that was launched with President Eisenhower's 1953 "Atoms for Peace" speech at the United Nations.[55] As is typically the case with public relations, in nuclear technology "image and reality were worlds apart."[56]

They provide numerous examples, including how Metropolitan Edison handled the PR when its Three Mile Island plant suffered a near-meltdown, starting with Met Ed's chief spokesman Don Curry announcing on "the first day of the crisis [that] 'there have been no recordings of any significant levels of radiation, and none are expected outside the plant.'"[57]

Stauber and Rampton tell of the still-continuing effort by the Department of Energy and nuclear industry through the American Nuclear Energy Council to have Yucca Mountain in

Nevada become a nuclear waste repository. They quote from a plan the council called its "Nevada Initiative" which called for a blanket of TV ads to provide "air cover" for the push, local reporters to be "hired" to present the "industry's side of the story." DOE scientists would act as a "scientific truth response team....With our 'campaign committee' of Nevada political insiders, our strategic response teams, the advertising program, and the polls that will provide us with a road map along the way, we believe that as each move is made, one or more of the targeted adversaries will begin to surface, move our way, fight us and then, eventually dialogue with the industry. It is through this strategic game of chess that the campaign will ultimately prevail and move to checkmate anti-nuclear forces in Nevada."[58]

They quote David Lilienthal, after he resigned as AEC chairman, complaining about the "many instances of the way in which public relations techniques—the not-so-hidden persuader—have been used to promote the appropriation of funds for the peaceful Atom."[59]

Nukespeak also closely examines the public relations push behind nuclear technology declaring that "the history of nuclear development has been profoundly shaped by the manipulation of information through official secrecy and extensive public-relations campaigns. *Nukespeak* and the use of information-management techniques have consistently distorted the debate over nuclear weapons and nuclear power."[60] *Nukespeak*, too, is chock full of examples.

Daniel Ford, former executive director of the Union of Concerned Scientists, in his book, *Cult of the Atom: The Secret Papers of the Atomic Energy Commission*, writes about the PR efforts by the U.S. government in the 1950s and 60s:

A public-relations effort on behalf of nuclear power was not merely an incidental activity of the [Atomic Energy] Commission. It was a fundamental part of what AEC officials,

at the highest level, saw as the agency's mission. Chairman
[Lewis] Strauss was mindful of the results of opinion surveys
that showed that postwar enthusiasm for nuclear power had
faded and that public support for the peaceful uses of atomic
energy was relatively weak. The Commission knew that it
would have to work systematically to win public support for a
large nuclear industry, and to lessen public fear of the hazards.
Strauss concluded that the national press—and science writers,
in particular—provided the AEC's "critical contact with the
public," as he termed it, and that the media would have to
serve as the conduit for the AEC's atomic power boosterism. In
a speech before the National Association of Science Writers in
September 1954, Strauss set out the themes that the AEC
wanted the media to present to the public. Electric power from
the atom, he said, could be available, according to the AEC's
experts, in "from five to fifteen years...It is not too much to
expect that our children will enjoy in their homes electrical
energy too cheap to meter."[61]

"Strauss invited the science writers to 'work together' with
the AEC and its scientists to educate the public about the
atom and its promise. From the laudatory articles on nuclear
energy that appeared over the next two decades—and the rarity
of any critical coverage of the potential hazards—it is evident
that the national media responded to the chairman's invitation
as he had intended," observed Ford. "With unquestioning support from the media, and unqualified endorsement by Congress
and the administration, the advocates of a large nuclear power
program proceeded, unchallenged, with their ambitious
enterprise."[62]

In my book, *Cover Up: What You Are Not Supposed To
Know About Nuclear Power*, I reproduced the DOE "Public
Information Plan" to push nuclear power by the Reagan
administration during the 1980s. The plan called for, among
other things, the DOE assistant secretary for nuclear energy "to
meet with selected editorial boards" of newspapers, to prepare

"articles about nuclear energy" or have "other qualified officials" write them and place them in publications including the *New York Times, Readers Digest* and *Time.* Various government departments would be utilized. "Defense and State could assert the effect on national security...The Departments of Commerce, Labor, and Treasury, as well as OMB [Office of Management and Budget}, could speak to the economic advantages. The Surgeon General and the President's Science Advisor might commission blue ribbon scientific panels to certify the negligible radiation effect of nuclear power reactors. The Departments of Interior might comment on the several environmental advantages of nuclear power."[63]

Moreover, many of the reporters covering nuclear technology—starting with Laurence—became cheerleaders for the technology, just like the reporters who cover the space beat have become uncritical space program boosters.

Laurence is a model for this. The only journalist allowed to witness the Alamogordo atomic bomb test, two months later, after A-bombs were dropped Hiroshima and Nagasaki, he wrote about the Alamogordo event in glowing terms in the *New York Times.* "The hills said 'yes' and the mountains chimed in 'yes,'" the newsman waxed poetic. "It was as if the earth had spoken and the suddenly iridescent clouds and sky had joined in one mighty affirmative answer. Atomic energy—yes."[64]

(Laurence tried hard to get on the Enola Gay for its atomic bombing of Hiroshima. He wasn't permitted to do that but was allowed to witness the bombing of Nagasaki from an observer plane—the only journalist to be present for the A-bomb attack on Japan.)

He would continue his verbal euphoria about nuclear technology for years afterward. "Laurence's reports were the backbone of the writing, reporting, filming, and editing that constituted a yea-saying to nuclear energy throughout three decades," notes *Time Bomb.*[65]

As Laurence wrote in a 1948 article for *Woman's Home Companion*, with nuclear energy humanity has "a chance to enter into a new Eden...abolishing disease and poverty, anxiety and fear." We might "learn to control weather and heredity...find the key to the riddle of old age." There would be "better, finer and more nourishing plants, better, cheaper and more abundant fertilizer; better and richer soils, farms, and gardens; better metals and machines; better and finer clothing and homes; better men and women." Nuclear plants would pump water and turn the world's deserts into "blooming gardens," turn swamps and jungles into "vast new lands flowing with milk and honey." Summing up this "turning point in the history of civilization," he claimed: "Such power plants could, in short, make the dream of the earth as a Promised Land come true in time for many of us already born to see and enjoy it."[66]

All the Nukes That's Fit to Print

Not only *Times*-man Laurence but the *New York Times* itself, as the U.S. "paper of record," is an important example of media handling—or mishandling—of nuclear power. With nuclear technology, as on other issues, the *Times* has been a model for the U.S. media.

Among those following Laurence's pro-nuclear bent at the *Times* was Roger Starr, a principal writer of hundreds of *Times'* editorials and essays under his own byline promoting nuclear power. He stressed in an interview with me in 1989 that the stance was fully accepted by others at the top at the *Times*. Between editors "and the publisher there is not a bit of disagreement" on the nuclear issue, Starr declared.[67]

It shows. On the tenth anniversary of Three Mile Island, then *Times* editorial page editor, Leslie Gelb, chose to publish only one op-ed on the nuclear plant accident: "Three Mile Island: The Good News." Thomas Pigford's piece contended the accident caused no ill health effects except for "the fright and trauma stemming from technical errors and public announcements" and was really "a positive development" because it prompted better nuclear utility management, which "means America's nuclear option can be stronger."[68]

Along with media boosterism of nuclear technology, suppression of critical stories on nuclear technology has been occurring at the *Times* (and much of the rest of U.S. media). When *Times* reporters have wanted to investigate nuclear issues, they've met stiff resistance. Frances Cerra resigned from the the *Times* after editors killed a story she had written about the Long Island Lighting Company facing "financial demise" because of its Shoreham nuclear plant project. A *Times* editor told her that publishing the piece "could adversely affect LILCO's financial well-being," said Cerra. "He further told me that I—at the time covering Long Island for the paper—should in the future consider LILCO out of my beat. When I told him that this was unacceptable, I was punished by being removed from Long Island coverage to dangle, uncomfortably, without portfolio and anything of substance to work on."[69]

Alden Whitman, a *Times* journalist for twenty-five years, said that "there certainly was never any effort made to do" in-depth or investigative reporting on nuclear power. Why? "I think there is stupidity involved," said Whitman, and further "the *Times* does regard itself as part of the establishment...They get very nervous when they attack industry. Certainly when they attack industry that is as heavily involved in finance and the banks as nuclear power, they would get very uptight. They don't want to attack the status quo."[70]

Anna Mayo speaks of having "built a full-time career on covering nuclear horror stories that the *New York Times* neglected." The long-time former *Village Voice* reporter notes that the *Times* has reporters "who are interested in this issue, and well able to report it...and have all the resources of the *Times*," but end up getting "reined in" or "put on other assignments." The story of the *Times* and nuclear power, says Mayo, is one of "constant cronyism, collusion and singleness of purpose" between the publication and those in government and industry who have been pushing nuclear power.[71]

Meanwhile, on the business side, a coming together of media and nuclear interests has been going on. On the board of directors of the *New York Times* is George B. Munroe, retired chairman and chief executive officer of the Phelps Dodge Corporation which, during his tenure, was deeply involved in uranium mining, and George Shinn, retired chairman of the First Boston Corporation, an investor in nuclear utilities. Board member Marian S. Heiskell, meanwhile, sister of former *Times* publisher Arthur Ochs Sulzberger and aunt of the current publisher, Arthur Ochs Sulzberger, Jr. has been a long-time member of the board of Consolidated Edison, the New York utility with nuclear interests.

Crooked TV

The business links of the *Times* to the nuclear industry pale in comparison to those of CBS, owned by Westinghouse, and NBC, owned by GE. (For decades before their network takeovers, both companies had run smaller, nevertheless substantial, chains of radio and TV stations.)

Both are deeply involved in determining content at their media holdings: GE's buy-out of NBC in 1986 and Westinghouse's acquisition of CBS in 1995 were no mere business decisions. "I think all the networks can do a better job of providing a more objective and balanced perspective," said Michael Jordan, the nuclear engineer who is the chair and chief executive of Westinghouse and personally arranged the $5.4 billion all-cash deal for Westinghouse to take over CBS.[72] Jordan has also said that he wants Westinghouse to "fully exploit all potential synergies among our business units."[73]

Westinghouse, the world's biggest manufacturer of nuclear plants and other nuclear equipment, has a record of stopping at nothing to push nuclear power. In 1988, the Phillipines filed a

$2.2 billion suit against Westinghouse accusing the company of bribing associates of the Marcos regime to build a nuclear plant "on the side of a volcano, beside an earthquake fault, on the Bataan peninsula," reported the *New York Times*.[74]

Westinghouse, the Number 3 U.S. nuclear weapons contractor, doing $3 billion-plus a year in nuclear weapons work, also runs nuclear facilities for the U.S. government, including its Savannah River, Fernald and W.I.P.P. nuclear operations.

GE has been a corporate outlaw virtually since its creation. GE and its officials have a long record of fraud and financial and environmental violations. One of its big activities has been corrupting public officials. Just consider the 1990s. An investigative article by Sam Husseini on GE in *Extra!* noted that in 1990 GE was convicted of defrauding the U.S. Department of Defense for overcharging the Army for a battlefield computer system. In 1992 it pleaded guilty to fraud, money laundering and corrupt business practices in the U.S. in connection with a sale of military jet engines to Israel. In 1992, anti-trust charges were brought against GE for working with the DeBeers diamond cartel to rig prices. Indeed, a "February 1994 report by the Project on Government Oversight found that GE had 16 instances of fraudulent activity against the government since 1990—the most of any company listed," noted the article titled "Felons On The Air: Does GE's Ownership of NBC Violate the Law?"[75]

GE and Westinghouse are companies that the media should be monitoring—not companies that should be owners of media. Indeed, the Federal Communications Commission, from the time it was created in 1934, has claimed it wants only "stewards of the community interest" to control the U.S. airwaves. Nevertheless, GE and Westinghouse are today giants of U.S. media and growing nationally and globally. After taking over CBS in 1995, Westinghouse, in a $3.9 billion deal, bought up the Infinity Broadcasting Corporation, a network of

83 radio stations. GE's NBC has been endeavoring to broadcast worldwide and move aggressively into cable TV with new
networks, including the 24-hour all-news channel MSNBC,
the 24-hour mainly talk-show channel CNBC and joint ownership in other cable TV channels.

If you work for GE's NBC or Westinghouse's CBS, you get
the message quickly about what you are *not* supposed to report
on. When an Emmy Award-winning report done at a Chicago
station on substandard bolts used in nuclear plants—including
those built by GE—was to go network and appear on the
Today show on GE's NBC, *Today* cut all reference to the
substandard bolts.[76]

Under such circumstances, one cannot expect to learn
much about nuclear power in space on NBC or CBS. And
don't hold your breath for the rest of mainstream U.S. media
to report on the issue either.

Thus, between the media failure to do critical reporting on
the U.S. space program and its dysfunction on nuclear technology, year after year, the matter of nuclear power in space
has ended up on the Project Censored list.

Voices of Integrity in the Desert of Venality

There are a few, a very few, media exceptions to this pattern. The *St. Petersburg Times*, for example, one of the distinct
minority of independently-owned newspapers remaining in the
U.S., stood virtually alone in editorializing against the Galileo
plutonium-fueled flight. It noted that "NASA speculates" that
the plutonium particles dispersed in an accident "could be
gathered up safely." But then why, asked the newspaper[77]

> if the Galileo is so safe, has the Florida Department of
> Health and Human Services assigned crews of radiation
> experts to the four-county region most likely to be affected
> by launch difficulties? Why have these crews already gath-
> ered data on existing radiation for comparison with readings

they plan to take after the launch? Why is Joel Reynolds, the space center's safety chief, entertaining plans for "emergency management" exercises? Despite the fancy euphemism, these plans sound distressingly familiar to baby-boomers trained in Cold War-era "civil defense" drills. "If we record high (radiation) doses leaving the space center, the state will recommend that people go inside their homes and turn off their air conditioners until the cloud passes," Reynolds says optimistically. As for the 100,000 who might gather outside to observe a shuttle take-off, "We'd never get them out of here," he admits.[78]

"The space agency may be ready to risk innocent lives in the name of science, and as a step toward developing the technology for the controversial Strategic Defense Initiative." There is no reason for Floridians to accept that risk as their own," declared the *St. Petersburg Times* in the 1989 editorial titled "Plutonium-238: A Risky Number."[79]

The *Los Angeles Times* in 1988 editorialized against nuclear-powered satellites in space. "The history of nuclear reactors in orbit gives great cause for concern," it noted. "Their safety record is not good."[80]

While this country does not currently use nuclear power for its satellites, it is planning to orbit as many as 100 nuclear reactors as part of the Strategic Defense Initiative. According to Lt. Gen. James Abrahamson, director of the 'Star Wars' project, without nuclear power "that's going to be a long, long lightcord that goes down to the surface of the Earth."[81]

The *Los Angeles Times* supported a proposal then being made by the Federation of American Scientists and a top Russian space scientist for a "ban on orbiting nuclear reactors...Prohibiting nuclear reactors in orbit is an idea that the United States and the Soviet Union should wholeheartedly pursue. The reentry of Cosmos 1900 will again focus the world's attention on the danger posed by radioactive material as it comes hurtling in from space. This continuing risk can be stopped by international agreement, and should be."[82]

Now and then, journalists will ask the hard questions of NASA (usually never reporters on the space beat, however). There is David Chandler of the *Boston Globe*. Or Bill Moyers, in a PBS program *The Truth About Lies*, in which there was a segment on NASA, lies and the Challenger tragedy. "Failure to look at the fearsome truth and the unwillingness to acknowledge the facts have been costly to our country," Moyers stated. "We've paid that cost in human life and mutual trust. Decisive moments in our recent past, unforgettable moments, reveal those pressures that drive people to deny the truth and distort reality." He interviewed those who tried to blow the whistle at NASA about shuttle problems before the Challenger disaster. "But NASA had other ideas," noted Moyers.[83]

And most other reporters have "other ideas" when it comes to space coverage. "NASA uses its RTGs only when there is no alternative," stressed Robert C. Cowen, a space enthusiast who writes on science for the *Christian Science Monitor*, accepting NASA's PR line.

It is not rare to see flat-out NASA PR lies published as news, such as the constant claims that the RTG canisters won't break—belied in the official documentation—or a statement published in the *Times* of London in 1995 in which the NASA projection of five to seven billion people being "exposed to the fallout" from a Cassini "flyby" accident was noted. The *Times*, the "paper of record" for the United Kingdom, stated: "A NASA spokesman emphasized that this was the absolute worst case scenario and highly unlikely because we plan to have Cassini miss the Earth by 10,000 miles."[84] In fact, as the *Final Environmental Impact Statement for the Cassini Mission* clearly states, Cassini is to fly over the Earth "at an altitude of 500 km [kilometers]" or 312 miles. The

NASA spokesman was off by 9,688 miles in his lie to the *Times* of London.[85]

Thus, the media treatment of the trouble-plagued Galileo flight as it arrived at Jupiter in 1995 was typical. "Jupiter Rendezvous Is A Marvel of Perfection," was the headline of John Noble Wilford's story in the *New York Times*. (No mention of the words plutonium or nuclear in the story, as usual.)[86]

The issue of nuclear power in space being chronically under-reported and a regular item on the Project Censored list has some "pretty clear components," says Mark Lowenthal of Project Censored. "The most obvious is the nature of media ownership—GE and Westinghouse," he states. Then there are the less direct ties, the "interlocking directorates" between media institutions and corporations involved in nuclear technology, members of the boards of directors of media on the boards of those corporations. Further, there is a similarity with the lack of vigilant reporting "on other areas of nuclear technology."[87]

The "critics of nuclear policy, those opposing the building of power plants or siting nuclear waste storage sites are on the outside. They don't have highly paid lobbyists or big advertising budgets. They don't have the ears of news producers; they don't run in similar social circles."[88]

Further, "there's a kind of national insecurity syndrome" when it comes to dealing with certain issues "in which the potential consequences can be very dramatic. There is a predisposition in media not to scare the public." And nuclear technology issues have "the potential to scare people. The press gravitates to stories that have a beginning, middle and end. There is no solution to the storage of nuclear waste or design flaws in nuclear plants. There is this great reluctance to alarm the public—despite the press having the job to point out serious public interest issues, serious public health issues. Nuclear issues are considered just too explosive." An examination could "create tremendous public unrest and anxiety. Noam Chomsky has written a great deal about this: how a major purpose of the press is to perpetuate the status quo and not delve into some of the realities that exist out there. Nuclear technology issues are something considered just too explosive. Although there is a big difference between fomenting public panic and having, at the least, a conversation on the issue."[89]

"You combine all these factors and you have a recipe for bad journalism, an abdication of press responsibility," said Lowenthal. "The press should serve as an early warning system. There is great journalism out there waiting to happen."[90]

CHAPTER SEVEN

SAVING
THE SPACE PROGRAM
FROM ITSELF

"We're here to save the U.S. space program from itself," declared Dr. Michio Kaku in May 1996 at the gates of the Cape Canaveral Air Station. As he spoke, 150 people held banners and posters with declarations such as: "No Plutonium In Space—Stop Cassini," "Absolutely No Nukes In Space," "PU-238 The Real Florida Lottery," "Just Say Solar On Cassini," "ESA Says Solar Works," "Why Fly Nukes In The Sky?" "Star Wars: Earth Is The Enemy," "Fund Human Needs Not Star Wars," "Plutonium Is Forever."[1]

The rally at the front gates of the U.S. Air Force facility—where the Cassini plutonium-powered space probe was to be launched the following year—was part of a three-day national meeting and protest organized by the Global Network Against Weapons & Nuclear Power in Space.

Dr. Kaku was warning of unprecedented catastrophe on the Cassini mission, describing the dangers of the launch and the 1999 "flyby." If during that "flyby" plutonium was dispersed, large numbers of people "could perish," said Dr. Kaku.[2]

Harvey Wasserman, senior advisor to Greenpeace U.S.A., walked up to the microphone and declared: "This is a survival issue—and it is a winnable issue."[3]

The meeting and protest were among a series of citizen actions against the use of nuclear power in space which have been happening in recent years both in the U.S. and abroad organized by the Global Network Against Weapons & Nuclear Power in Space.

The Movement at Ground Zero

The gathering began with Bill Sulzman, the Global Network's co-coordinator and director of Colorado-based Citizens for Peace in Space, declaring that the U.S. military is seeking to dominate space—"to put outer space in the hands of the 'warfighter'"—and to utilize nuclear technology for this. "I can't think of a more failed technology." He noted the motto of the U.S. Space Command is "'Master of Space'...That gives you an idea of the attitude." The military and NASA have made an "unholy alliance" in the military's quest for space domination, said Sulzman, a former Roman Catholic priest.[4]

Now "people-power" and a commitment to "compassion and conscience" must be brought "into an area where it is not wanted and where it is lacking," said Sulzman. "There must be "resistance" to the U.S. push "to weaponize and nuclearize space," he said in the main hall at a Holiday Inn in Cocoa Beach, Florida down the road from Cape Canaveral.[5]

There were workshops spread through meeting rooms of the Holiday Inn, workshops with unholiday-like titles: "U.S. Space Command: Spying & War Planning" with Loring Wirbel of Citizens for Peace in Space, and "HAARP in Alaska: Not a Pretty Sound," at which Cory Bartholomew and Bonnie Urfer of the Madison, Wisconsin-based Nukewatch spoke on the U.S. military's space-focused program called the High Frequency Active Auroral Research Project (acronomymed HAARP). In this scheme, high frequency radio waves would be used as weapons. There was "Theatre as Resistance and Resistance as Theatre" with Mary Sprunger-Froes of the First Strike Theatre of Colorado Springs; "U.S. Spy Satellites and

Florida Facilities" with John Pike of the Federation of American Scientists along with Sulzman; and "ABC's of Direct Action/Civil Disobedience" with Mary Lynn Sheetz and Donna Johnson of Citizens for Peace in Space. Dr. Johnson, a psychologist, was stressing how important it is, in therapy and life, to not be "in denial" but to deal with reality and commit to changing things that are wrong.[6]

The conference reconvened and heard from Bruce Gagnon, also co-coordinator of the Global Network, who spoke about the U.S. government being a "renegade government" spending "massive amounts of money" to nuclearize and weaponize space, "and at the same time saying no money is available for schools" and other social needs. "This issue is not about losing our democracy—we have lost it," said Gagnon. "There is a dictatorship running out of buildings with no signs" that would like to "direct the lives of the people of the world." Gagnon said "the time has come for us to take bolder action" and "stop this stuff."[7]

There was a panel discussion on "Organizing an International Cassini Campaign" and then the trip to the Cape Canaveral Air Station and the protest. It began with a prayer from Bobby C. Billie, spiritual leader of the Independent Traditional Seminole Nation. "We need to be serious so future generations can survive," he said somberly. "We have to come back to Earth to heal the Earth."[8]

Gagnon, at the May 1996 demonstration, noted that the week before NASA officials had advised Florida residents that if there is an accident during the launch of the Cassini probe and plutonium is dispersed, people should "just stay inside."[9]

"Forever!" commented Gagnon.[10]

Fred Hitchcock, commander of the Florida chapter of the Atomic Veterans of America, told the protesters that "if they launch Cassini....I'll be in California. You don't know unless you've been there—I've been there." He told of being parachuted, as a nineteen-year-old soldier, into the mushroom cloud of an atomic bomb test. As a result, he and his children have suffered severe medical problems, he said. If there is an accident involving Cassini, it "will affect generation after generation," said Hitchcock.[11]

At the dinner that night, Dr. Kaku said "we are the makers of history" with the power to make "space a nuclear-free zone." There is no "force more powerful than the force of love, the force of people united," said Dr. Kaku, and with that "social change is possible."[12]

Those at the event in Florida came from ten states and Europe. Among the attendees was Byron Morgan, a twenty-two-year NASA veteran who traveled from California. "I love NASA," he said. "But it's like being the father of an alcoholic. Nuclear energy in space is like alcohol to NASA."[13]

The Global Network Against Weapons & Nuclear Power in Space was formed at a "National Organizing Meeting on Space Nuclear Power and Weapons" held in Washington, D.C. in July 1992. At that time, the Galileo space probe, which many of the 200 people present had been involved in trying to stop from being launched, was hurtling back at the Earth for its second "flyby." Dr. Kaku told this gathering, in the chambers of the District of Columbia City Council, that Galileo was a "harbinger" of things to come. He detailed the structure of Star Wars—"a gigantic space-based system based on nuclear power"—and other plans to deploy nuclear energy in space.[14]

Sydney Bowman, who had come from England, voiced her concerns about the "nuclearization" of space by the U.S.[15]

Suzanne Marinelli of the Sierra Club of Hawaii told of the opposition on the island of Kauai, where she lived—"it's really paradise"—to Star Wars (later to be renamed Stars) test launches there.[16]

Chris Brown of Citizens Alert in Nevada, where plans were being made at the time to test the "Timberwind"/Space Nuclear

Thermal rocket said in the 1950s and 60s "nine out of ten" tests of atomic weapons "resulted in fallout over Nevada, Utah and Montana. It was a mess." It was now high time, said Brown, "to stop making the citizens" of the western U.S. "victims of the country's addiction to nuclear weapons and nuclear power."[17]

Steven Aftergood of the Federation of American Scientists scored the U.S. government secrecy he had encountered—"somewhere between ridiculous and completely offensive"—in examining the use of nuclear power in space. The government has been seeking, he said, to "insulate" its space nuclear programs from the "democratic process."[18]

Canadian scientist Walter Dorn outlined international standards on the use of space. The U.S. was resisting United Nations guidelines on space activity where nuclear power was involved. Indeed, the year before, *Space News* had reported in a front-page story that the U.S. had "withdrawn its support for the United Nations draft guidelines for the use of nuclear power in space because of Defense Department and NASA fears that space missions might be hindered by the proposed standards." The article went on to note that "U.S. Defense Department officials complained to the State Department that the draft guidelines could pose obstacles to a nuclear-powered ballistic missile defense system...NASA managers said the document could put constraints on interplanetary and robotic missions, and the White House called for a more thorough technical and policy review of the issue."[19]

Sulzman said that the U.S. "is gearing up to dominate space the way the military has tried to control oceans. It wants to weaponize it, nuclearize it."[20]

Harvey Wasserman spoke of the "terrible" U.S. plans to send up "Chernobyls in the sky" for military and civilian purposes.[21]

A press conference was held after the two-day session, at which the founding of the Global Network was announced. "We're going to educate, mobilize, activate and influence the whole space policy program and turn the U.S. away from weaponizing and nuclearizing space," said Gagnon at the press conference.[22]

An "action" platform was outlined. It called on the U.S. Congress to "zero out space-based weapons funding" and the Strategic Defense Initiative Organization and its multi-billion dollar budget and "zero out the budget for nuclear propulsion programs such as 'Timberwind.'" It called on the Democratic candidates for president and vice president that year—Clinton and Gore—"to continue their opposition," as voiced in the campaign, "to a space arms race." It declared opposition to the the placement of nuclear power systems in space and support of Iowa Senator Tom Harkin's Outer Space Protection Act to ban weapons from space. (Harkin's bill has never passed Congress.) The platform said the Global Network would work "to remove the secrecy and expose the misinformation presented to the public regarding these issues." It concluded by saying that the organization would seek "to build international cooperation in space and urge the reallocation of resources to benefit all humanity and to protect the planetary environment."[23]

A series of Global Network meetings and protests in the U.S. followed. The group met at Colorado College in 1993, and demonstrated as Dr. Edward Teller spoke before the National Space Foundation in Colorado Springs. And it also picketed the U.S. Space Command's headquarters at the Falcon Air Force Base, outside of Colorado Springs. In 1994, it held a meeting at the University of New Mexico and demonstrated at one of the annual symposia on Space Nuclear Power and Propulsion in Albuquerque. In 1996, Florida was the site of its meeting and demonstration.

And in 1997, the Global Network truly went global with a series of meetings in Europe. Gatherings were held in The Netherlands in cooperation with the Amsterdam-based World Information Service on Energy and in Belgium with the organization For Mother Earth. Meetings were held in the United

Kingdom with the Menwith Hill Women's Peace Camp and the Campaign for Nuclear Disarmament. In Germany, gatherings were organized, including a two-day conference at the Technical University of Darmstadt, with the Mutlangen-based Center for Peace and Contact, the International Network of Engineers and Scientists Against Proliferation (INESAP) and other groups.

"I was not aware that the nuclear industry was going upwards," commented Albert Beale of the Housmans Peace Resource Project at the March 1997 presentation of the Global Network held in Conway Hall in London, a room bedecked with sculptures and paintings of English thinkers and activists who had spoken there through the years, including George Bernard Shaw and Bertrand Russell.[24]

I'm O.K., You're Glowing...and It Ain't My Problem

Of special interest—and concern—in Europe was the way the U.S. has limited its financial liability in the event of an accident involving one of its nuclear space systems. In 1991, NASA and the DOE entered into a "Space Nuclear Power Agreement" to cover U.S. space nuclear activities under the Price-Anderson Act. That law, passed in 1957, supposedly on a temporary basis to spur the development of commercial nuclear power in the U.S., limits liability for property damage, illnesses or death caused by a nuclear accident.

Utilities in the 1950s had been resisting the building of nuclear plants out of concern for their financial "exposure"— damages they would have to pay in an accident. So nuclear proponents got Congress to pass the Price-Anderson Act restricting the total liability in the event of a nuclear accident to $560 million, with the U.S. government paying the first $500 million, the utility as owner of the nuclear facility the remaining $60 million. That would be how much, in total, people could collect—despite the real damages. The liability limit was raised amid the controversies through the decades as the Price-Anderson Act was renewed, three times so far. It is currently $8.9 billion, still a fraction of what a Chernobyl-level nuclear plant accident, or worse, is projected by the U.S. Nucelar Regulatory Commission as causing in damage.

But that's only for damage within the U.S. The limit for all damages to other countries and their people was set at $100 million in 1962—and remains *unchanged.*[25]

By placing U.S. space nuclear power programs under the Price-Anderson Act, NASA and the DOE limited the liability for all other nations and all other people a U.S. nuclear space device might impact to that $100 million.

"It is obvious by this that we care less about other nations than we do about ourselves," comments Michael Mariotte, director of the Nuclear Information and Resource Service, about that move.[26]

Europeans were amazed during the Global Network series of meetings in 1997 to hear about and examine the documentation of the "Space Nuclear Power Agreement."

And if nuclear power in space is "safe," as the U.S. government claims, why does its use need to be covered under the Price-Anderson Act?

The New "Nuclear Umbrella"
Or... How to Dominate the Planet

In Darmstadt, in part of the city leveled in World War II as a practice bombing run for the fire-bombing of Dresden, Gagnon stressed the military aspect of the U.S. move into space. It was in 1982, he said at the Technical University of Darmstadt, that he got his first indication of the U.S. military push into space. He said he had been watching a television report on a demonstration against the deployment of U.S. Pershing and cruise missiles in Europe when the programming switched to a conference at which Lt. General Daniel Graham, of the Reagan administration Star Wars notoriety, was speaking. Graham was being asked, said Gagnon, about the protesters and replied that he was not concerned because "they're demonstrating against ICBMs and we're moving into space—and they don't have a clue."[27]

Further, the U.S. was approaching space in the tradition of Columbus conquering the New World, Gagnon went on. Columbus brought "a bad seed" when he came to the Americas, "slicing native people down to nothing" in order to exploit the riches. Now, "as we go out to explore space," said Gagnon, "we're taking a bad seed—nuclear power and nuclear weapons." Again, "greed" is central—to "mine the skies" for helium-3 and other resources. To protect its operations, the U.S. was following imperial Great Britain which "ruled the seven seas with their armada. Thus, now it was the U.S. military talking about being 'master of space.'"[28]

Loring Wirbel of Citizens for Peace in Space, a technical writer who has focused on U.S. military strategy for space, revealed that the "military overlay in space has become more and more pronounced"—with officials of the Clinton administrations regularly speaking in terms of "force multipliers for the domination of the planet."[29]

"Nukem"

And giving a presentation on how solar power could substitute for plutonium-fueled energy system in space was Dr. Gerhard Strobl, manager of the development of high efficiency solar cells for the company whose work was the subject of the 1994 European Space Agency (ESA) announcement of a "technology milestone" in building solar power systems for deep space probes. Strobl's presentation during the 1997 Global Network Europe meetings, said much about the technology—and realpolitiks—of space power.[30]

Under a contract with the "science department of ESA," his company, Deutsche Aerospace (DASA), worked on high-efficiency solar systems because "ESA wants to make deep space missions and does not have RTGs," the plutonium power source. Also, Dr. Strobl said, RTGs are "very, very expensive" and there is an issue of "safety and social acceptance." The contract, which ran from 1991 to 1996, was for $3 million and the result was development of solar cells with 25% efficiency, the highest ever achieved.

But as for their use on Cassini, initially in his presentation Dr. Strobl said it might be "difficult"—despite the 1994 European Space Agency announcement and in contradiction to the comment of ESA physicist Carla Signorini in *Florida Today* the following year that, given funding and a few years, a solar system with the new cells could be ready for a mission to Saturn.[31]

Gagnon challenged Dr. Strobl to explain his hesitance about the use of his company's new solar cells on a Cassini mission, considering what had transpired.

Meanwhile, I noticed in the documents Dr. Strobl had shown with an overhead projector a new name in connection with his company: "Nukem."[32]

"Nukem" followed the company name.

What, I asked Dr. Strobl, was "Nukem?" What connection did it have with his company?

Nukem, he said, had acquired his company in 1995.

I explained that I did not speak German but did Nukem have a link to nuclear power? He acknowledged, a bit red-faced, that, in fact, Nukem was the "nuclear power arm" of the state utility in Germany that provides all the nation's electric power, Rheinisch-Weolfalische Elektrizitatatswerke or RWE. Nukem, he said, runs the nuclear power operations of RWE.

I said it surely stretched credibility for him, after the European Space Agency announcement of the solar technology breakthrough involving his company in 1994, the declaration in 1995 that its solar system could be used to power a Saturn mission and then the takeover of the company by Nukem that same year, to now come to the conference and be hesitant about the use of solar energy for the Cassini mission.

Dr. Strobl then changed his approach.

He said his company could produce a solar system for the Cassini mission. The Cassini probe would have to be redesigned to be fitted for solar energy, he said, but that was just a matter "of satellite design." Still, Cassini could make use of solar power, he said. "We solved the basic problem of high efficiency solar cells for space," said Strobl. And, he noted, his company was building a solar system to power the European Space Agency's Rosetta space probe which is to be launched in 2003 to "go beyond the orbit of Jupiter," into deep space, and observe the comet Wirtanen in the year 2011. "There will be no RTG on Rosetta," he said, and his company's solar system for the space probe would be producing 500 watts of electricity. [33] (That would be about the same wattage produced by the two plutonium-fueled RTGs used on Galileo on its flight to Jupiter.)

He said his company has done work for NASA in the past, producing solar cells used on the Hubble space telescope. "We'd greatly appreciate work from NASA," said Dr. Strobl.[34]

But, I asked him, would his company's owner, Nukem, be happy with its small 100-person subsidiary creating solar systems that could displace nuclear power?

"Space is no problem," Dr. Strobl replied.[35]

Meanwhile, others at the conference told me that Nukem was not only the prime company producing commercial nuclear power in Germany but has also been deeply involved with plutonium, having sought several years ago to build a plutonium reprocessing facility.[36]

Building a Movement

The presentations at the Darmstadt conference concluded with physicist Jürgen Sheffran, a professor at the university and a leader of INESAP. It summed up the conference—and the situation well. The slides Dr. Sheffran flashed on a screen began with what he considered should be the "Objectives and Demands" of the space program.

- "Apply space technology to social needs" topped the list. Needs such as economic betterment, environmental preservation, development and education were noted.
- "Solve problems of Planet Earth instead of creating new imbalances and causes of conflict."
- "Prevent confrontation, enhance international cooperation."
- "Ban space weapons by international law." Dr. Sheffran, commenting as the slide was presented, said that as it is now, "international law is deficient" in dealing with space. Essentially, he said, "we only have the Outer Space Treaty."
- "Avoid oversized, costly and risky space projects."
- "Explore alternative technology paths."

And then there were "Criteria for Future Space Technology Use."

- "Impossibility for severe catastrophe" topped this list.
- "Proliferation resistance" came next.
- "Minimization of long-term effects."
- "Sustainability."
- "Benefit-cost effectiveness compared to alternatives."

And as for "Conditions for Space Technology Assessment," the list consisted of:

- "Comprehensive assessment of spaceflight and alternatives."
- "Independent expert opinion."
- "Public debate."

"The focus must not be only on the technical side. Technology is not the solution to everything," said the German scientist.[37]

The conference also included a day and evening of political strategizing. Bill Sulzman was saying at one strategy session that "as we know, nuclear technology from the very beginning has been a curse on humankind. Over the years, it has been found that breaking down the energy of the atom can kill people with a massive explosion or break down one cell at a time. Part of the reason that nuclear power is still alive despite all the awareness, is the continuing push for it. In the U.S., the history of nuclear technology is tied to the large national laboratories which have a vested interest in the use of nuclear power." Meanwhile, the nuclear enterprise has been cloaked in "secrecy. Our challenge is to demand the truth," he said, and further "to act together in a non-violent way to stop this."[38]

The Global Network Against Weapons & Nuclear Power in Space is "trying to build a constituency of people around the world who don't want to see nuclear power in space." An alternative vision is needed, he said.[39]

"We must have a vision for the next century, the next millenium," said Martin Koppold, whose job title for the Center for Peace and Contact is "peaceworker." The choice, he said, is between "hell or heaven on Earth. The nuclear hell on Earth has already started," he went on, "for those [workers] at Los Alamos [National Laboratory] who have been contaminated with plutonium for the Cassini project." The Cassini project, the use of space for purposes which "only a few will profit from," the increasing militarization of space, this all must be stopped, said the German safe-energy and peace activist. "We in the peace movement want to see space used for a different purpose."[40]

Plans were made that included postcard-writing to President Clinton and other political officials in the U.S. and abroad, direct actions and protests, putting pressure on the U.S. Congress and the European Parliament, and bringing lawsuits—including the possibility of going to the World Court.

Going Home

On the airplane returning from Europe, I gazed out the window of the Boeing 747 at the beautiful Earth unfolding below. I had been reduced to writing on a pad I had bought at the airport in Munich, the power source for my laptop computer having burned out in a hotel room in Brussels. Ah, technology...and a very tiny example of the reason why the use of nuclear power in space is so dangerous: technology fails. As Dr. Sheffran had said back in Darmstadt, it is critical to restrict activities that can lead to "severe catastrophe" especially where innocent people are concerned.

And the key, as Sulzman had stressed the night before, is for people to know what is happening—so they can act on matters that can so profoundly affect their lives.

I was thinking on the jet that in the coming week, Project Censored would be announcing that my journalism on the use of nuclear power in space was its selection for the "most under-reported," "best-censored" story of 1996. How much, I thought, I would rather not to get that award and instead have the issue fully reported. For I am convinced that if people knew about the push to deploy nuclear power and weapons in space, that would be the end of it.

At John F. Kennedy Airport, a friendly immigration officer looked at my passport and said, nicely, "Welcome home."

I was home. But what was my homeland up to?

Gofman: "I Am Appalled"

Upon reaching my home, topping the pile of faxes that had come while I was away was one from Dr. John Gofman. A giant of science, a man of great conscience, a former high figure in the government's nuclear establishment as associate director of Lawrence Livermore Laboratory, who as a matter of integrity resigned that post rather than continue in what he concluded was a death-dealing enterprise, had reviewed the NASA projections of Cassini consequences.

"I am appalled after reading the June 1996 *Final Environmental Impact Statement for the Cassini Mission* to think that serious consideration is being given to going ahead with the use of some 72.3 pounds of Plutonium-238 on that mission," Dr. Gofman said beginning the letter. He said that just the amount of Plutonium-238 NASA admits will likely be dispersed as vapor or respirable particles in an Earth flyby accident—not the full load of Plutonium-238 Cassini will be carrying—"represents an astronomical quantity of a potent alpha-emitting cancer producer. The number of cancer doses is so high as to make calculation extraneous."[41]

His letter went on: "Scientists and engineers in control of their faculties would surely have eliminated this project from their agenda. Yet it appears that is not the case."[42]

Dr. Gofman continued: "And releases contemplated as possible would likely end the space program. That would be a shame since the space program produces such remarkable and interesting feats. I do not believe that what may be the world's largest recent dissemination of potent carcinogens will enhance the stature of NASA."[43]

The View from Inside the Industry:
Worries are Overblown

Indeed, boosters of the U.S. space program should realize that a disaster involving a nuclear mission would be *The End* of the U.S. space program. A disintegration of Cassini in a "flyby" accident and a dispersal of plutonium onto the Earth, a nuclear-propelled rocket crashing to Earth, a catastrophic accident involving any other of the many civilian and military nuclear devices being proposed for placement in space, would mark *The End*.

The fight against a nuclear Cassini mission, the challenge to the nuclearization and weaponization of the U.S. space program, is a fight, as Dr. Kaku said, to save the space program from itself. It is also a fight to save the Earth from what the U.S. space program has become.

Vested interest can be blinding—especially to people without the conscience, without the independence, without the sensitivity of a Dr. John Gofman.

Before leaving for Europe, I interviewed, at length, the man who co-discovered plutonium. I had obtained correspondence between the Clinton administration and Dr. Glenn Seaborg, former chairman of the U.S. Atomic Energy Commission and a longtime promoter of nuclear technology, for a project being pushed by Seaborg to irradiate food on a huge scale in the U.S. In the correspondence, Seaborg said a company in which he had "an interest" wanted to acquire most of the government's stockpile of the deadly radioisotope Cesium-137 (the principal poison emitted in the Chernobyl nuclear plant accident) and use it in a massive food irradiation program. Food irradiation extends the shelf life of food. However, opponents charge serious health impacts—including cancer—can result from eating radiation-exposed food. From nuclear in space to nuclear power zapping food, there would seem to be no end, and for Dr. Glenn Seaborg, that's the way it should be.

Dr. Seaborg, now in his 80s, recounted how it was also at Lawrence Berkeley Laboratory in Berkeley, California, where he was speaking from, that more than a half-century before he discovered not only Plutonium-239 but, a month earlier, Plutonium-238—the power source for Cassini and other space missions involving nuclear energy.

It was "here" in the middle of the night between February 23 and 24, 1941 "we made the chemical identification" of Plutonium-238, said Seaborg. "It was me, Joseph W. Kennedy and Arthur C. Wahl." Then, the next month, "we discovered the other plutonium," Plutonium-239. For this identification, made on March 28, 1941, he vividly recalled, "we were joined by Emilio Sagre."[44]

Ever since, Dr. Seaborg has promoted applications of the element he discovered and other uses of nuclear technology. After working on the Manhattan Project and seeing Plutonium-239 turned into a fuel for atomic bombs, he shifted to the chairmanship of the AEC and through the years has advocated the most extreme uses of nuclear technology. In *Man and Atom*, which he co-authored in 1963, he declared that nuclear power could fix up a "slightly flawed planet."[45]

He advocated using nuclear devices to blast out "instant harbors" around the planet, cut a canal across the isthmus of Panama—dubbed the "Panatomic Canal" when Seaborg pushed it—and carve out with nuclear detonations a network of waterways linking the Atlantic, Gulf of Mexico and the Pacific.[46] Also in *Man and Atom* he called for using a nuclear explosion to close the Straits of Gilbraltar which, he said, would cause the Mediterranean to rise and freshen to the point that it could be used to irrigate the Sahara Desert. Dr. Seaborg observed that "of course, the advantages of a verdant Sahara would have to be weighed against the loss of Venice and other sea-level cities."[47]

In our interview, after boosting the use of nuclear technology to irradiate food, he moved on to the space program. Seaborg declared: "The whole space program is possible because of Plutonium-238. The Plutonium-238 isotope furnishes the electricity." Of any risk to life on Earth from using nuclear-powered space devices, Seaborg said "I think the danger is not at all serious" and "the advantages far outweigh the risks...The planet flybys, the landing on the moon, they use that [Plutonium-238] as an energy source. The success of all of this depended on use of Plutonium-238."[48]

As to plutonium being an extremely toxic substance, "that's nonsense," Seaborg insisted. "The people who have ingested plutonium are going to die some day just like you and I." And there are "all kinds of biological agents more toxic" than plutonium, said Dr. Seaborg, such as Black Plague bacilli. If someone ingests plutonium, "the worst that can happen is that it will shorten your life expectancy from 50 years to 49 years." He said that "many of the people who ingested plutonium one way or the other 50 years ago" are still alive today.[49]

I noted, however, that the big problem with plutonium is inhalation, not ingestion. Seaborg's inflection changed, indicating he was surprised that I knew this. "Well," he said, "if you deliberately put it into somebody's lung...the recipient will eventually develop cancer." But that is "a very unusual case," people wouldn't ordinarily inhale plutonium, said Dr. Seaborg.[50]

What if the Cassini space probe explodes on launch and spreads plutonium, or on its "flyby" disintegrates and disperses plutonium dust all over the world—couldn't that, I asked, lead to people inhaling plutonium? The chances of an accident on launch "is very small" and if there is an accident in the minutes after that, the probe "would plunk down in the ocean somewhere." As for a "flyby" accident, the plutonium "is in a container" which should, said Dr. Seaborg, prevent it from dispersing in a "flyby" mishap. And, he stressed, there would be "one chance in several hundred" that this would occur and the plutonium would be spread. Then he added that this might be "closer to one in a thousand."[51]

Of opponents of nuclear technology, Dr. Seaborg said that they "don't realize that there is radioactivity in everybody, everybody has a little radioactivity in them."[52]

What, Me Worry? It Can't Happen Here

The interview with Seaborg was reminiscent of one I had a few years before—having gone to Brookhaven National Laboratory to hear Dr. James Powell, the principal developer of the "Timberwind" nuclear-propelled rocket design, give a lecture on why nuclear-propelled rockets were good. "The Particle Bed Reactor: Nuclear Rockets and Beyond," was the title of his talk.

It was 1993 and Dr. Powell began by telling 200 other scientists packed into the auditorium about how $200 million had been spent on the "Timberwind"/Space Nuclear Thermal Program up to then and how $800 million more in government money would be spent in the near future. The excitement in the room was palpable. (It was a few months before the "Timberwind"/ Space Nuclear Thermal Propulsion Program was to be cancelled.)[53]

On a briefing chart, Dr. Powell, senior nuclear engineer heading the Reactor Systems Division in Brookhaven National Laboratory's Department of Nuclear Energy, had mapped the history of U.S. efforts to develop nuclear rockets.

The chart started with the NERVA project, went on to other early nuclear rocket programs and then there was a point which was listed on the chart as "The Great Die-Off"—the stoppage of the nuclear rocket program. After that, activity picked up again in the 1980s with the Space Nuclear Thermal Propulsion project (the codename "Timberwind" didn't appear on the chart nor was it uttered during the presentation).[54]

Dr. Powell explained that a nuclear rocket would be far preferable to a conventional one on a trip to Mars—that an atomic rocket could make the trip in six months, while it would take a year on a conventional rocket. He explained in detail the mechanics of the system using a "particle bed reactor" for rocket propulsion.

There were a couple of scientists in the audience who had some concerns. "In light of Challenger," asked one, couldn't a nuclear rocket pose a danger if "it fell back" to Earth?

Dr. Powell replied by making a comparison. Because of the high level of radiation produced by Plutonium-238, the radioactive load of the 24 plutonium-fueled space probes already launched by the U.S. "far exceeds the amount of radioactivity" that might be released in an accident involving a rocket propelled with a nuclear reactor, he said. He said if a nuclear rocket disintegrated and fell back to Earth and its radioactive poisons were "uniformly dispersed," the result to many people would be the radiation equivalent of an X-ray and that it would be nothing to worry about. If, however, the nuclear rocket stayed together until it slammed into the ground and then broke apart, the radioactivity would be "back to natural background" levels beyond "a couple of kilometers," he said.

I went up to Powell after his lecture and asked him about the problem if the nuclear rocket crashed down on midtown Manhattan or another heavily populated part of the planet. What if the "couple of kilometers" was a population center?

"What we say if people ask us that," said Dr. Powell, "is that the probabilistic risk of that happening is very low."[55]

"It's like the craziest part of the human psyche is running amok here and is trying to expand our very worst karma to the far corners of the universe," comments Harvey Wasserman of Greenpeace on the use of nuclear power in space. "The arrogance and the inability to learn from past mistakes is staggering. It's staggering that after the Titanic, the Challenger, Bhopal,

Three Mile Island, the Thresher [a nuclear-powered submarine which sank], Chernobyl—how many disasters do we need before we learn anything? Here is the question: is there a learning curve, a learning capability on the part of NASA, DOE and the nuclear industry? With every passing month, it looks like these agencies just should be put out of our misery."[56]

Vested interest, however, can be blinding—can, as Dr. Gofman notes, allow certain scientists and engineers to not be "in control of their faculties," and government agencies and corporations to be out of touch with reality, too.

Illegal

The push to use nuclear power in space is illegal. The Outer Space Treaty of 1967, of which the U.S. was a principal initiator and original signator, says that states shall not "place in orbit around the Earth any objects carrying nuclear weapons or any other kinds of weapons of mass destruction...or station such weapon in outer space in any other manner."[57] Yet in its *New World Vistas: Air and Space Power for the 21st Century*, the U.S. Air Force speaks of the "fielding of space-based weapons of devastating effectiveness"—preferably nuclear-powered—in the next twenty years.[58]

As for nuclear devices in space, the Outer Space Treaty declares that states are to avoid uses of space which will lead to "harmful contamination and also adverse changes in the environment of Earth."[59] What could produce more more "adverse changes in the environment of Earth" than nuclear poisons raining down on the planet?

Also, the Outer Space Treaty declares that "each state party to the treaty that launches or procures the launching of an object into outer space...is internationally liable for damage to another state party."[60] Meanwhile, the U.S., through the 1991 "Space Nuclear Power Agreement" between NASA and DOE, has limited U.S. liability to just $100 million for all other nations and all other people beyond U.S. residents in the event of an accident involving a U.S. space nuclear device. This is obviously not being "internationally liable for damage" as the Outer Space Treaty requires.

Further, the military use of space being planned by the U.S. is in total contradiction to the principles of peaceful international cooperation that the U.S. likes to espouse. The aim is to develop a world in which it would literally be U.S.A. *uber alles*.

"World *Dominance*"

I also came home to the publication of a new book articulating U.S. space military strategy: *The Future of War*, subtitled *Technology & American World Dominance in the 21st Century*. Yes, *American World **Dominance** in the 21st Century*.

"He who controls space controls the battlefield," George Friedman, a co-author of the book was quoted as saying. The U.S. will be dominant in the 21st Century and beyond because of its space-age weaponry, he contended. Other nations, including Russian, Japan and China are just "passing blips" since they lack the money or technology to compete with the U.S.[61]

George and Meredith Friedman write in *The Future of War*:

> While warfare will continue to dominate and define the international system, the manner in which wars are waged is undergoing a dramatic transformation, which will greatly enhance American power.[62]

> The United States is expanding war and its power into space and to the planets. Just as European power redefined relations among nations, so American power is redefining those relations. Just as Europe shaped the world for half a millenium, so too the United States will shape the world for at least that length of time. For better or worse, America has seized hold of the future of war, and with it—for a time—the future of humanity.[63]

As for nuclear power, the Friedmans see it as a "solution" for space military power needs "not only to provide internal power...but also to provide propulsion power."[64]

Despite the claim that only the U.S. could exploit space militarily—that's only jingoistic wishful thinking. Once the U.S. begins to implement its plans to weaponize and nuclearize space, just watch Russia and China—and whoever—follow suit. The heavens would be armed, as has been the Earth.

The deployment of nuclear power in space is colossally dangerous. "With nukes in space, the problem is technology is not perfect. Indeed, the space program is an example of that," comments Michael Mariotte of the Nuclear Information and Resource Service. "What you have are two essentially experimental technologies. The failure of either one causes a disaster. The failure of both could cause a catastrophe."[65]

"Our Risk and Their Management"

As this book was readied for publication, I received a telephone call from Alan Kohn, a career NASA official involved with safety issues in the use of space nuclear power systems. He noted he had been NASA's emergency preparedness officer at its Kennedy Space Center for the Galileo and Ulysses launches. He said he had read in the *Orlando Sentinel* about a presentation I had given in Orlando on the dangers of the Cassini mission. "You're right," he said.[66]

He explained that he "did not agree with the decision at the time" to use plutonium-fueled power systems on the Galileo and Ulysses missions "and I still do not believe in their use. Radioisotopes should not be used as power or heating source in spacecraft launched from the Earth's surface."[67]

"They call it risk management—but it's our risk and their management," said Kohn, who worked for NASA for thirty years, from 1964 to 1994.[68]

He noted that "we just went through" the apology by President Clinton to hundreds of men with syphillis left untreated by government researchers in the Tuskegee experiments, as well as revelations of the government using people as radiation guinea pigs. "Who the hell gives the government the right to make a decision that can and, in some cases, does cause the loss of life of some people?" demanded Kohn.[69]

The matter of informed consent is involved, said Kohn. "When you get in an automobile and drive, you are voluntarily putting yourself at risk," said Kohn. With space nuclear devices, people "are being put to risk without their knowledge."[70]

He said:

This exceeds the government's right in a democratic society. Democracy depends on informed judgement. I don't think the government has provided the public with sufficient information on which to make an informed judgement. I don't think that Congress understands the risk either. NASA as a bureaucracy has made a decision without the consent of the public or their representatives in Washington. Administrations have rubber-stamped these decisions. This is supposed to be a democracy, not a dictatorship. The public and its representatives are supposed to have the information and the opportunity to contribute to what decisions are made. We have been denied this right.[71]

Kohn recounted how, during the Galileo and Ulysses launches, he arranged for buildings at the Kennedy Space Center to be "converted to fall-out shelters" to protect personnel in the event of the dispersal of plutonium in an explosion of the shuttles lofting the plutonium-fueled probes. "But I could not do anything to protect the public outside the gates." he said. "Unless you evacuated the public before these kind of launches, there is no way to protect the people. But they don't want to evacuate the public for they know this would alarm the public, which would then move to prevent the launch."

Preparations NASA makes for emergency preparedness for nuclear space shots, said Kohn, are "cosmetic attempts.

Nothing could hold back the plutonium fall-out from dropping on nearby communities—Titusville, Cocoa, Cocoa Beach, the City of Cape Canaveral. They are all in extreme danger." A spread of plutonium in an accident on launch could "render the area unliveable."

As to the Cassini Earth "flyby," Kohn said that considering the speed at which it is to be flying, if it dips down and interacts with the atmosphere, he expects "it will completely disintegrate" and the plutonium will fall out. He called the "flyby" scheme "unconscionable."

No space mission, said Kohn, is "as important as the lives and health of the public."

"The government," concluded the long-time NASA official, "seems not to have any sense."

Initially in our conversation, Kohn was not sure he wanted his name to go public with his information. Then, as we talked, he said that because the gravity of the issue, he felt obligated to stand up by name—despite any personal cost.

"The Job of the Government is to Protect the People"

Kohn subsequently spoke at an anti-Cassini rally in June 1997 organized by the Florida Coalition for Peace & Justice at the gates of the Cape Canaveral Air Station. "I haven't given a public speech for a long time," he began, as rain pelted down and lightning bolts flashed in the surrounding sky. "In the favorite biblical phrase of the late President Johnson, 'Come, let us reason together.'"[72]

That morning's *Orlando Sentinel* had carried a story about Kohn turning whistleblower which quoted Joel Reynolds, NASA safety director at its Kennedy Space Center, taking issue with Kohn, insisting the plutonium on Cassini would be in a containment that is "like a bank vault." The story also said "NASA estimates the chance that the rocket would explode on launch and release plutonium into the air at 1 in 1,500."[73]

"I have great respect for Joel Reynolds, the safety director at KSC," Kohn told the protesters. "He is a real gentleman; he was a pleasure to work with. And I want to tell you that the pressure doesn't come from the Kennedy Space Center to launch Cassini. They're obeying orders from higher up. This is not a little story, this is a national or even an international story. The pressure comes from NASA headquarters. The orders come down—and when the orders come down, if you work for a bureaucracy, particularly a government bureaucracy, you do what you're told, you say what you're told to say, and you even think, despite your intelligence, the way you're taught to think. I've never understood the voluntary surrendering of intelligence and I certainly can't put up with surrendering the moral requirements of justice and protection for each other."[74]

Kohn went on:

Specifically, I was the emergency preparedness operations officer—in NASA-ese I was called the EPO—on the Galileo and Ulysses missions…I was also a member of the Radiological Emergency Force Group and the RTG Contingency Working Group. My responsibilities were as already defined: I was responsible for the safety of the government employees on both sides of the river: CCAFS [Cape Canaveral Air Force Station] right over here and KSC right over there. Let me tell you, they didn't even let me do that job. I was told that the job was cosmetic, that nothing was going to happen and I should just sit and counsel everyone in the radiation control center and do nothing, and in case of disaster, the unlikely event of disaster would take place, I would take all protective measures real time. The only protective measure I could have taken at that time, of course, would have been to wet my pants. And my own immediate management told me: lay off, keep a low profile, don't let the public know, above all don't let the protest groups know that there is any danger at all. I disobeyed orders. I provided that all the buildings should be turned into fall-out shelters, that air conditioning be shut off, that buildings be sealed, the doors be sealed, that people who were going to work outside would be put in bunny suits and given gas masks with HEPA filters. I provided washdowns. I told them no visitors. They brought visitors out anyway. And by the way, in the mission control center when I said no visitors, I got an ovation from the people.[75]

His fellow NASA employees "applauded me because they agreed with me. They didn't agree with me publicly but the applause was enough to show me that on the government side of those fences, there are a lot of people who agree with *you*, but out of misguided loyalty they don't have the freedom—they think they don't have the freedom—to speak out. I disagree. The first loyalty is to the public. The first loyalty is to the taxpayer. The first loyalty is to each other, to our own families. These are your friends and neighbors here. They feel the same way you do but they're not going to say so."

Kohn said that "we were told by NASA that the odds against the Cassini blowing up and releasing radiation [are] 1,500 to one. Those are pretty poor odds. You bet the lottery and the odds against you there are one in 14 million—1,500 to one are unacceptable odds," he said.[76]

"You can't in good conscience do a thing like that," Kohn said. "I call for the people who live in this community to protect themselves, their families and their children, to protect their neighbors. And I call on the people on the other side of the fence, the government side of the fence, who have families and friends and neighbors in the area also: don't let this launch go forward with 72-plus pounds of plutonium. That is not really a sane alternative.[77]

"I expect people to speak out regardless of what the cost is. If you're going to keep quite about an issue like this, then your jobs aren't worth a bucket of warm spit. If you're going to give up your soul and your conscience just to keep your jobs, the jobs aren't worth it," said Kohn.[78]

"Now I'm going to tell you: they think their hands are tied, their hands are not tied. They have a freedom to speak out, too. I had resistance from many in management when I converted the buildings to fall-out shelters and when I did all the other work I did to protect the government workers. But I had a lot of support also. The support unfortunately was quiet. I got away with doing the job I did against opposition and then I got rewarded with all kinds of awards and thank-yous after I had done the job. That didn't take away the fact that we were willing to risk the public doing these launches. How would we have protected the public? We had representatives from, I forget whether it was fourteen or seventeen government agencies including the FEMA and Brevard Emergency Management associations, and what they were going to do was they were going to go out there and they were going to monitor the fall-out as the plutonium fell on your heads, you here in Brevard County. And what could they have done to stop that plutonium from falling on your heads if it was a real-time emergency? Exactly nothing. They couldn't have erected an umbrella like [those] I see out here over all of Titusville, for example. And I saw the footprints of potential fall-outs which depended on wind, speed and direction and height at which the explosion took place.[79]

"They call the RTGs indestructible," said Kohn. "They're indestructible just like the Titanic was unsinkable. And they are committing the lie, the sin of omission, in not telling you the whole truth. There should be public hearings. I don't see the Congress holding public hearings. I don't see NASA holding public hearings. I don't see anyone addressing the issues. They figure if they keep it quiet, if they just pacify everyone, they can get away with everything they want to do. And they have gotten away with everything they wanted to do up until now.[80]

"It is time to put a stop to their freedom to threaten the lives of the people here on the Earth and particularly the people here in the vicinity of the space centers," said Kohn of

NASA. "I don't know how they can do this. I don't know what in a democracy they think gives them the right to do a thing like this. They have no such right. This is not a combat situation. You are not soldiers. You cannot be put at risk because someone makes a decision that nothing is going to happen.[81]

"As I said, they themselves say the odds are 1,500 to one, wherever they got those numbers from—I don't believe any numbers they give me because they're all speculations. I've been in weapons systems analysis groups. I've done figures, too," said Kohn. "The figures are always phony. They're just pulled out of a series of formulas which are nothing but pre-sumptions. The Titan IV has blown up before. If it blows up this time and if it releases plutonium, it will be too late to do anything about it whatsoever.[82]

"I call on my former co-workers to speak up. I call on the people who know the truth to speak up. If it means your jobs, so what? Who cares about a job? Health and the lives of the public are more important than any job on this Earth including the presidency of the United States. The job of the government is to protect the people, not to put the people at risk," stated Kohn. "I expect better from my co-workers and my former employers. I expect honesty, I expect complete hearings, I expect testimony, and after that I expect them to cancel this launch until they can do it safely." [83]

When the cheers for Kohn subsided, Bruce Gagnon declared: "It takes courage to come here and say those things."[84]

"Federal Employees Take an Oath"

Also as this book went to press, another veteran NASA employee called declaring opposition to a nuclear-fueled Cassini mission but said because he is employed by NASA he needed anonymity. He followed up with a detailed written statement in which he questioned "the assumptions, methods and conclusions" of NASA in its reports on, and analyses of, the Cassini mission:[85]

As a NASA employee I have a responsibility to express my concerns. NASA employees have insight into our nation's space program and how it functions. I am deeply concerned about a potential catastrophic failure that could release Plutonium-238 into the Earth's atmosphere. Federal employees take an oath to uphold and defend the U.S. Constitution and the general welfare. I question NASA's proposal to risk exposing millions of people to carcinogenic, vaporized Plutonium-238.

NASA relies on probalistic risk assessment to determine probability of mission success. NASA completely disregards evidence from recent spacecraft missions. Since 1990, NASA has launched four planetary spacecraft: Galileo, Mars Observer, Mars Surveyor and Mars Pathfinder. Three of the four have already suffered mission-threatening or mission-limiting failures. The Mars Observer suffered a catastrophic failure shortly before Mars orbit insertion. Thus the catastrophic failure rate is one in four. If Cassini suffers a similar failure in preparing for the Earth flyby maneuver, it could reenter the Earth's atmosphere.

The NASA studies discuss atmospheric dispersal of plutonium particles, but there is no evidence that they have used adequate atmospheric transport models. Particles from Chernobyl were detected worldwide about three weeks after the accident. It appears that NASA has oversimplified the health effects of plutonium—probably the most toxic substance on Earth. Plutonium-238 continues to emit radiation for years after a human body absorbs it.

NASA claims that solar power is not feasible for missions to the outer planets. However, the example they gave takes an only moderately efficient design and scales it to Saturn distances. More efficient designs are possible and should have been considered even if it means delaying the launch date.

Previously, NASA concealed data demonstrating the feasibility of solar power for planetary spacecraft.

As a NASA employee, I am disturbed by these dubious conclusions presented without adequate scientific justification. I am very concerned about the Cassini mission. The probability of an inadvertent reentry may be small, but the consequences are catastrophic.

This NASA source urged that the Cassini mission "be postponed to allow further investigation and consideration of alternatives" including "the use of solar power. NASA employees support planetary exploration," he stressed, "if it is done responsibly without accepting unnecessary catastrophic risks."

Unnecessary

Beyond the huge danger and issues of legality and cost, the use of nuclear power in space is unnecessary. "No one has yet shown me a use of nuclear material in space that is justified," declares Dan Hirsch.[86]

Safe solar energy can do the job. Of course, if companies like Nukem continue to gobble up developers of solar energy systems, maybe solar won't be allowed to do it—but it sure can. And what spin-offs back on Earth the expanded development of solar energy for space use would have. (With a mix of other safe, renewable energy forms, solar can replace lethal nuclear power on Earth, too—again as long as the Nukems of the world don't prevent that from happening, which is the big question, not the issue of whether it can be done technologically.)

Safe energy alternatives are here now for the Cassini project and for other space missions—especially if a national and global commitment is made to energy forms other than nuclear power. The new high-efficiency solar cells for deep space probes were developed over a five-year period in Europe on a $3 million budget—the budget for a few weeks' worth of office supplies for NASA.

NASA Ineptness

NASA, meanwhile, as I have gotten to know well in more than a decade on the nuclear-in-space story, is no clean-as-a-whistle, efficient agency, by any means.

As Congressman John Conyers of Michigan said in 1993, after chairing hearings by the House Government Operations Committee into a string of NASA screw-ups in the early 1990s: "It is no wonder that many people seem to have lost faith in NASA." Of NASA ineptness, Frank Conahan, an assistant U.S. comptroller general, had testified before the committee that "some of these problems are embedded in the culture of the organization. If we are going to see real improvement, we have to turn this culture around."[87]

Screw-ups by NASA and its contractors and in the military space program—big and small screw-ups—have continued. Some are as dopey (yet potentially dangerous) as the unauthorized use of "super-glue" for six years to make repairs on shuttles. The "dabs of glue" came from "the kind sold at most model shops," reported the Associated Press in 1994.[88] Some of the screw-ups are as potentially dangerous as Challenger-like O-ring problems. A 1995 *Newsday* headline said "O-ring troubles again" when the launch of the shuttle Endeavor was indefinitely postponed.[89] Or there were the admitted launch "horror" stories. "Horner Calls Launch Record a 'Horror Story,'" was the front-page headline in Space News in 1993 over a story about Charles Horner, then commander of the U.S. Space Command, telling "aerospace officials" that "widespread inefficiencies and frequent launch delays may have cost U.S. taxpayers more than $3 billion in recent years." Horner was quoted as saying: "I can tell you horror story after horror story." According to *Space News*, he was especially bothered about launches of the Titan IV.[90]

Cassini: One of a Series

The Cassini space probe mission is an awesome space danger ahead—and it is one of a series of planned nuclear space missions. Bruce Gagnon appeared before the Cape Canaveral City Council to discuss Cassini on March 6, 1997. The governmental body of the municipality closest to the U.S. Cape Canaveral launch site had wanted Air Force and NASA representatives and Gagnon to appear together for a debate. "The Air Force and NASA said no. They didn't want to face us publicly," said Gagnon. [91]

So the Cape Canaveral City Council had to arrange for the Air Force and NASA representatives to appear on March 5 and Gagnon the following night. In their presentation, the Air Force and NASA sought to assure the city officials by declaring that the Cassini mission would be "the last" plutonium-fueled space shot from Cape Canaveral. Gagnon, however, had with him a list he obtained from the government of twelve plutonium-fueled space shots the U.S. planned between 1997 and the year 2009. It included three "outer solar system" missions: Cassini in 1997, "Comet Nuclear Mission" in 2002 and "Pluto Flyby" with a 2003 date. Various missions to Mars involving plutonium-fueled devices were listed, including three "MESUR" shots, in 1999, 2001 and 2003, and the "Mars SR" missions in 2007 and 2009. In addition, six plutonium-fueled missions involving the moon were listed: "Site Rover" in 1998, "Telescope" in 1999, and two "Network" missions in both 2001 and 2002. [92]

There was "anger" on the Cape Canaveral City Council, recounted Gagnon, that NASA and the Air Force "didn't give the full story." [93]

If an accident does not occur on Cassini, it could happen on any one of the other nuclear space shots planned. It is just a matter of odds.

And as to odds, the government changed the odds of a nuclear accident on Cassini in April 1997 in a *Supplemental Environmental Impact Statement for the Cassini Mission*. It radically increased its prediction of the chances of an accident "that could threaten" the plutonium-powered system to 1 in 36 and put the odds at 1 in 345 "of an accident predicted to release" plutonium.[94]

What You Can Do

What can be done? One part of the stategy of the Global Network Against Weapons & Nuclear Power is to seek presidential intervention. The approval process for a nuclear space shot requires a go-ahead from a presidential panel with which the U.S. president can intervene. In the end, on decisions on space nuclear power, the buck stops at The White House. Will Bill Clinton have the sense and the courage to cancel Cassini? The postcards being distributed by the Global Network and affiliated groups to President Clinton ask him to "please cancel this mission and order NASA to pursue alternative power sources. We cannot allow nuclear power to proliferate in space. One accident with space plutonium could harm the whole world."

The most lethal aspect of the mission involves the 1999 "flyby." Cassini can still be diverted anytime between launch and the outrageously dangerous August 16 Earth "flyby." And it *must* be diverted because if there is an accident and plutonium comes raining down on Earth, as Dr. Gofman says, "the number of cancer doses" would be "so high as to make calculation extraneous."

Grassroots political action is occurring. On March 25, 1997 the Marin County Board of Supervisors in California unanimously passed a resolution "expressing Marin County's serious concern to the inclusion of plutonium as part of the Cassini spacecraft project due to dangers of nuclear radiation" and demanding that President Clinton, the California congressional delegation and state legislators "thoroughly investigate the potential health hazards associated with the Cassini launch as presently designed" and "to delay the launch" pending further study.[95] The board acted on the request of the Marin County Peace Conversion Commission whose chairperson, Dr. William Rothman, stressed in his letter that "even as the Cassini probe project enters its final pre-launch phase, a new, high-efficiency solar cell can, without plutonium's terrible dangers, provide ample electrical generating power to do what Cassini's plutonium is intended to do. NASA, however, appears to be proceeding with inadequate caution."[96]

A variety of challenges to Cassini and other nuclear space missions, including protests in front of The White House and at the United Nations, are moving ahead, as of this writing.

To get involved in the situation, to learn about the activities going on and being planned around the world, readers are urged to contact: The Global Network Against Weapons & Nuclear Power in Space, c/o the Florida Coalition for Peace & Justice, P.O. Box 90035, Gainesville, Florida 32607. Phone: (352) 468-3295. E-mail: fcpj@afn.org. Web site: www.afn.org/~fcpj/space.

With Cassini on the horizon, and the other nuclear space missions planned—for which Cassini is very much an ice-breaker—sooner or later, disaster will occur. It is inevitable, if these dangerous missions are allowed to happen. In launches of chemically propelled rockets there is a 1 percent failure rate. Such a failure rate is unacceptable when nuclear poisons are involved. There can be no chance of failure when death-dealing nuclear technology is involved and that is why, simply, it cannot be involved. Only a nuclear-free space program is sustainable, sensible, possible.

That, however, is not the direction of things.

The "Linchpin" of the U.S. Space Program

The drive continues—the headlong dash to nuclearize and weaponize space.

"Nuclear energy in outer space," says Dr. Kaku, "is the linchpin" of the U.S. space program. "What we are headed for is a nuclear-propelled rocket and nuclear-propelled lasers in outer space. That's what the military and that's what NASA would really like to do. With a "Timberwind" rocket, a booster rocket to hoist large payloads into outer space, we are talking about the ultimate goal of this madness. First, we have small reactors called SNAP reactors. Then we have the RTGs and Galileo and Cassini. Then we have the big "Timberwind" projects. And ultimately what they would like to do is to have nuclear-powered battle stations in outer space. That's what all of this is leading up to."[97]

The U.S. wants to put into space "weapons and nuclear power plants and attain mastery of outer space with the atom," says Dr. Kaku. "We have nuclear weapons on the land. We have nuclear weapons in the ocean. We have nuclear weapons in the air. And now they would like to have nuclear weapons in outer space in order to take the high ground."[98]

"And that's why we, as environmentalists, as activists, as concerned citizens, have to stop this now before it reaches the point of militarization of outer space," says Dr. Kaku. "We have to stop these Cassinis. We have to stop these Ulysses now before we have full-blown 'Timberwinds,' before we have Alpha lasers, before we have genuine nuclear booster rockets and nuclear power plants in outer space. We have to send a signal to NASA and a signal to the United States Pentagon that we're not going to tolerate the nuclearization of outer space, and it stops now."[99]

It is up to all of us to make that happen.

It's Not Worth the Risk

If the Cassini launch does take place, it—hopefully—will be without accident. The 1999 Cassini "flyby" of Earth, if it is to happen, will—hopefully—occur without global disaster. But with the U.S. planning to continue to launch nuclear payloads, to expand its nuclear space program which includes the development of nuclear-propelled rockets, and to deploy nuclear-powered weapons overhead, catastrophe—an unprecedented nuclear catastrophe—is inevitable.

It may or may not happen on the Cassini mission but, sooner or later, it will happen. We are on a countdown to nuclear space disaster.

One need not be a rocket scientist to know that putting nuclear poisons on a rocket is stupid: rockets *can* and *do* blow up on launch and if nuclear material is on board, that stuff will come out. Newton's Law of Gravity remains operable: what goes up can easily come down, and on our heads. With nuclear materials at issue, we are talking about radioactive poisons descending on us.

And schemes like an Earth "flyby" with a space device containing plutonium is just asking for it: nuclear Russian roulette with the gun pointed at the Earth.

The use of nuclear power in space devices is not worth the risk.

To destroy a portion of life on Earth in order to explore space makes no sense.

Solar energy is now available to substitute for nuclear power in space.

As for space weaponry, we are living at an historic juncture. We have an opportunity now to halt the expansion of a new round of the arms race into space. The Star Wars of the Reagan era is clearly not over, as the U.S. military seeks to attain the "ultimate high ground" and, with nuclear-powered weaponry, to dominate space and the Earth below. We have a chance to stop something wrong and dangerous before it happens, before it is too late.

In each and every generation, it seems, a choice is presented. "I have set before you life and death, blessing and curse," it is stated in Deuteronomy. "Therefore choose life, that you and your descendants may live."

We are now at that crossroads again.

We must choose life.

NOTES

Chapter One: "Canberra…We've Got a Problem"

1. Cable News Network, November 17, 1996.
2. Emergency Management Australia is an agency under the Department of Defense originally established in 1974 and then called Natural Disasters Organization; its name was changed to Emergency Management Australia in 1993. "EMA performs its emergency management functions in relation to natural, human-caused and technological hazards," it says in a description of itself provided to Australian journalist Peter Cronau in February 1997. Its SPRED plan involves coordination "and control" of the activities of Australian commonwealth, state and territory officials "in locating, recovering and removing radioactive space debris and the monitoring and neutralizing of any radiological contamination threat arising from the reentry of space debris." Cronau was told by Emergency Management Australia: "The plan was originally developed back in 1988 in response to a possible impact onto Australia from Cosmos 1900."
3. *Florida Today*, "Crippled Mars Probe Crashes Harmlessly to Earth in South Pacific Waters," based on Associated Press dispatch, November 17, 1996.
4. "Australia Calls Russian Rocket Crash 'Happy Ending,'" Xinhua News Agency, November 18, 1996.
5. Cable News Network, November 18, 1996.
6. "Reentry of Russian Space Probe," Statement by the Press Secretary, The White House, November 17, 1996.
7. Cable News Network, November 17, 1996.
8. "Russians Try To Put Space Probe On Course," Reuters, November 17, 1996.
9. Ibid.
10. Roxana Dascalu, "Parts of Space Probe Could Hit Earth—TV," Reuters, November 17, 1996.
11. Ibid.
12. Brian Donaghy, "Mars Probe Crash Puts Australia on Red Alert," *The Irish Times*, November 18, 1996, p. 1.
13. "Crippled Mars Probe Crashes Harmlessly to Earth in South Pacific Waters," op. cit.
14. Cable News Network, November 17, 1996.
15. "Russian Space Probe Crashes Near Australia," Rossiiskiye Vesti, November 19, 1996.
16. Veronika Romanenkova, "Experts Uncertain About Causes of Mars 96

Crash," ITAR-TASS, January 21, 1997. Koptev also was quoted in that ITAR-TASS dispatch as saying: "Since a ship could in no way influence the flight itself and would only provide information, it was decided not to send it."

17. Todd S. Purdum, "Russian Space Probe Falls Back to Earth," *The New York Times,* November 18, 1996, pp. A-1, A-3.

18. "Russian Space Probe Lands in South Pacific Ocean," Reuters, November 18, 1996.

19. Veronika Romanenkova, "Russia Says Probe's Debris Pose No Threat To Any State," ITAR-TASS, December 18, 1996.

20. Paul Hoverstein, "U.S., Russia Differ By Day On Crash of Mars 96 Probe," *USA Today,* November 19, 1996.

21. "Australia Calls Russian Rocket Crash 'Happy Ending,' " op. cit.

22. Script, KFC-TV Channel 2 Late News, November 17, 1996.

23. Cable News Network, November 17, 1996.

24. *Florida Today,* November 18, l996.

25. David Hoffman and Peter Baker, "Errant Russian Spacecraft Crashes Harmlessly After Scaring Australia," *The Washington Post,* November 18, 1996, p. A18.

26. "Update on Russian Space Probe," Directorate of Public Affairs, United States Space Command, Release No. 41-96, November 29, 1996.

27. David L. Chandler, "Eyewitnesses In Chile Shed Light On Russian Probe's Spectacular Fall," *The Boston Globe,* December 5, 1996, p. A2.

28. Chris Bryson, "How Safe Are Nuclear-Powered Space Missions?" *Christian Science Monitor,* December 17, 1996, p. 12.

29. Ibid.

30. Ibid.

31. Chandler, "Eyewitnesses In Chile Shed Light on Russian Probe's Spectacular Fall," op. cit.

32. David L. Chandler, "U.S. Said To Fumble Space Debris Alert," *The Boston Globe,* December 4, 1996, p. 1.

33. Ibid.

34. Reuters, "Russian Mars Craft Said To Have Fallen In Bolivia," *The New York Times,* December 14, 1996, p. 7.

35. Dr. Barrera, interview by the author, January 1997.

36. Sergio Velasquez, "Por Eventual Caida de Sonda Rusa: Piden Investigar Posible Radiacatividad en Norte," *El Mercurio,* January 3, 1997.

37. Ibid.

38. Sergio Monivero Brunz, "Se Informo En Iquique: Sonda Rusa Cayo En Suelo Boliviano," *El Mercurio,* December 13, 1996, p. C08.

39. Franklin Bustillos, press attache, Bolivian Embassy to the United States, interview by the author, Washington, D.C., February 1997.

40. Gordon Bendick, interview by the author and Terry Allen, editor of *CovertAction Quarterly*, February 1997.

41. Ibid.

42. Ibid.

43. Leonard David, "Mars 96 Mishap Highlights Weak Coordination," *Space News*, January 20-26, 1997, p. 18.

44. Ibid.

45. Ibid.

46. Steven Aftergood, interview by the author, January 1997.

47. Leonard David, op. cit.

48. *Emergency Preparedness for Nuclear-Powered Satellites*, Organisation for Economic Cooperation and Development and Swedish National Institute for Radiation Protection, Paris, 1990, p. 17.

49. "U.S. History of RTG Power Source Use," Contained in *Draft Environmental Impact Statement for Project Galileo*, National Aeronautics and Space Administration, Washington, D.C., 1990, pp. 3-4.

50. *Emergency Preparedness for Nuclear-Powered Satellites*, op. cit., p. 21.

51. Dr. John Gofman, interview by the author, January 1997.

52. *Emergency Preparedness for Nuclear-Powered Satellites*, op. cit., p. 21.

53. Helen Caldicott, *Nuclear Madness* (New York: Norton, 1994), p. 80.

54. Ibid., p. 81.

55. After ten half-lives there would be only about one thousandth of the original amount of radioactivity being emitted from a radioactive substance. So the total time it remains radioactive—what is termed its "hazardous lifetime"—is calculated by multiplying its half-life by a figure of from ten to twenty. Thus the "hazardous lifetime" of Plutonium-238 is 87.8 to 1,756 years, the "hazardous lifetime" for Plutonium-239 is 245,000 to 490,000 years. Although Plutonium-238 is the major portion of the fuel used in RTGs, there are smaller amounts of other plutonium isotopes included as well—among them Plutonium-239. The fuel mix, for example, on the Cassini space probe is, according to NASA's *Final Environmental Impact Statement for the Cassini Mission* (p. 2-18), to consist of: 70.8 percent Plutonium-238, 12.8 percent Plutonium-239 and a combination of Plutonium-240, Plutonium-241 and Plutonium-242 totalling 2 percent. Further, 2.4 percent of the Cassini fuel is to include "long-lived actinides" and other "impurities" and 11.8 will be oxygen. So, says the *Final Environmental Impact Statement for the Cassini Mission*, "the term plutonium dioxide" is used to refer "to the mixture of the oxides of several plutonium isotopes, with Pu-238 as the dominant isotope" of the fuel.

56. Joseph A. Angelo, Jr. and David Buden, *Space Nuclear Power* (Malabar, Florida: Orbit Book Company, Inc., 1985), p. 140.

57. Ibid., p. 17.

58. Giovanni Caprara, *The Complete Encyclopedia of Space Satellites* (New York: Crown Publishers, 1986), p. 35.

59. *Emergency Preparedness for Nuclear-Powered Satellites*, op. cit., p. 22.

60. "U.S. History of RTG Power Source Use," op. cit., pp. 3-4.

61. Jim Lovell and Jeffrey Kluger, *Lost Moon, The Perilous Voyage of Apollo 13* (Boston: Houghton Mifflin Company, 1994), pp. 294-96.

62. Ibid., p. 295.

63. Ibid., pp. 295-296.

64. "U.S. History of RTG Power Source Use," op. cit., p. 3-4.

65. *Emergency Preparedness for Nuclear-Powered Satellites*, op. cit., p. 22.

66. Michael Rosenberg, interview by the author, August 1995. See Karl Grossman and Judith Long, "Apollo Outtakes," *The Nation*, September 11, 1995.

67. Craig Covault, "First U.S. Mars Rover Launched to Red Planet," *Aviation Week and Space Technology*, Vol. 145, No. 24, December 9, 1996, p. 24.

68. *Assessment of the Topaz International Program*, National Research Council, National Academy Press, Washington, D.C., 1996, pp. 61-62; "Fallen Waste," *The Christian Science Monitor*, December 17, 1996, p. 12; and Douglas Hart, *The Encyclopedia of Soviet Spacecraft* (New York: Exeter Books, 1987), p. 47.

69. According to Joseph A. Angelo, Jr. and David Buden's *Space Nuclear Power*, op. cit., p. 245: "After successful startup and operation at power in its permitted orbit for 43 days, a series of spurious electronic signals accidentally shut down the SNAP-10A. Because of aerospace safety design features, it was not possible to restart the reactor system using groundbased commands. Consequently, this reactor remains quiescent in its 4,000 year orbit...When the SNAP-10A finally reenters the Earth's atmosphere several millenia from now, the radioactivity level of its core will be negligible. Then, as designed, it will harmlessly disperse itself during a final fiery plunge through the Earth's upper atmosphere." The claim that even after 4,000 years the radioactive waste remaining on SNAP-10A will be insignificant is debatable. Many fission products have "hazardous lifetimes" during which they remain radioactive exceeding 4,000 years.

70. Douglas Hart, op. cit., pp. 35-36.

71. *Emergency Preparedness for Nuclear-Powered Satellites*, op. cit., p. 22.

72. Ibid.

73. Douglas Hart, *The Encyclopedia of Soviet Spacecraft* (New York: Exeter Books, 1987), p. 43.

74. Ibid.

75. *Emergency Preparedness for Nuclear-Powered Satellites*, op. cit., p. 22.

76. Ibid., p. 24.

77. Ibid., pp. 24-25.

78. Ibid., p. 25.

79. Douglas Hart, op. cit., p. 43.

80. *Assessment of the Topaz International Program*, op. cit., p. 61; "Fallen Waste," op. cit.; Douglas Hart, p 47.

81. Douglas Hart, p. 47.

Chapter Two: "The Mother of All Accidents"

1. *Fact Sheet: The Cassini Mission*, National Aeronautics and Space Administration, Washington, D.C., 1995, pp. 2-3.

2. Tim Weiner, "Lost Titan Missile Carried 3 Satellites, U.S. Officials Report," *The New York Times*, pp.1A and 1B.

3. "Workhorse, My Foot," *Space News*, August 9-15, p. 14.

4. *Final Environmental Impact Statement for the Cassini Mission*, National Aeronautics and Space Administration, Solar System Exploration Division, Office of Space Science, June 1995, pp. 4-76.

5. *Baltimore Gas & Elec. v. Natural Resources Defense Council*, 462 U.S. 87, 97 (1983).

6. *Final Environmental Impact Statement for the Cassini Mission*, pp. 4-51.

7. Ibid.

8. Dr. Horst Poehler, interview by the author, January 1997.

9. Ibid.

10. *Final Environmental Impact Statement for the Cassini Mission*, p. D-18.

11. Chris Bryson, "How Safe Are Nuclear-Powered Space Missions?" *The Christian Science Monitor*, December 17, 1996, p. 12.

12. Ibid.

13. Marilyn Meyer, "Risks Of Plutonium Launch Debate, Scientists Again Line Up To Oppose 1997 Blastoff," *Florida Today*, May 21, 1995, p. 17A.

14. Dr. Michio Kaku, interview in *Nukes In Space, The Nuclearization and Weaponization of the Heavens*, EnviroVideo, Box 311, Ft. Tilden, N.Y. 11695 1-800-ECO-TV46.

15. *Final Environmental Impact Statement for the Cassini Mission*, op. cit., p. 4-76.

16. Dr. Ernest Sternglass, Interview in *Nukes In Space, The Nuclearization and Weaponization of the Heavens*, op. cit.

17. Dr. Ernest Sternglass, interview by the author, January 1997.

18. Dr. Helen Caldicott, interview by the author, January, February 1997.

19. Ibid.

20. Byron Morgan, interview by the author, March 1997.

21. Dr. Alice Stewart, interview by the author, March 1997.

22. Dr. Richard E. Webb, interview by the author. His *The Accident Hazards of*

Nuclear Power Plants was published the University of Massachusetts Press in 1976.

23. Liz Tucci, "Goldin Subjects Cassini To Cost, Risk Reductions," *Space News*, March 14, 1994, pp. 1 and 21.

24. William Harwood, "NASA Studies Cassini Launch on Shuttle," *Space News*, March 6, 1994, pp. 1 and 21.

25. "Keep Cassini on Titan," *Space News*, March 14-20, p. 7.

26. Ibid.

27. Sean Holton, "GOP Swings Ax at Saturn Craft," *Orlando Sentinel*, July 26, 1995, pp. A-1 and A-4.

28. "Full Committee Print" or draft of bill of Committee on Appropriations. *Departments of Veterans Affairs and Housing and Urban Development, and Independent Agencies Appropriation Bill*, 1996, 104th Congress, 1st Session.

29. Interview August 1995.

30. Charles Manor of Lockheed Martin's Corporate Communications office, interview by the author, February 1997, said Lockheed Martin, headquartered in Bethesda, Maryland, did $14.3 billion of business with the U.S. Department of Defense in 1996, out of total business of $26.9 billion. He said that the Titan IV has been used "almost exclusively for military missions" with, up until Cassini, "a few NASA and commercial missions."

31. NASA's *Final Environmental Impact Statement for the Cassini Mission* states that each of the RTGs on Cassini "is designed to provid 285 watts of electrical power" for a total of 855 watts (p. 1-14). However, according to NASA's Cassini web site (http://www/jpl.nasa.gov), they will be generating "628 watts at the end of the mission." This averages to 745 watts of electricity during the mission. The web site further outlines the Cassini "spacecraft and instrument power demand of between 600-700 watts." In addition to the three RTGs, some 157 tiny cylinders (which NASA calls Radioisotope Heat Units or RHUs), each containing 2.7 grams or .006 pounds of Plutonium-238 fuel—for a total of slightly less than a pound—are to be scattered on board the Cassini probe to furnish heat. Dr. Horst Poehler says of the plutonium-filled RHUs: "Their packaging is minimal, and their distribution all over the spacecraft makes them highly vulnerable to spilling their deadly contents in case of an accident."

32. "New Solar Cells With Record Efficiency," Press Information Note No. 07-94, European Space Agency, Paris, April 19, 1994.

33. Ibid.

34. Ibid.

35. Ibid.

36. Meyer, "Risks Of Plutonium Launch Debate, Scientists Again Line Up To

Oppose 1997 Blastoff," op. cit.

37. Dr. Michio Kaku, interview by the author, November, 1996.

38. *Draft Environmental Impact Statement for the Cassini Mission*, National Aeronautics and Space Administration, Solar System Exploration Division, Office of Space Science, October 1994, pp. 2-54.

39. *Final Environmental Impact Statement for the Cassini Mission*, op. cit., p. D-7.

40. Dr. Michio Kaku, interview by the author, February 1997, op. cit.

41. D.E. Rockey, R. Bamford, M.G. Hollars, R.W. Klemetson, T.W. Koerner, E.L. Marsh, H. Price, C. Uphoff, *The Systems Impact Of A Concentrated Solar Array On A Jupiter Orbiter*, Jet Propulsion Laboratory, California Institute of Technology, Pasadena, California, 1981, p. 445. Prepared under Contract No. NAS7-100, National Aeronatics and Space Administration.

42. Keith Easthouse, "Radioactive Mishaps Rising At LANL," *The New Mexican*, July 29, 1996, pp. A-1-A-4.

43. Ibid.

44. Ibid.

45. Robin Suriano, "Emergency Plans Being Drawn Up For Oct. Launch," *Florida Today*, January 27, 1997, pp. A-1 and A-6.

46. Ibid.

47. Todd Halvorson, "Delta 2 Rocket Explodes," *Florida Today*, January 18, 1997, p. A-1.

48. Frank Oliveri, "Residents Take Shelter From Toxic Cloud," *Florida Today*, January 18, 1997, p. A-1.

49. Ibid., p. A-1.

50. Ibid., p. A-1, and Bruce Gagnon, interview by the author, January 1997.

51. Ibid., p. A-1 and A-7.

52. Ibid., p. A-7.

53. R.C. Heaton, J.H. Patterson, K.P. Coffelt, *Behavior of Plutonium Oxide Particulates in a Simulated Florida Environment*, Los Alamos National Laboratory, Los Alamos, N.M., LA-10498-MS, UC-33A, August 1985, p 1.

54. Ibid., pp. 1-2.

55. Ibid., pp. 12-13.

56. *Final Environmental Impact Statement for the Cassini Mission*, op. cit., p. 4-35.

57. Ibid.

58. Ibid.

59. Ibid., pp. 4-36 to 4-37.

60. Ibid., p. 4-37.

61. Ibid.

62. Ibid., p. 4-37 to 4-38.

63. Ibid., p. 4-38.

64. Ibid.
65. Ibid.
66. Ibid., pp. 4-38 to 4-39.
67. Ibid., p. 4-49.
68. Ibid.
69. Ibid.
70. Ibid., p. 4-51.
71. Ibid.
72. Ibid.
73. Ibid., p. 4-54
74. Ibid.
75. Ibid., p. 4-67.
76. Ibid.
77. Ibid.
78. Ibid., p. 4-72.
79. Ibid.
80. Ibid.
81. Ibid.
82. Ibid.
83. Ibid.
84. Ibid.
85. Ibid.
86. "Transuranium Elements, Volume 2, Technical Basis for Remedial Actions," U.S. Environmental Protection Agency, U.S. Office of Radiation Programs, Washington, D.C., Report No. EPA/520-1-90-016, June 1990. Cited in *Final Environmental Impact Statement for the Cassini Mission*, op. cit., p. 8-11.
87. *Final Environmental Impact Statement for the Cassini Mission*, op. cit., p. 4-70.
88. Ibid., pp. 4-71 and 4-73.
89. Ibid., p. 4-73.
90. Ibid.
91. Ibid.
92. Ibid., p. 4-74.
93. Ibid.
94. Ibid., p. 4-76.
95. Ibid.
96. Ibid.
97. Ibid., p. 4-75.
98. Ibid.
99. Ibid., p. 4-76.
100. Ibid., p. 4-77.
101. Ibid.

102. Ernest Sternglass, *Secret Fallout: Low-Level Radiation from Hiroshima to Three Mile Island* (New York: McGraw Hill, 1981) is the expanded version of Dr. Sternglass's earlier *Low-Level Radiation* (New York: Ballantine Books, 1972).

103. Dr. Ernest Sternglass, interview, op. cit.

104. Ibid.

105. Ibid.

106. Ibid.

107. Ibid.

108. Ibid.

109. Dr. Caldicott, interview op. cit.

110. Ibid.

111. Ibid.

112. Ibid.

113. Ibid.

114. Ibid.

115. Ibid.

116. Dr. Stewart, interview op. cit.

117. Ibid.

118. Ibid.

119. Dr. Edward Lyman, interview by the author, March 1997.

120. Ibid.

121. Dan Hirsch, interview by the author, March 1997.

122. Ibid.

123. Ibid.

124. Dr. Steven Wing, interview by the author, March 1997.

125. Ibid.

126. Dr. Helen Caldicott interview, op. cit.

127. *Final Environmental Impact Statement for the Cassini Mission*, op. cit., p. 4-90.

128. Ibid., p. B-8.

129. Dr. Michio Kaku speech at National Space Organizing Meeting and Protest, Cocoa Beach, Florida, May 26, 1996.

130. Ibid.

131. Ibid.

132. Dr. Michio Kaku, interview in *Nukes In Space: The Nuclearization and Weaponization of the Heavens*. Dr. Kaku, professor at the City University of New York for more than 20 years, earlier taught at Princeton University. An internationally recognized authority on Einstein's unified field theory, his books include: *Hyperspace: A Scientific Odyssey Through Parallel Universes, Time Warps, and the 10th Dimension* (New York: Oxford University Press, 1994); *Beyond Einstein: The Cosmic Quest for the Theory of the Universe* (New York: Bantam Books, 1988);

Nuclear Power: Both Sides (New York: W.W. Norton, 1983).

Chapter Three: One-in-100,000 Becomes One-in-76

1. "DOE's Nuclear Power Sources Scheduled For Shuttle Missions to Jupiter and the Sun," *Energy Insider*, U.S. Department of Energy, Washington, D.C., January 1983, Vol. 6, No.1, pp.1-5.

2. Ibid., p.1.

3. Karl Grossman, *Cover Up: What You Are Not Supposed To Know About Nuclear Power* (Sag Harbor, N.Y.: Permanent Press, 1980).

4. TV programs and documentaries written and hosted by Karl Grossman in recent years about nuclear power are available through EnviroVideo, Box 311, Ft. Tilden, N.Y. 11695, 1-800-ECO-TV46. The videos include: *Three Mile Island Revisited; Dr. Vladimir Chernousenko: The Truth About Chernobyl; Solar Energy Now; Second Wind; The Push to Revive Nuclear Power; Millstone: A Millstone; Millstone at the Crossroads; Life, Death and the Nuclear Establishment; The Whistle-Blowers; Hydrogen: Abundant Clean Energy; Reactor Watchdog Project; Food Irradiation; Loose Nukes; Robert Pollard; Prairie Island Coalition; Michael Mariotte: Nuclear Information and Resource Service;* and *Nukes In Space: The Nuclearization and Weaponization of the Heavens.*

5. *Energy Insider*, op. cit., p. 5.

6. "Only One Will Go," NASA Journalist In Space, Journalist In Space Program, University of South Carolina, College of Journalism, Columbia, SC 29208.

7. Karl Grossman, *Nicaragua: America's New Vietnam* (Sag Harbor, NY: Permanent Press, 1985).

8. Letter, Karl Grossman, Freedom of Information Act Request, January 9, 1995.

9. *Energy Insider*, op. cit., p. 1.

10. Letter, Karl Grossman, January 9, 1995, op. cit.

11. Letter from Nell M. Hayes, FOIA and Privacy Acts Activities Branch Specialist, Division of Reference and Information Management, U.S. Department of Energy, Washington, D.C., January 18, 1985.

12. Letter, Karl Grossman, February 1, 1985.

13. Letter from Ronald R. Turner, Director of Reference and Information Management, Office of Administrative Services, U.S. Department of Energy, Washington, D.C., March 14, 1985.

14. Letter, Karl Grossman to Director, Office of Hearings and Appeals, U.S. Department of Energy, Washington, D.C., March 29, 1985.

15. Ibid.

16. Decision and Order of the Department of Energy, Case Number HFA-0285, George B. Breznay, Director, Office of Hearings and Appeals,

U.S. Department of Energy, May 20, 1985.

17. Letter from Ronald R. Turner, May 28, 1985.

18. Dan Butler, interviews by the author, May 1985 to February 1986.

19. Karl Grossman, "Government Cover-Up Is Illegal," *Review* newspapers, August 8, 1995. Column also appeared in *The East Hampton Star, The Southampton Press* and other newspapers.

20. *Updated Safety Analysis Report for the Galileo Mission and the International Solar-Polar Mission*, Prepared for the U.S. Department of Energy, General Electric Advanced Energy Programs Department, General Electric Company, Document No. GESP-7186, April 1984.

21. Ibid., p. 2-2.

22. Ibid., pps. 2-2 to 2-3.

23. Ibid., pps. 2-2 to 2-4.

24. Ibid., p. 2-5.

25. Ibid., pp. 2-9 to 2-10.

26. Ibid., pp. 2-18 and 2-20.

27. *Updated Safety Analysis Report for the Galileo Mission and the International Solar-Polar Mission*, Volume III, Nuclear Risk Analysis Document, Prepared for the U.S. Department of Energy, Advanced Energy Programs Department General Electric, Document No. GESP-7187, May 1984.

28. Letter from James J. Lombardo, Acting Director, Division of Special Applications, Office of Defense Energy Projects and Special Applications, Office of Nuclear Energy, U.S. Department of Energy, Washington, D.C., September 17, 1985.

29. *Updated Safety Analysis Report for the Galileo Mission and the International Solar-Polar Mission*, Volume III, op. cit., p. 5.

30. *Draft Environmental Impact Statement for Project Galileo*, Prepared by Jet Propulsion Laboratory, Pasadena, CA and NASA Headquarters, 1985, p. iii.

31. Ibid., p. 3-4.

32. *Updated Safety Analysis Report for the Galileo Mission and the International Solar-Polar Mission*, Volume III, Nuclear Risk Analysis Document, op. cit., p. 6.

33. Karl Grossman, *Power Crazy: Is LILCO Turning Shoreham Into America's Chernobyl?* (New York: Grove Press, 1986).

34. Dan Butler, interview by the author, January 29, 1986.

35. William Harwood, "NASA Officials Calculate Shuttle Risks," *Space News,* January 29-February 4, 1996. "The odds of a catastrophic failure across all mission phases range from a worst-case estimate of 1-in-76 to a best-case 1-in-230," according to the article which quoted Bryan O'Connor, NASA'S deputy associate administrator for space science as saying

"that's an indication it's not a precise science." The article also noted that "in 1988, NASA commissioned a study to determine the odds of a launch failure as the agency approached returning to flight after Challenger's destruction in 1986. At that time, ignoring post-Challenger safety improvements, the median odds of a failure during launch were estimated to be 1-in-78." The article quoted space analyst Joan Johnson-Freese as saying "everyone's doing everything they possibly can to prevent" another shuttle catastrophe "but again, hardware wears out."

36. "The Lethal Shuttle," *The Nation*, February 22, 1986, p. 1.

37. "The Plutonium Cover-Up?" *The Nation*, March 15, 1986, p. 1.

38. James Gleick, "NASA's Russian Roulette," *The New York Times*, p. 16.

39. Ibid.

40. Richard P. Feynman, *What Do You Care What Other People Think?* (New York: W.W. Norton & Company, 1988), pp. 179-180. In the book, Feynman also amusingly discussed "the crazy acronyms that NASA uses all over the place: 'SRMs' are the solid rocket motors, which make up most of the 'SRBs,' the solid rocket boosters. The 'SSMEs' are the space shuttle main engines; they burn 'LH' (liquid hydrogen) and 'LOX' (liquid oxygen), which are stored in the 'ET,' the external tank. Everything's got letters. And not just the big things: practically every valve has an acronym, so they said, 'We'll give you a dictionary for the acronyms—it's really very simple.' Simple, sure, but the dictionary is a great, big, fat book that you've gotta keep looking through for things like 'HPFTP' (high-pressure fuel turbopump) and 'HPOTP' (high-pressure oxygen turbopump)," p. 126.

41. Ibid., p. 180.

42. Elliot Marshall, "Feynman Issues His Own Shuttle Report, Attacking NASA's Risk Estimates," *Science*, Volume 232, June 27, 1986, p. 1596.

43. Ibid., p. 1596.

44. Ibid., p. 1596.

45. David E. Sanger, "Challenger Report Is Said to Omit Some Key Safety Issues for NASA," *The New York Times*, June 8, 1986, pp. 1 and 36.

46. Lawrence C. Levy and Earl Lane, "Rogers Recommends Against Prosecuting Shuttle Officials," *Newsday*, June 11, 1986, p. 5.

47. Feynman, *What Do You Care What Other People Think?*, op. cit., p. 236.

48. Ibid.

49. Letter, Karl Grossman, February 7, 1987.

50. Ibid.

51. Letter from John H. Carter, Chief of FOI and Privacy Acts, U.S. Department of Energy, Washington, D.C., February 20, 1987.

52. Letter from Shirley M. Green, Deputy Associate Administrator for

Communications, National Aeronautics and Space Administration, to *The Nation*, May 17, 1988. The new studies listed by Green in which DOE participated were *Safety Evaluation Report for GLL/ULS*, February 1, 1986 prepared by the Inter-Agency Nuclear Safety Review Panel whose members are DOE, NASA and the Department of Defense, and *Assessment of the Safety Documentation for the Galileo and Ulysses Missions*, May 23, 1996, co-authored by DOE.

53. Karl Grossman, "Nuclear Shuffle," *Our Right to Know*, Winter/Spring 1988, pp. 7-9.

54. Bruce Murray, *Journey Into Space: The First Three Decades of Space Exploration* (New York: W.W. Norton & Company, 1989), p. 235.

55. "Giotto: The First Ever Earth Gravity Assist Manoeuvre," European Space Agency, Paris, June 22, 1990, News Release #31. The Giotto "flyby" occurred on July 2, 1990. "Using the Earth's gravitational force to redirect Giotto will be a first in the history of space exploration," said the statement. "Following Giotto, at the end of the year in December 1990, the NASA Galileo spacecraft will also exploit our planet's gravitational force to gain speed for its flight to Jupiter."

56. The first Galileo "flyby" occurred on December 8, 1990 and the second on December 8, 1992. After the 1992 "flyby," NASA announced that the "Galileo spacecraft flew by the earth this morning at 10:09 a.m. EST at an altitude of 189 miles (304 kilometers) above the South Atlantic Ocean" and this had "added about 8,300 miles per hour (13,300 kilometers per hour) to the spacecraft's speed and changed its direction slightly so that its elliptical orbit now will reach to the orbit of Jupiter." "Galileo Cruises By The Earth," press release, National Aeronautics and Space Administration, Washington, D.C., December 8, 1992.

57. *Supplemental Draft Environmental Impact Statement for the Galileo and Ulysses Missions*, National Aeronautics and Space Administration, Office of Space Science and Applications, Solar System Exploration Division, Washington, D.C., November 1987, p. 4-17.

58. Letter from Patricia Riep, Freedom of Information Act Officer, National Aeronautics and Space Administration, Washington, D.C., April 18, 1989.

59. Karl Grossman, Letter to Patricia Riep, February, 1989.

60. Karl Grossman, Letter to Richard Truly, February, 1989.

61. Letter from Patricia Riep, Freedom of Information Act Officer, National Aeronautics and Space Administration, Washington, D.C., July 20, 1989.

62. *Final Safety Analysis Report for the Galileo Mission*, NUS Corp., "Prepared for the U.S. Department of Energy," Volume III (Book 1) Nuclear Risk Analysis Document, NUS5126, Rev. 1, General Purpose Heat Source

Radioisotope Theromelectric Generator Program, Contract DE-AC01-87NE32134, January 13, 1989, p. 2-10. Actually, the document stated: "Analysis of these accident environments and their probabilities indicate that given an accident, a release of RTG fuel will occur about 83 times in 100." It turned out, NASA officials later said, that the decimal point was accidentally left out between the 8 and the 3.

63. *Final Safety Analysis Report for the Galileo Mission*, General Electric, Astro-Space Division, Spacecraft Operations, Valley Force Space Center, Philadelphia, PA, "Prepared for U.S. Department of Energy," Document No. 87SDS4213, General Purpose Heat Source Generator Program, Contract DE-AC01-79ET32043, December 15, 1988, p. 6.

64. *Galileo Earth Avoidance Study Report*, Jet Propulsion Laboratory, California Institute of Technology, JPL D-5590, Rev. A., November 4, 1988, p. 4-8.

65. Ibid., p. 1-5.

66. *Florida Coalition for Peace and Justice, et al.*, v. *George Herbert Walker Bush, et. al*, Civil Action No. 89-2682 OG, U.S. District Court, Washington, D.C., 1989. Declaration of Karl Z. Morgan, Plaintiff's Exhibit C, p. 2.

67. Ibid.

68. Ibid.

69. *Florida Coalition for Peace and Justice, et al.*, v. *George Herbert Walker Bush, et al*, op. cit., Declaration of Dr. Michio Kaku, Plaintiff's Exhibit W, p. 2.

70. Ibid.

71. Ibid., p. 5.

72. Ibid., p. 9.

73. Dennis E. Powell, "The Death of a Whistleblower," *The Miami Herald*, July 29, 1990, p. 16.

74. *Florida Coalition for Peace and Justice, et al.*, v. *George Herbert Walker Bush, et al*, op. cit. Declaration of John R. Casani, Defendant's Exhibit 2, p. 6.

75. Ibid., p. 4.

76. Ibid., p. 6.

77. Ibid., Memorandum of Justice Oliver Gasch, October 1989.

78. *Florida Coalition for Peace and Justice, et al.*, v. *George Herbert Walker Bush, et al*, United States District Court for the District of Columbia, Case No. 89-2682, Motion to Intervene and Memorandum of Points in Authorities in Support of Intervention, Oct. 10, 1989.

79. Ibid.

80. *Florida Coalition for Peace and Justice, et al.*, v. *George Herbert Walker Bush, et al.*, No. 89-5372, Circuit Court of Appeals for the District of Columbia, Exhibit 6.

81. D.E. Rockey, R. Bamford, M.G. Hollars, R.W. Klemetson, T.W. Koerner, E.L. Marsh, H. Price, C. Uphoff, *The Systems Impact of a Concentrated*

Solar Array on a Jupiter Orbiter, op. cit., p. 440.

82. Ibid., p. 445.

83. Interoffice Memo, Jet Propulsion Laboratory, August 11, 1986, "Subject: Presentation on Alternative Power Sources for Planetary Exploration."

84. Paul M. Stella, *Interplanetary Exploration—A Challenge for Photovoltaics*, Jet Propulsion Laboratory. "Carried out by the Jet Propulsion Laboratory...under contract with the National Aeronautics and Space Administration." Undated.

85. Ibid., p. 3.

86. Ibid., p. 7.

87. Dudley G. McConnell, Memorandum, August 23, 1988.

88. Lanny Sinkin, interview by the author, October 1989.

89. Bruce Gagnon, interview by the author, October 1989.

90. Lanny Sinkin, "In Memoriam: William E. McInnis, 1936-1990," *Convergence*, Fall 1990, p. 14.

91. Ibid.

92. Robert Cooke, "Stray Signals Shuts Down Jupiter Craft," *Newsday*, March 30, 1991, p. 17.

93. John Noble Wilford, "Move Seeks to Salvage Space Mission," *The New York Times*, August 12, 1991, p. A-11.

94. Kurt Loft, "Galileo Failure May Devastate NASA," *The Tampa Tribune*, September 9, 1991, pp. 1 and 6.

95. "Stuck Antenna Limits Jupiter Probe," *Newsday*, December 24, 1991, pp. 63 and 65.

96. Robert Cooke, "Galileo's Tangled Mission," *Newsday*, June 23, 1992, pp. 53 and 55.

97. Associated Press, "NASA Will 'Hammer' Probe's Stuck Antenna," *The New York Times*, December 29, 1992.

98. John Noble Wilford, "Scientists Set to Give Up on Galileo's Antenna," *The New York Times*, January 21, 1993.

99. William Harwood, "Galileo Antenna Resists Latest Repair Attempt," *Space News*, January 25-31, 1993, p. 7.

100. Ben Iannotta, "Galileo Recorder Jams," *Space News*, October 16, 1995, pp. 1 and 28.

101. John Noble Wilford, "Jupiter Rendezvous Is a Marvel of Perfection," *The New York Times*, December 9, 1995, p. 12.

102. *Final Environmental Impact Statement for the Ulysses Mission (Tier 2)*, National Aeronautics and Space Administration, Office of Space Science and Applications, Solar System Exploration Division, Washington, D.C., June 1990.

103. Associated Press, "Groups Seek to Prevent Nuclear Space Probe," *The New York Times*, September 9, 1990.

104. *Final Environmental Impact Statement for the Ulysses Mission (Tier 2)*, op. cit., p. E-37.

105. Karl Grossman and Judith Long, "NASA Nonsense," *The Nation*, May 14, 1990.

106. *Florida Coalition for Peace and Justice, et al.* v. *George Herbert Walker Bush, et al.*, op cit., Joint Brief of Amici Curiae, Committee to Bridge the Gap, Los Angeles Physicians for Social Responsibility, Southern California Federation of Scientists. Filed September 28, 1990.

107. Letter from Lynn W. Heninger, NASA Assistant Administrator for Congressional Relations to U.S. Senator Harry Reid of Nevada. July 14, 1989. A similar letter went to many members of Congress.

108. Karl Grossman and Judith Long, op. cit.

109. L. K. Brown, "150 Protest Ulysses Launch," *Florida Today*, September 23, 1990, p. 1-A.

110. Ibid., p. 2-A.

111. Associated Press, "Problem Reported With Solar Explorer Spacecraft," *Knoxville-News Sentinel*, December 15, 1990.

Chapter Four: "Ultimate High Ground"

1. David E. Lilienthal, *Change, Hope, and The Bomb* (Princeton, N.J.: Princeton University Press, 1963), p. 112.

2. Ibid., p. 72.

3. Ibid., p. 73.

4. John W. Simpson, *Nuclear Power from Underseas to Outer Space* (La Grange Park, Illinois: American Nuclear Society, 1995), p 122.

5. By Phillips Laboratory Public Affairs, "Taking the High Ground: The Space Advantage," *Focus*, January 17, 1997, p. 5.

6. Ibid.

7. Ibid.

8. Ibid.

9. *United States Air Force Phillips Laboratory*, a brochure published by Office of Public Affairs, Phillips Laboratory, 3550 Aberdeen Avenue SE, Kirtland AFB, New Mexico.

10. William B. Scott, "USSC Prepares for Future Combat Missions in Space," *Aviation Week & Space Technology*, August 5, 1996, p. 51.

11. Ibid.

12. U.S. Air Force Advisory Board, *New World Vistas: Air and Space Power for the 2lst Century*, "Space Technology Volume," 1996, pp. xviii and 29.

13. Ibid., p. 29.

14. Ibid.

15. Ibid.

16. Ibid.

17. Ibid., pp. 29-30.

18. Byron Splice, "SDI Looks to Nuclear Power, Orbiting Reactor Essential, Director Says," *Albuquerque Journal*, January 12, 1988, pp. A-1 and A-9.

19. William J. Broad, *Star Warriors: A Penetrating Look into the Lives of the Young Scientists Behind Our Space Age Weaponry* (New York: Simon and Schuster, 1985), p. 21.

20. Ibid., p. 59.

21. Ibid., p. 16.

22. Jack Manno, *Arming the Heavens: The Hidden Military Agenda for Space, 1945-1995* (New York: Dodd, Mead & Company, 1984), p. 3.

23. Ibid., p. 62.

24. Eisenhower comment quoted in George Robinson, "Space Law, Space War, and Space Exploration," *Journal of Social and Political Studies*, Fall 1980, #3, p. 170.

25. U.S. Congress, *Investigation of Government Organizations for Space Activities*, p. 333, and Manno, op. cit., p. 63.

26. Ibid., p. 116.

27. Ibid.

28. Dr. Michio Kaku, interview in *Nukes In Space: The Nuclearization and Weaponization of the Heavens*, op. cit.

29. Ibid.

30. Gar Stoller, "Star Wars in Paradise, Hawaiian Missile Firings Raise Safety Concern," *Conde Nast Traveler*, July 1994, p. 46.

31. Interview in *Nukes In Space, The Nuclearization and Weaponization of the Heavens*, op. cit.

32. Hearst Newspapers, "'Star Wars' Over Florida? Pentagon Ponders Missile-Testing Program," *The Gainesville Sun*, May 22, 1995, p. 1-2B.

33. Jenny Staletovich, "Tempers Fly High in the Keys Over Air Force Missile Test Plan," *The Palm Beach Post*, January 12, 1997, pp. 1A-16A.

34. Defend America Act of 1996, 104th Congress, 2d Session, H.R. 3144, S.1635, March 21, 1996.

35. Eric Schmitt, "Now, After $36 Billion Run, Coming Soon: 'Star Wars II,' New G.O.P. Plan Is Smaller, but Still Costly," *The New York Times*, February 7, 1995, p. A20.

36. Michio Kaku, *To Win a Nuclear War* (Boston: South End Press, 1992).

37. Anna Eisele, "Nuclear Research Initiated, NASA'S Marshall, Pentagon Advance Propulsion Concepts," *Space News*, October 14-20, 1996, p. 1.

38. Statement issued by The White House, "National Policy on Space Power and Propulsion," August 17, 1993.

39. Ibid.

40. Ibid.

41. Anna Eisele, "Nuclear Research Initiated, NASA'S Marshall, Pentagon

Advance Propulsion Concepts," op. cit.

42. Ibid.

43. Stephen Hilgartner, Richard C. Bell, Rory O'Connor, *Nukespeak: The Selling of Nuclear Technology in America* (New York: Penguin Books, 1983), p. 47.

44. Ibid.

45. John W. Simpson, *Nuclear Power from Underseas to Outer Space*, op. cit., pp. 133-134.

46. "The Nuclear Space Age," *Nucleonics*, vol. 19, no. 4, April 1961, p. 156.

47. Robert E.L. Adamson, "Washington Foresees Major Role for Nuclear Space Power," *Nucleonics*, vol. 19, no. 4, April 1961, p. 55.

48. Norman Gerstein, interview by the author, December 1996. Since leaving NASA, he has been in business and is president of NJG, Inc., an engineering consulting company, based in Germantown, Maryland.

49. *Nukespeak: The Selling of Nuclear Technology in America*, op.cit., p. 49.

50. Ibid.

51. Ibid., p. 47.

52. Kenneth F. Glantz, Lieutenant Colonel, United States Air Force, *Nuclear Flight: The United States Air Force Programs for Atomic Jets, Missiles, and Rockets* (New York: Duell, Sloan and Pearce, 1960).

53. Ibid., p. 5.

54. Ibid., p. 6.

55. Ibid., p. 10.

56. Ibid.

57. Ibid., p. 11.

58. Ibid., p. 12.

59. Ibid.

60. Ibid., pp. 168-169.

61. Ibid., pp. 190-194.

62. "Remarks of Senator Albert Gore on the Floor of the U.S. Senate, March 20, 1962" are contained in *Proceedings of the Subcommittee on Research, Development, and Radiation of the Joint Committee on Atomic Energy, Congress of the United States, Eighty-Seventh Congress, Second Session on Space Nuclear Power Applications, September 13, 14 and 19, 1962* (Washington, D.C.: U.S. Government Printing Office, 1962), p. 352.

63. Ibid.

64. Ibid., pp. 352-353.

65. Ibid., p. 10.

66. According to NASA's "U.S. History of RTG Power Source Use," the first RTG launched was a SNAP-3A launched on a navigational satellite (Transit 4A) on June 29, 1961. It is one of the four SNAP satellites with "dispersable plutonium" systems still in relatively low orbit and

thus expected to fall to Earth in several centuries.

67. Quoted in Nigel Flynn, *War In Space* (New York: Exeter Books, 1986), p. 6.

68. Ibid., p. 8.

69. Gregg Herken, *Counsels of War* (New York: Oxford University Press, 1987), p. 397.

70. William J. Broad, *Teller's War: The Top-Secret Story Behind the Star Wars Deception* (New York: Simon & Schuster, 1992), p. 105.

71. Ibid.

72. Ibid., p. 106.

73. Nigel Flynn, p. 8.

74. Ibid.

75. William J. Broad, p. 108.

76. Ibid., p. 138.

77. Ibid., p. 73.

78. Testimony of General James Abramson, *Space Nuclear Power, Conversion and Energy Storage for the Nineties and Beyond,* Hearings before the Subcommittee on Energy Research and Production of the Committee on Science and Technology, U.S. House of Representatives, Ninety-Ninth Congress, First Session, Oct. 8, 9, 10, 1985. Contained in record of the hearing, U.S. Government Printing Office, Washington, D.C., p. 9.

79. Ibid.

80. Ibid.

81. Ibid.

82. Byron Spice, "SDI Looks to Nuclear Power, Orbiting Reactor Essential, Director Says," op. cit., p. 1.

83. Steven Aftergood, "Background on Space Nuclear Power," *Science & Global Security,* Vol. l., Nos. 1-2, 1989, p. 104.

84. Quoted in Ibid., pp. 104-105. Original citation, "Debate on APS Directed-Energy Weapons Study," *Physics Today,* November 1987, pp. 52-53.

85. Ibid., p. 104.

86. Testimony of Dr. Robert Rosen, Deputy Associate Administrator for Aeronautics and Space Technology, National Aeronautics and Space Administration, *The SP-100 Space Reactor Power System,* Hearing before the Subcommittee on Investigations and Oversight of the Committee on Science, Space, and Technology, U.S. House of Representatives, One Hundred Second Congress, Second Session, March 12, 1992, Contained in record of the hearing, U.S. Government Printing Office, Washington, D.C., 1992, p. 121.

87. *SP-100 Space Reactor Safety,* U.S. Department of Energy, DOE/NE-0083, May 1987, p. 1.

88. Ibid., p. 10.

89. Ibid., p. 2.

90. Ibid., p. 3.

91. Robert L. Park, *On the Horizon* (a sidebar to Park's article "Do We Want Chernobyls in the Sky?"), *The Washington Post*, February 26, 1989.

92. David C. Morrison, "Space Nukes," *National Journal*, June 4, 1988, p. 1511.

93. Steven Aftergood, interview by the author, January 1997.

94. R. Jeffrey Smith, "U.S. Developing Atom-Powered Rocket," *The Washington Post*, April 3, 1991, pp. A-1 and A-6.

95. William J. Broad, "Rocket Run by Nuclear Power Being Developed for 'Star Wars,' Secret Pentagon Program Revealed in Documents," *The New York Times*, April 3, 1991, pp. A-1 and B-6.

96. "Probability of Impacting NZ," Sandia National Laboratory, Undated. The analysis was in the form of a series of charts. The chart headed "Probability of Impacting NZ [New Zealand]" stated as its last line that the "Results" showed "NZ Impact Probability, Given A Failure Is" 4.34 x 104 which is 4.34-in-10,000 or one-in-2,325.

97. Bob Davis, "Nuclear-Powered Rocket Is Studied By Project in Pentagon's SDI Office," *The Wall Street Journal*, April 3, 1991, p. A-22.

98. Dr. Kendall, interview by the author, April 1992.

99. John Fleck and Rex Graham, "City Selected Test Site For Soviet, Leaders Say Move Evidence State's Future Tied to Space," *Albuquerque Journal*, January 8, 1991, p. A3.

100. Yeltsin statement included in transcript of comments made at "summit meeting" of the UN Security Council, *The New York Times*, February 1, 1992.

101. John Noble Wilford, "Reactor Test in Orbit Is Opposed," *The New York Times*, Jan. 13, 1993, p. C-7.

102. Vincent Kiernan, "Topaz Reactor Test May Foul Up gamma Ray Observatory Work," *Space News*, Sept. 7-13, 1992, p. 9.

103. Albert S. Marshall, "Status of the Nuclear Safety Assessment for the NEPSTEP (Topaz II) Space Reactor Program," Sandia National Laboratories, Albuquerque, NM, 1993. The report's acknowledgements note it was funded by the Strategic Defense Initiative Organization and, in addition to Marshall, contributors include seven other scientists from Sandia; six from Los Alamos National Laboratory; three from Advanced Sciences, Inc.; and two from the University of New Mexico.

104. Ned S. Rasor, "Topaz, More Topaz," *Space News*, letter, April 4-10, 1994, pp. 18-19.

105. Vincent Kiernan, "Agencies May Fight for Topaz," *Space News*, Jan. 18-24, 1993, p.1 and 20.

106. *Cosmos 1900 and the Future of Space Nuclear Power*, Hearing before the Committee on Natural Resources, United States Senate, one

Hundredth Congress, Second Session, September 13, 1988, U.S. Government Printing Office, Washington, 1989, p. 57.

107. "NASA to Establish Office For Nuclear Propulsion," *Aviation Week & Space Technology*, Jan. 7, 1991, p. 34.

108. William J. Broad, "Shuttle Is Off at Last, on 8-Day Military Mission Without Secrecy," *The New York Times*, April 29, 1991, p. B-6.

109. Joseph J. Trento, *Prescription For Disaster, From the Glory of Apollo to the Betrayal of the Shuttle* (New York: Crown Publishers, 1987), p. 215.

110. Ibid., p. 216.

111. Ibid., pp. 218-219.

112. Anne Eisle, "Air Force, NASA Will Consolidate Space Efforts," *Space News*, March 10-16, 1997, p. 5.

113. Ibid.

114. Ibid.

Chapter Five: "Nukes Forever!"

1. Dr. Robert Park, interview by the author, March 1997.

2. John J. O'Connor, "Will the Asteroids Destroy Kansas City? Guess," *The New York Times*, February 14, 1997, p. B-16.

3. Diane Werts, "Watch Out Below! Asteroid-Mania Hits the Tube," *Newsday*, February 9, 1997, pp. C-14 and C-15.

4. From Shoemaker's appearance on *Today* show, February 26, 1996.

5. Diane Werts, op. cit.

6. Kathy Sawyer, "The Sky *Is* Falling," *The Washington Post National Weekly Edition*, March 3, 1996, pp. 1 and 6.

7. William J. Broad, "Earth Is Target for Space Rocks at Higher Rate Than Thought," *The New York Times*, January 7, 1997, pp. C-1 and C-8.

8. Theresa Foley, "Scientists Leery of Nuclear Defense Against Asteroids," *Space News*, February 28-March 6, 1996, p. 8.

9. Dave Cravotta, "Killer Asteroids, Can Scientists Prevent Doomsday?," *Final Frontier*, March/April 1996, p. 23.

10. Robert L. Park, "Star Warriors on Sky Patrol, Edward Teller Wants to Nuke Asteroids," *The New York Times*, March 25, 1992, p. A-23.

11. Ibid.

12. Ibid.

13. Ibid.

14. Ibid.

15. Ibid.

16. Ibid.

17. Ibid.

18. Ibid.

19. Ibid.

20. Ibid.

21. Ibid.

22. Dr. Park interview op. cit.

23. Ibid.

24. Ibid.

25. Ibid.

26. Fran Smith, "Killer Asteroid Dooms Earth! And If You Believe That, Edward Teller and Friends Have Several Billion Dollars' Worth of Space Weaponry to Sell You," *West*, the magazine of *The San Jose Mercury News*, March 22, 1992, pp. 12-19.

27. Ibid., p. 18.

28. Warren E. Leary, "Quayle's Influence Seen in NASA Shake-Up," *The New York Times*, February 15, 1992.

29. Ibid., p. 12.

30. Ibid., p. 13.

31. Ibid., p. 18.

32. Gerrard is a partner in the New York law firm of Arnold & Porter, former chair of the Environmental Law Section of the New York State Bar Association, general editor of the six volume *Environmental Law Practice Guide*, and adjunct professor at Columbia Law School and the Yale School of Forestry and Environmental Studies. Ms. Barber is an associate at Arnold & Porter.

33. Michael B. Gerrard and Anna Barber, *Asteroids and Comets: U.S. and International Law and the Lowest-Probability, Highest-Consequence Risk*, presented at the New York University Colloquium on Outer Space Law, February 20, 1997. To be published later in 1997 in the *New York University Environmental Law Journal*.

34. Ibid.

35. Theresa Foley, "Scientists Leery of Nuclear Defense Against Asteroids," *Space News*, op. cit.

36. Lawrence Spohn, "Sandia Studies Nuke-Powered TV Satellites, The Project Has the Potential to Dominate the Entire Communications Industry, One Scientist Says," *Albuquerque Tribune*, January 15, 1994, pp. A-1-A-2.

37. Ibid., p. A2.

38. Ibid.

39. Ibid.

40. Vincent Kiernan, DoD Cancels Plan for Nuclear Rocket," *Space News*, May 17, 1993, p. 6.

41. *America at the Threshold*, Report of the Synthesis Group on America's Space Exploration Initiative, Synthesis Group, Arlington, Virginia, May 3, 1991, p. 66.

42. Dr. Stanley K. Borowski, "Nuclear Propulsion: The Key to Economical Access Through Space," *Ad Astra*, September /October 1996, p. 38.

43. Ibid., p. 41.

44. Dr. Robert Zubrin, *The Case for Mars*, (New York: The Free Press, 1996).

45. Dr. Robert Zubrin, "Question of Power," *Ad Astra*, November/December 1994.

46. Ibid., p. 67.

47. Ibid., pp. 67-68.

48. Ibid., p. 68.

49. Ibid.

50. Kathy Sawyer, "Build Nuclear-Powered Rocket For Mars Mission, Panel Urges," *The Washington Post*, June 12, 1991.

51. Ibid., p. 66.

52. Rex Graham, "Astronauts May Rocket to Mars, Trips Will Be Powered with Nuclear Energy," *Albuquerque Journal*, January 14, 1992, p. A-1.

53. Ibid., p. A-3.

54. *Final Environmental Impact Statement Space Nuclear Thermal Propulsion Program, Particle Bed Reactor Propulsion Technology Development and Validation*, Department of the Air Force, Washington, D.C., May 1993, Cover Sheet.

55. Ibid., S-8-S-12.

56. Chuck Broscious, *Comments on Space Nuclear Thermal Propulsion Program Environmental Impact Statement*, Submitted on Behalf of Environmental Defense Institute, Moscow and Troy, Idaho, September 14, 1992.

57. James Coates, "Environmental Fears Could Ground Nuclear-Powered Rocket," *Chicago Tribune*, April 12, 1992.

58. Ibid.

59. Letter from Lt. Colonel Roger X. Leonard, Chief, Concepts/Exploration division, U.S. Air Force, to Institute for Security and Cooperation in Outer Space, March 29, 1993.

60. Ibid.

61. Vincent Kiernan, "DoD Cancels Plan for Nuclear Rocket," op. cit.

62. "U.S.-Soviet Study Finds Mars Base Feasible Within 21 Years," press release from Stanford University News Service, June 26, 1991, p. 4.

63. Glenda Chi, "U.S.-Soviet Mission Touted as Cheaper, Quicker Way to Mars," *San Jose Mercury News*, June 27, 1991.

64. "U.S.-Soviet Study Finds Mars Base Feasible Within 21 Years," op. cit.

65. Douglas Isbell, "Stanford Mars Mission Scenario Uses Soviet Energy," *Space News*, July 8-14, 1991, p. 24.

66. Ibid.

67. Ibid.

68. William J. Broad, "Russian Rockets Get Lift in U.S. From Cautious and

Clever Design," *The New York Times*, Oct. 29, 1996, p. C-1.

69. Ibid.

70. Ibid., p. C-6.

71. Ibid.

72. Ibid.

73. John Noble Wilford, "NASA Plans New Series of Cheaper Spacecraft," *The New York Times*, December 19, 1995, p. C-1.

74. Ibid., p. C-13.

75. Theresa Foley, "Air Force Launches $2 Million Study of Space Reactor Needs," *Space News*, February 6, 1994.

76. Ibid.

77. Ibid.

78. Hiroshi Takahashi and An Yu, "Use of Irons Thruster to Dispose of Type II Long-Lived Fission Products into Outer Space," Presentation at the Fourteenth Annual Symposium on Space Nuclear Power and Propulsion," Albuquerque, NM, January 28, 1997.

79. Ibid.

80. Hiroshi Takahashi and Xinyi Chen, "Alternative Way to Dispose of High-Level Waste in Outer Space," Presented at American Institute of Physics Conference, 1995, Proc. 324, p. 347.

81. Ibid., p. 349.

82. Ibid., p. 352.

83. Ibid.

84. Theresa Foley, "Firms Consider Nuclear Powerplant in Communications Satellite Concept," *Space News*, January 10, 1994.

85. Ibid.

86. "Lunar Mining Could Provide Future Energy Source for Earth," National Aeronautics and Space Administration, Washington, D.C., Release: 90-139, October 17, 1990.

87. Ibid.

88. From classified AEC documents disclosed during U.S. Congressional hearings led by Senator Edward Kennedy in April 1979 on the federal government's responsibility for cancers caused by the testing of atomic weapons. Cited in Grossman, *Cover Up: What You Are Not Supposed To Know About Nuclear Power*, p. 251.

89. Lawrence E. Joseph, "Who Will Mine the Moon?," *The New York Times*, January 19, 1995, p. A-23.

90. Ibid.

91. Ibid.

92. Ibid.

93. Ibid.

94. Ibid.

95. Ibid.
96. Ibid.
97. Leonard David, "LunaCorp Looks for Route to Moon via Japan," *Space News*, June 10-16, 1996, p. 20.
98. John S. Lewis, *Mining the Sky, Untold Riches from the Asteroids, Comets, and Planets* (Reading, MA: Helix Books, Addison-Wesley Publishing Company, Inc., 1996), p. 208.
99. Ibid., p. 197.
100. Ibid., p. 163.
101. Ibid., p. 209.
102. Ibid., p. 211.
103. Ibid., p. 212-213.
104. Pat Dasch, "Space Summit Forum, Mars and the Future of the U.S. Space Program," *Ad Astra*, January/February 1997, pp. 8-9.
105. Ibid., p. 9.

Chapter Six: Censored

1. Mark Lowenthal, interview by the author, March 1997.
2. William Boot, "NASA and the Spellbound Press," *Columbia Journalism Review*, July/August 1986, pp. 23-29.
3. Ibid., p. 24.
4. Ibid.
5. Ibid.
6. Ibid.
7. Ibid., p. 28.
8. Ibid.
9. Ibid.
10. Ibid., p. 29.
11. Ibid.
12. Ibid.
13. Ibid.
14. Ibid.
15. Coverage of and interview with Wilford at his presentation, entitled "Science and the Media," Brookhaven National Laboratory, July 19, 1990.
16. Ibid.
17. Ibid.
18. John Noble Wilford, "Galileo Spacecraft Loops by Earth for Gravitational Boost to Jupiter," *The New York Times*, December 9, 1990, p. 9.
19. John Noble Wilford, "Planetary 'Slingshot' Aims Craft at a Rendezvous with Jupiter," *The New York Times*, December 8, 1992, pp. C-1 - C-10.

20. Ibid.

21. John Noble Wilford, *Mars Beckons: The Mysteries, the Challenges, the Expectations of Our Next Great Adventure in Space* (New York: Alfred A. Knopf, 1990), pp. 191-192.

22. M.L. Stein, "Could The Media Have Prevented Shuttle Disaster," *Editor & Publisher,* July 12, 1986, pp. 11-12.

23. Ibid., p. 11.

24. Ibi., p. 12.

25. Bruce Gagnon, interview by the author, November 1996.

26. Ibid.

27. Bruce Gagnon, interview by the author, January 1997.

28. Ibid.

29. Ibid.

30. Ibid.

31. Ibid.

32. Hirsch, interview by the author, January 1990.

33. Ibid.

34. James Skardon, "The Apollo Story: What the Watchdogs Missed," *Columbia Journalism Review*, Fall, 1967, p. 11.

35. Ibid.

36. Ibid.

37. Ibid., pp. 11-12.

38. Ibid., p. 13.

39. James Skardon, "The Apollo Story: The Concealed Patterns," *Columbia Journalism Review*, Winter, 1967, p. 34.

40. Ibid.

41. Ibid., p. 37.

42. Ibid.

43. Bruce Murray, *Journey Into Space, The First Thirty Years of Space Exploration* (New York: W.W. Norton & Company, 1989), p. 363.

44. Hilgartner, Bell and O'Connor, *Nukespeak: The Selling of Nuclear Technology in America*, op. cit., p. 33.

45. Corrine Browne and Robert Munroe, *Time Bomb: Understanding the Threat of Nuclear Power* (New York: William Morrow and Company, 1991), p. 27.

46. Ibid., p. 34.

47. James W. Kunetka, *City of Fire: Los Alamos and the Birth of the Atomic Age* (Englewood Cliffs, New Jersey: Prentice-Hall, Inc., 1978), p. 153.

48. Hilgartner, Bell and O'Connor, *Nukespeak, The Selling of Nuclear Technology in America*, op. cit., p. 33.

49. Ibid., p. 34.

50. James W. Kunetka, *City of Fire*, op. cit., pp. 170-171..

51. Ibid., p. 170.

52. Ibid.

53. Ibid., p. 171.

54. *PR Watch*, a quarterly, is published by the Center for Media & Democracy, 3318 Gregory Street, Madison, Wisconsin 53711.

55. John C. Stauber and Sheldon Rampton, *Toxic Sludge Is Good For You, Lies, Damn Lies and the Public Relations Industry* (Monroe, Maine: Common Courage Press, 1995), pp. 34-35.

56. Ibid., p. 35.

57. Ibid., p. 39.

58. Ibid., p. 41.

59. Ibid., p. 35. Quote from David Lilienthal, *Change, Hope, and the Bomb*, pp. 111-112.

60. Hilgartner, Bell and O'Connor, *Nukespeak: The Selling of Nuclear Technology in America*, op. cit., p. xiv.

61. Daniel Ford, *The Cult of the Atom: The Secret Papers of the Atomic Energy Commission* (New York: Simon & Schuster, 1982), p. 35.

62. Ibid.

63. Karl Grossman, *Cover Up: What You Are Not Supposed To Know About Nuclear Power* (Sag Harbor, N.Y.: Permanent Press, updated edition, 1982), pp. xviii-xix.

64. William L. Laurence, *The New York Times*, September 26, 1945.

65. Browne and Munroe, *Time Bomb, Understanding the Threat of Nuclear Power*, op. cit. pp. 37-38.

66. William L. Laurence, "Paradise or Doomsday?", *Woman's Home Companion*, May 1948, p. 33.

67. Roger Star, interview by author, March 1989.

68. Thomas Pigford, "Three Mile Island: The Good News," *The New York Times*, March 29, 1989, p. 16-A.

69. Frances Cerra's troubles over the nuclear issue at *The New York Times* is chronicled in Grossman, *Power Crazy, Is LILCO Turning Shoreham Into America's Chernobyl*, (Grove Press: New York, NY, 198) pp. 305-306. They are also discussed in the 1996 video *Fear and Favor in the Newsroom*.

70. Alan Whitman, interview by author, October 1979. Included in Grossman, *Cover Up: What You Are Not Supposed to Know About Nuclear Power*, (Sag Harbor, NY: Permanent Press, 1980), p. 190.

71. Anna Mayo, interview by the author, October 1979 and March 1989.

72. Tom McGrath, "Talking With: Michael Jordan," *USAir Magazine*, May 1996, p. 14.

73. Westinghouse Electric Corporation, *1994 Annual Report*.

74. Fox Butterfield, "Phillipines Expected to File Suit Against Westinghouse,"

The New York Times, December 1, 1988, pp. D-1 and D-8.

75. Sam Husseini, "Felons on the Air: Does GE's Ownership of NBC Violate the Law?" *Extra!*, November-December 1994.

76. Karl Grossman, "20/20 Out of Focus on Nuclear Issues." *Extra!*, January/February, 1994, p. 14.

77. "Plutonium-238: A Risky Number," St. Petersburg Times, May 29, 1989.

78. Ibid.

79. Ibid.

80. "Let's Ban Nuclear Satellites," Los Angeles Times, July 25, 1988.

81. Ibid.

82. Ibid.

83. *The Truth About Lies, The Pubic Mind With Bill Moyers*, A co-Production of Public Affairs Television, Inc., New York. Presented by WNET/New York and WETA/Washington, D.C. Aired Nov. 29, 1989. Quotes from transcript of program.

84. Giles Whittell, "Aborted Apollo 13 Mission 'Risked Nuclear Disaster,'" *The Times*, September 9, 1995.

85. *Final Environmental Impact Statement*, op. cit., p. 4-40. The NASA document acknowledges that "during the VVEJGA trajectory"—the "flyby" route taking the Cassini twice around Venus, once past the Earth and then on to Jupiter and Saturn—"the spacecraft would fly past the Earth at an altitude of 500 km (1,6000,000 ft) and at a velocity of 19.1 km/s (62,700 ft/s)." That speed translates to 42,300 miles per hour. For a discussion of the vital importance for reporters, when doing environmental stories to ask hard questions, to get to the fundamentals of the story because of an "unusual responsibility as messengers who raise issues which directly affect the health and survival of humankind and the biosphere," see the chapter "Media and Journalism" authored by Professor Ann Filemyr and Karl Grossman in *Greening the College Curriculum: A Guide to Environmental Teaching in the Liberal Arts*. It is edited by Jonathan Collett and Stephen Karakashian (Washington, D.C. and Covelo, CA.: Island Press, 1996). We call our approach to environmental journalism "Deep Journalism." We stated: "It is not acceptable simply to poke a microphone in front of the face of the spokesperson for Exxon and be told that the mess in Prince Edward Sound is not *that bad*, and then write an article which simply juxtaposes the ecological destruction with the corporation's denial. These journalists should be prepared to dig, to seek to determine what really happened, how things really work. That is the necessary direction, the start toward Deep Journalism. And some may be fortunate and work at media locations where they will be fully free to practice Deep Journalism in environmental reporting."

86. John Noble Wilford, "Jupiter Rendezvous Is Marvel of Perfection," *The New York Times*, December. 9, 1995, p. 12.

87. Mark Lowenthal, interview by the author, February 1997.

88. Ibid.

89. Ibid.

90. Ibid.

Chapter Seven: Saving The Space Program From Itself

1. Coverage of the event held May 25-27, 1996.

2. Ibid.

3. Ibid.

4. Ibid.

5. Ibid.

6. Ibid.

7. Ibid.

8. Ibid.

9. Ibid.

10. Ibid.

11. Ibid.

12. Ibid.

13. Byron Morgan, interview by the author, May 1996.

14. Coverage of the event July 18-19, 1992.

15. Ibid.

16. Ibid.

17. Ibid.

18. Ibid.

19. Andrew Lawler, "U.S. Backpedals on Nuclear Rules," *Space News*, March 6, 1991, p. 1.

20. Coverage of the event July 18-29, 1992, Ibid.

21. Ibid.

22. Ibid.

23. Global Network statement issued at press conference July 20, 1992, Washington, D.C. Coverage of press conference.

24. Coverage of the event, March 18, 1997, Conway Hall, London.

25. "Memorandum of Understanding between the Department of Energy and the National Aeronautics and Space Administration Concerning Radioisotope Power Systems for Space Missions," signed July 26, 1991, by then NASA Administrator Richard Truly and DOE Secretary James Watkins.

26. Michael Mariotte, interview by the author, July 1991.

27. Coverage of the conference, March 20, 1997, Damstadt, Germany.

28. Ibid.

29. Ibid.

30. Ibid.

31. Ibid.

32. Ibid.

33. Ibid and interview with Dr. Strobl.

34. Ibid.

35. Ibid.

36. Nukem, according to the files of the German newspaper, *Die Tageszeitung*, has a long and messy history in nuclear technology and specifically with plutonium. Articles on Nukem in *Die Tageszeitung* include stories of 20 Nukem workers being contaminated with plutonium in March 1987, the company being suspected of diverting nuclear materials to Libya and Pakistan in January 1988, 4.2 kilograms of plutonium reported missing from Nukem in September 1988, Nukem being accused of falsified testing systems to check radioactive contamination in February 1990 and the revelation in 1990 that Nukem had sold enriched uranium to Iraq.

37. Coverage of the conference, March 20, 1997, Damstadt, Germany.

38. Coverage of strategy session, March 20.

39. Ibid.

40. Ibid.

41. Faxed letter from Dr. John Gofman, March 17, 1997.

42. Ibid.

43. Ibid.

44. Dr. Glenn T. Seaborg, interview by the author, March 1997.

45. Dr. Glenn T. Seaborg and William R. Corliss, *Man and Atom* (New York: E.P. Dutton and Co., Inc., 1971), p. 174.

46. Ibid.

47. Ibid., p. 188-194.

48. Dr. Glenn T. Seaborg, interview by the author, March 1997, Ibid.

49. Ibid.

50. Ibid.

51. Ibid.

52. Ibid.

53. Coverage of lecture by James Powell, "The Particle-Bed Reactor: Nuclear Rockets and Beyond," Brookhaven National Laboratory, February 10, 1993.

54. Ibid.

55. Ibid.

56. Harvey Wasserman, interview by the author, March 1997.

57. Treaty on Principles Governing the Activities of States in the Exploration and Use of Outer Space, including the Moon and Other Celestial

Bodies, also referred to as the Outer Space Treaty. The treaty was "largely based," according to the United Nations, "on the Declaration of Legal Principles Governing the Activities of States in the Exploration and Use of Outer Space" and adopted by the General Assembly in 1962. "A few new provisions" were subsequently added, and "the treaty was opened for signature by the three depository governments," the Soviet Union, the United Kingdom and the U.S., in January 1967 and entered into force in October 1967. "The Outer Space Treaty provides the basic framework on international space law," according to the UN.

58. Ibid.
59. Ibid.
60. Ibid.
61. Jane Ciabattari, "Why the 21st Could Be the American Century," *Parade*, April 6, 1997, p. 8.
62. George and Meredith Friedman, *The Future of War: Power, Technology & American World Dominance in the 21st Century*, (New York: Crown Publishers, 1996), p. ix.
63. Ibid., p. 420
64. Ibid. p. 367
65. Michael Mariotte, interview by the author, March 1997.
66. Alan Kohn, interview by the author, June 1997.
67. Ibid
68. Ibid
69. Ibid.
70. Ibid.
71. Ibid.
72. Coverage of the demonstration held June 14, 1997.
73. Seth Borenstein, "Ex-NASA Official Protests Cassini," *The Orlando Sentinel*, June 14, 1997, p. A-6.
74. Coverage of demonstration, June 14, 1997.
75. Ibid.
76. Ibid.
77. Ibid.
78. Ibid.
79. Ibid.
80. Ibid.
81. Ibid.
82. Ibid.
83. Ibid.

84. Ibid.

85. Veteran NASA employee, interview by the author, June 1997. Also, the employee, who requested anonymity, sent a written statement.

86. Dan Hirsch, interview by the author, March 1997.

87. Associate Press, "NASA's Problems in Space, on Land," *Newsday*, October 7, 1993, p. A-15.

88. Associated Press, "Glue Used for Repairs of Shuttle, NASA Says," *The New York Times*, February 13, 1994, p. 13.

89. Earl Lane, "Endeavor Lift-Off Postponed, O-ring Troubles Again," *Newsday*, July 29, 1995, p. A-8.

90. William Harwood, "Horner Calls Launch Record a 'Horror Story,'" *Space News*, June 3, 1993, p. 1.

91. Bruce Gagnon, interview by the author, March 1997.

92. "Plutonium-238 Requirements," undated DOE report. Subsequently, Jeff Lawrence, NASA Associate Administrator for Legislative Affairs, wrote Representative Michael Forbes of New York, who inquired about the report, that "since the chart was created" the Comet Nuclear Mission and the Mars Environmental Survey listed on it were cancelled. (Jeff Lawrence, letter to Representative Forbes, June 26, 1997). However, after NASA's subtraction of two of the missions involving nuclear power from the DOE list, *Space News* reported in June 1997 a NASA plan to send two nuclear power plants to Mars in separate launches in 2007 to be used on manned missions to Mars. There would be a series of trips in 2007 bringing equipment to Mars. The "second cargo mission" in 2007 "would deliver" the first nuclear power plant, "the final cargo mission of 2007 would deliver…a second nuclear power plant," according to the article by Anne Eisele, "Mars Planners Struggle to Lower Costs," *Space News*, June 9-15, p. 1

93. Bruce Gagnon, interview by the author, op. cit.

94. *Nuclear Safety Analyses for Cassini Mission Environmental Impact Statement Process*, Haliburton NUS Corporation, Gaithersburg, MD, Prepared for U.S. Department of Energy, Space and National Security Programs, Office of Nuclear Energy, Science and Technology, p. 2-2.

95. "Resolution of the Marin county Board of Supervisors Expressing Marin County's Serious Concern to the Inclusion of Plutonium as Part of the Cassini Spacecraft Project Due to Dangers of Nuclear Radiation," approved unanimously, March 25, 1997.

96. Dr. William Rothman, Chairperson Marin County Peace Conversion Commission, letter to Marin County Board of Supervisors, February 26, 1997.

97. Dr. Michio Kaku, interview in *Nukes in Space: The Nuclearization and Weaponization of the Heavens*, op. cit.

98. Ibid.

99. Ibid.

INDEX

A

Abrahamson, James, 106, 123-124, 145, 187

accident/failure record, 17-18, 71, 72, 74, 174, 220, 224. *see also* names of individual flights

Aftergood, Steven, 11, 125, 126-127, 195

agricultural area decontamination, 46, 47

Air Force Space Command. Partnership Council, 133

airplane, nuclear-propelled, 116

Alamogordo atomic bomb test, 181

alternative power source, 86, 89, 90, 221. *see also* solar energy systems

Alvarado, Leo, 7

American Astronomical Society, 129

America's Space Exploration Initiative, 144

Ananyev, Vladimir, 3

Anti-Ballistic Missile Treaty (1974), 123

anti-missile system tests, 110-111

Apollo 13 mission, 15-17, 71

Armstrong, Neil, 61, 75

Ashy, Joseph W., 104

Askers, Jim, 165

asteroids, 134-142, 159

Astrofuel, 156

Atomic Energy Commission, 100, 180

atomic explosion, first, 176-178

atomic weapons tests, 195

atomic-powered airplane, 116

Australia and Mars 96, 1-5

B

Babcock and Wilcox, 127, 149

Bailey, Sterling, 155

Ballistic Missile Defense, 110

Baquedano, Manuel, 8

Barber, Anna W., 141-142

Barrera, Luis, 7, 8-9

Bartholomew, Cory, 192

beagles as test animals, 56

Beale, Albert, 197

Behavior of Plutonium Oxide Particulates in a Simulated Florida Environment, 37-38

Belcher, Phil, 176, 177

Bell, Robert, 2-3

Bendetsen, Karl R., 122

Bendick, Gordon, 9-10

Benedict, Howard, 166

Biddle, Wayne, 166-167

Billie, Bobby C., 193

bi-modal reactors, 152-153

Bolivia and Mars 96, 6-7, 9

Boot, William, 164-165, 166

Borowski, Stanley K., 144

Bowman, Sydney, 194

Boylan, Steve, 10-11

Breznay, George B., 64

Broad, William J., 106, 121-122, 123, 151

Broscious, Chuck, 147

Brown, Chris, 147, 195

Buden, David, 153

Butler, Dan, 65, 73-74

Byars, Carlos, 165

C

Caldicott, Helen, 13, 27-28, 53-54

Canavan, Gregory, 135

ACKNOWLEDGEMENTS

The author wishes to thank the folks at Common Courage Press: typesetter Tara Townsend, publicist Liz Keith, proofreader Karen Steward, and publisher Greg Bates—whose idea this book is; Dr. Michio Kaku, professor of nuclear physics at the City University of New York who was so kind as to review the manuscript; Louise Mills, Sue Mermelstein and Mary Cunnane for their great help with the manuscript; Bruce Gagnon, Brian Keaney, Mary Beth Sullivan, Ele Kenyon, Jan Longwell-Smiley, and John and Sheila Stewart of the Florida Coalition for Peace & Justice; Bill Sulzman, Loring Wirbel and Donna Johnson of Citizens for Peace in Space. Thanks to Steve Jambeck and Joan Flynn, my partners in EnviroVideo. To Dr. Ralph J. Herbert, professor of environmental studies at Southampton College. To Dr. Helen Caldicott. With much appreciation to Terry Allen of *CovertAction Quarterly* and Judith Long of *The Nation*, publications which have had the guts to publish my articles on this issue. Thanks to the former hands at NASA and to its contractors, who, as a matter of conscience, have been—and are—speaking out on the use of nuclear power in space: Alan Kohn, Dr. Horst Poehler and Byron Morgan. And thanks to the whistleblowers at NASA who have provided me with information, yet remain anonymous. With much appreciation to: Harvey Wasserman of Greenpeace; Carol S. Rosin of the Institute for Security and Cooperation in Outer Space; webmasters Russell Hoffman and Robert Cherwink; Bill Smirnow; Wes Thomas; Mark Elsis of Lovearth; Carol Brouillet; Regina Hagen; World Information Service on Energy; Nuclear Information and Resource Service; WBAI radio. To Greg Ruggiero of the Learning Alliance; Rob Cotter; journalists Chris Bryson and Peter Cronau; Dr. Ernest Sternglass; Dr. John Gofman; Frank Melli of Green Sphere, Inc.; Jeff Keating; Robert Anderson; videomaker Gloria Walker; radio program host David Barsamian; Dan Hirsch, of the Committee to Bridge the Gap; Pol D'Huyvetter and Tom Keunen of For Mother Earth; Bruce David, editor-in-chief of *Rage* magazine; writer Sara Shannon; Karin Westdyk; and John Stauber and Sheldon Rampton of *PR Watch*. And, as always, great thanks to my wife, Janet Grossman.

About the Author

For almost 30 years, Karl Grossman has pioneered combining investigative reporting and environmental journalism in a variety of media. He is the narrator and host of award-winning environmental TV documentaries and the author of three books on environmental and energy issues. Karl Grossman's articles have appeared in *The New York Times*, *Newsday*, *The Nation*, *Columbia Journalism Review*, *E, The Environmental Magazine*, *Covert Action Quarterly*, *Extra!* and in numerous other publications. He is the recipient of numerous honors for journalism, including the George Polk Award.

His journalism on the use of nuclear power in space has been repeatedly cited in the annual judging of Sonoma State University's Project Censored of the issues most "censored" or "under-reported" by the national news media. In 1997, Project Censored selected Grossman's articles on the subject as its "top censored story of 1996."

He is a full professor of journalism at the State University of New York / College at Old Westbury where he teaches Investigative Reporting and Environmental Journalism.